Praise for *Sowing Seeds*

"With Robert Bly leading the charge, and with stakes made extraordinarily high because of the war raging in Vietnam, our generation fed not only on poetry and literature but on impassioned discussions of politics, sex, race, music, feminism, and ideas; we read aloud from works in progress, saw a proliferation of underground and small presses, and trusted one another enough to give companionship, support, love and occasionally, criticism. In the process, Minnesota's poets, booksellers and small presses gave birth to an important cultural renaissance, the effects of which are still being felt today. Mark Gustafson has brilliantly and meticulously chronicled this time and has set it in amber, a gift for all who experienced it and a handbook for generations of readers and writers who believe that many voices are better than a few, and that art and poetry matter."

Marly Rusoff, literary agent and founder of The Loft Literary Center, which celebrated its 50th Anniversary in 2024

"Mark Gustafson is the unselfish keeper of the Robert Bly seed bank. This sparkling book shares the fruit grown from those heirloom seeds."

Timothy Young, author of *Herds of Bears Surround Us*, *Building in Deeper Water*, and other books

"In *Sowing Seeds*, Mark Gustafson gives us an erudite, beautifully written chronicle of the decades when Minnesota came into its own as a center for literature of the highest order. The 'sower' himself is, of course, Robert Bly. As Gustafson observes, Robert Bly is as central to American poetry as Whitman. Bly was a catalyst, as are all heroes, and through his own poetry and his translations, he transformed the literary landscape. Gustafson writes beautifully, with first-hand knowledge as well as thorough research, about the half century during which Robert Bly brought the literary world to Minnesota. Poetry dissolves borders, and as Bly said, '…can live anywhere.'"

Connie Wanek, author of *Rival Gardens: New and Selected Poems*, *On Speaking Terms*, and other books

"What a brilliant idea to write a book that traces the roots (and the flowering) of the Minnesota poetry community! Of course, Robert Bly was at the center of this community and Gustafson does a wonderful job of showing why this was the case. But the book—with its central metaphor of 'sowing'—goes far beyond Bly's remarkable gifts, influence, and generosity: it speaks eloquently to the necessity of community. Without it, the book suggests, we wither and die. But with it, whole new worlds open, not just in the present, but also for the future. *Sowing Seeds* is a kind of handbook for how to protect and nurture the poetic spirit. Read it and delight!"

Jim Moore, author of *Prognosis, Underground: New and Selected Poems*, and other books

"*Sowing Seeds* traces how a flyover landscape with sub-zero temperatures has fostered an impressive creative community through friendships, human generosity, and reading poetry out loud. The Minnesota literary ecosystem is a small miracle, and this book is a must-read for those interested in nurturing and maintaining arts communities into the future."

Lynette Reini-Grandell, author of *Wild Things: A Trans-Glam-Punk-Rock Love Story* and *Wild Verge*

"Scholar Mark Gustafson knows more about 20th century Minnesota literary history and culture than anyone. Thank God he has written it down in *Sowing Seeds* for all to remember. He is particularly acute on the pivotal role of poet Robert Bly who returned from Harvard and New

York to his prairie roots to sow the seeds of the vibrant literary culture now flowering across Minnesota and the nation."

James P. Lenfestey, author of *Time Remaining: Body Odes, Praise Songs, Oddities and Amazements* **and other books**

"Robert Bly appears in this book as if he were an early settler in a newly discovered continent. He didn't just build himself a house there; he invited scores of others to join him until a new and thriving nation arose on fields no one previously thought to cultivate. Deeply researched and clearly written, *Sowing Seeds* is a solid contribution to the history of American letters."

Lewis Hyde, a MacArthur fellow, and author of *A Primer for Forgetting, Trickster Makes This World* **and other books**

"Robert Bly is arguably the most important poet from the United States. Nobody has covered his journey with as much intelligence and enthusiasm as Mark Gustafson. *Sowing Seeds* is Mark's newest installment and without a doubt the most interesting book ever written about Bly. After the first 50 pages I realized Mark was more than a great writer, he was my hero."

Klecko, author of *A Bakeable Feast* **and** *Hitman-Baker-Casket Maker: Aftermath of an American's Clash with ICE***, and other books**

"Mark Gustafson's recounting of how Minnesota's great poetry community was built is thorough, well documented, and fascinating. And, for those of us who were there, a treasure trove of fond memories. A must read for poets and booklovers everywhere."

David Unowsky, founder of the legendary Hungry Mind Bookstore (later, Ruminator), which spun off its own literary magazine and press

"Mark Gustafson's *Sowing Seeds: the Minnesota Literary Renaissance & Robert Bly* accomplishes what few literary histories do: with breadth and precision, this book renders an entire artistic landscape in all its vigor and diversity. Beginning in the 'profound social, political, and cultural transformation' of the Sixties and arriving at this day, Gustafson traces the development of a vital strain of American literary life. His own gifts as a storyteller and prose writer make *Sowing Seeds* a beautiful and just contribution to the major work he honors."

Peter Campion, professor of creative writing at the University of Minnesota, author of *Radical as Reality: Form and Freedom in American Poetry* and other books

"No one knows Robert Bly's work and its influence better than his biographer Mark Gustafson. *Sowing Seeds*, a much-needed survey of a brilliant yet undersung period in Minnesota literary history, thoroughly illuminates those thrilling decades when Bly acted as a powerhouse of community, seeming to gather all of Minnesota poetry, in one way or another, in his generous reach."

Thomas R. Smith, author of *Medicine Year* and *Poetry on the Side of Nature: Writing the Nature Poem as an Act of Survival*, and other books

Sowing Seeds

Minneapolis

FIRST EDITION SEPTEMBER 2024
Sowing Seeds: The Minnesota Literary Renaissance & Robert Bly
Copyright © 2024 by Mark Gustafson
All rights reserved.

No part of this book may be used or reproduced in any manner whatsoever without written permission except in the case of brief quotations used in critical articles and reviews.

For information, write to Calumet Editions,
6800 France Avenue South, Suite 370, Edina, MN 55435

10 9 8 7 6 5 4 3 2 1
ISBN: 978-1-962834-24-7

Cover and interior design: Gary Lindberg
Cover photo © Gerard Malanga

"All flourishing is mutual."

–Robin Wall Kimmerer, *Braiding Sweetgrass*

For Sarah, again,
animae dimidio meae

TABLE OF CONTENTS

PREFACE 1
Setting the scene: Where we find ourselves now, our inheritance, the largesse.

CHAPTER 1—INTRODUCTION: GENEROSITY AND GENERATIVITY 5
Bly as the original sower and a gift giver, and how he got that way. Within the wider context of the Cold War period. The purpose, character, and structure of this book.

CHAPTER 2— SWEET HOME, MINNESOTA 27
The nature of the state of Minnesota, good and bad (including the weather), and writers who had left (Lewis, Fitzgerald, Eberhart) and those who stayed (Le Sueur, McGrath, Manfred). Bly's farming background and decision to stay. The negative and positive connotations of "regional."

CHAPTER 3— GOOD SOIL AND ROCKY GROUND 45
The first germination in this larger story happened with a receptive poet, JamesWright, at the University of Minnesota, where also was the most resistant poet, Allen Tate. The *Minnesota Review* has its origins there, under Tate's influence. But University students on the staff of the *Ivory Tower* (Keillor, Hyde, Moore, Hampl, and others) were very responsive, becoming new sowers in turn.

CHAPTER 4— HOMEGROWN POETRY 61
Two books, Bly's *Silence in the Snowy Fields* and Wright's *The Branch Will Not Break* were the most important models to young poets in the Upper Midwest, as they testify, showing that great and important new poetry could arise in and even acknowledge an apparently ordinary locale.

CHAPTER 5— A RIVER RUNS THROUGH IT 81
An examination of the settings for the growth of the counterculture in Minneapolis in the 1960s, Dinkytown and the West Bank, where poetry also took root. Bob Dylan, folk music, McCosh's book store, Savran's Paperback shop. Focus on Marv Davidov and Dave Morton's magazine *Region*—the little known but first evidence in Minnesota of the "mimeograph revolution."

**CHAPTER 6—BREAD & ROSES:
MINNESOTA RADICAL/RADICAL MINNESOTA** **99**

Bly got down to the roots, even before the antiwar movement started moving, showing that poetry could supply both bread and roses, that it had a role in artfully taking on political topics and struggles, with the obvious example of Neruda. Also, his support of the Honeywell Project, especially. It was so important for younger, draft-age poets and others to see the impassioned resistance of this Navy veteran. Here I single out poet Jim Dochniak's vision as a secondary development.

**CHAPTER 7—STIRRING THE AIR, SHATTERING
THE GLASS, AND A SUDDEN FEELING: THE LOFT**. **125**

Marly Rusoff's links with Bly (and Neruda) are all-important in this illuminating and sometimes surprising narrative of the origins and early history of this essential, far-reaching, and still vibrant local institution.

CHAPTER 8—INDIGENOUS CULTURE IN THE NORTH COUNTRY. **147**

Minneapolis was a central site for this nationally important cultural revival (including various literary and artistic activities, the formation of the American Indian Movement, and of the U of M's Department of American Indian Studies, the first of its kind). Bly led the way in drawing attention to the grim and violent mistreatment of Native Americans, also by giving a significant boost to a young Native American poet at the beginning of his career.

CHAPTER 9—A NEW CROP OF LITERARY MAGAZINES: TWIN CITIES . . **171**

The bar Bly's own magazine set was high, but still inspiring. Examples considered in detail include: *Plainsong, Nickel & Dime Quarterly, Black Flag, The Lamp in the Spine, the North Stone Review, Moons and Lion Tailes, Lake Street Review, Sing, Heavenly Muse, Preview.*

CHAPTER 10—POETRYAPOLIS: POETRY READINGS TWIN CITIES **197**

The public poetry reading, outside the confines of colleges/universities, was a new phenomenon and another powerful means of building community. Its dramatic local development is traced. Again, Bly led the way.

CHAPTER 11—POETRYAPOLIS: OTHER URBAN GATHERINGS. **221**

Several poet collectives, most importantly the Women Poets of the Twin Cities, gave rise to many poetry readings and other in-person engagements, as did Roy McBride, Etheridge Knight's Free People's Poetry Workshop, the Hungry Mind Bookstore, the Amazon Bookstore, the

Great Midwestern Book Fair, and the Black Market Book Fair. All these contributed mightily to the well-being of our literary ecosystem.

CHAPTER 12—THE CROP OF LIT MAGS: GREATER MINNESOTA 243
Again, strong poetry communities in Moorhead, Duluth, Marshall, and elsewhere around the state, usually with a nod to Bly, produced these and other magazines: *Crazy Horse, Dacotah Territory, Steelhead, North Country Anvil, Lake Superior Journal, Great Circumpolar Bear Cult, Loonfeather, Great River Review*.

CHAPTER 13—BUILDING BRIDGES OUTSTATE: POETRY OUTLOUD . . . 265
An extraordinary and inspiring account of how poetry was brought to small towns across rural Minnesota, especially via Poetry Outloud, an intrepid troupe of young poets. Bly was deeply involved in bridging the urban-rural divide, too. Also, the Bookbus covered the Upper Midwest.

CHAPTER 14—SMALL-SCALE FARMING/A COUNTERPOETICS 287
As the small press revolution was happening throughout the nation, so it happened in Minnesota, where, again, Bly had set the example with his own small Sixties and Seventies press. Another important means of knitting together the poetry community. Noted in detail are Minnesota Writers' Publishing House, Nodin Press, Territorial Press, Knife River Press, Ox Head Press, Prairie Gate Press, Vanilla Press, Red Studio Press, Holy Cow! Press, Ally Press, New Rivers Press, and other smaller ones.

CHAPTER 15—LOOKING AHEAD & SPREADING THE WORD. 319
The impressive and essential work, with Bly in the early forefront, of getting contemporary poetry into schools statewide and making it accessible and meaningful to students. The Poets in the Schools Program, the Urban Arts Program, and the further expansion to other populations via COMPAS (Community Programs in the Arts). At the same time the programs provided jobs for poets, allowing them to pursue their own poetry writing.

POSTSCRIPT— 333
Back to the present with a contemporary poem by Danez Smith.

ACKNOWLEDGMENTS. 337
INDEX. 339
ABOUT THE AUTHOR 351

Sowing Seeds

The Minnesota Literary Renaissance
& Robert Bly, 1958–1980

Mark Gustafson

Minneapolis

Also by Mark Gustafson

The Odin House Harvest: An Analytical Bibliography of Robert Bly's Fifties, Sixties, Seventies, Eighties, Nineties, and Thousands Press

Born Under the Sign of Odin: The Life & Times of Robert Bly's Little Magazine & Small Press

Preface

Once upon a time, Minnesota was not home to a remarkably lively and mutually supportive literary culture. There was no Loft Literary Center, one of the nation's leading such independent literary organizations. The Minnesota Center for Book Arts, the largest and most comprehensive of its kind in the country, had not yet been born. Three of the nation's most renowned non-profit independent literary presses—Milkweed Editions, Coffee House Press and Graywolf Press—did not yet exist here. Nor was there Rain Taxi, including its quarterly *Rain Taxi Review of Books* and the enormously popular annual Twin Cities Book Festival.

But that was in the past. Today, in addition to all the above, several noteworthy small presses, an amazing plenitude of reading series, many independent bookstores, numerous college and university creative writing programs, and countless local and homegrown efforts (publications, collectives, clubs, groups, and other resources) provide enrichment based on the written and spoken word. And they keep on generating more and more words. Indeed, a brief look at the online Twin Cities Literary Calendar gives a sense of the almost overwhelming amplitude of the Minnesota literary ecosystem, packed with events (mostly readings) on nearly every day of the month. The exciting ramifications of this extraordinary confluence of interconnected activity are magnified by the certitude that untold thousands of individual participants have benefited over the years—

writers and readers, teachers and students, mentors and advisees and others on the periphery.

This ecosystem, comprised of so many interconnected organisms, may seem better described as—to use another in vogue botanical term—a rhizome, that is, a sort of enormous plant, manifestations of which pop up out of the ground here and there over an ever-expanding area. Beyond the first impression of many separate plants randomly emerging in the same vicinity, careful investigation of a rhizome shows that in fact they are all interconnected underground, invisibly. The postmodern theorists Deleuze and Guattari proposed: "Any point of a rhizome can be connected to anything other, and must be."[1] That sounds fitting for a diverse, extensive and mutually supportive literary community like ours.

Until one reads further, that is, where the authors also state: "The rhizome is an anti-genealogy."[2] For in this book I am seeking answers to genealogical questions, these and others: How did we get here? How did our exciting and diffuse literary scene come to be what it is? Who was responsible? Why did this literary flourishing happen? And why did it happen when it did? And where it did? Why up here in Minnesota and not elsewhere in the Midwest, in Chicago, Milwaukee, Des Moines, Omaha, St. Louis, Kansas City, Indianapolis, Cleveland or Detroit, for example?

In recent years, the oft-repeated wisdom—in answer to all of these questions—has been that philanthropy in Minnesota (especially on the part of foundations, corporations, and state government) in support of all arts, including the literary, has been primarily responsible for this renaissance. Disputing that view was Don Olsen, a career university librarian, poet and letterpress printer, who had been a student in English at the University of Minnesota in the early 1960s, when that department was a national powerhouse. On the

---

1   Gilles Deleuze and Felix Guattari, *A Thousand Plateaus: Capitalism & Schizophrenia*, tr. Brian Massumi (University of Minnesota Press, 1987), 7.

2   Ibid., 21.

topic of the writing community in Minnesota, he told me, bluntly: "I have a feeling that the grantmonger culture that came about in the 1980s and 90s and now permeates everything tends to think that they started it all. That's bullshit."[3]

Now wait a minute, you might say. But Olsen's dismissive remark should not for a moment be construed to ignore or belittle the importance of the extraordinary growth in philanthropic financial support benefiting the literary and other arts, a boon that started cropping up here in the early to mid-1970s, escalated in the 1980s and continues.[4] It rather serves to ensure that we do not succumb to a common misapprehension, but that we get the history right, the chronology straight, that we accurately establish the line of descent: who begat whom, and what begat what.

As most of the literary organizations listed above formally began or took root here in the 1980s, this book's investigation looks further back, concentrating on the previous two decades, 1958 to 1980. That was the exciting period when Minnesota's largely dormant literary ecosystem was reinvigorated and began to proliferate anew. The thriving in turn elicited the widespread enthusiasm that then led to the materialization of financial support, an essential component of its furtherance ever since. It was the early phase of a mini-renaissance, a rebirth, a revival, and it took place not just in the

---

3   Don Olsen to Mark Gustafson (hereafter MG), 2 September 2000. I should acknowledge this communication as one (long dormant) seed of this book.

4   A fine brief summation of what was happening then in the local book world is Robert Rulon-Miller's introduction to his *Quarter to Midnight: Gaylord Schanilec & Midnight Paper Sales: A Discursive Bibliography* (Rulon-Miller Books, 2011), 1-4. A broad and useful survey of writers and writing in the Upper Midwest at the end of the period 1980-2000 is by Patricia Kirkpatrick, "Where Dakota Drifts Wild in the Universe: Writing in the Northern Territory," *Hungry Mind Review* 52 (Winter 1999-2000), 14-20.

Of course, since 2008, the Arts and Cultural Heritage fund of the Clean Water, Land and Legacy Amendment to the Minnesota Constitution has been an extraordinary benefit to artists and arts organizations.

Twin Cities, but across greater Minnesota and the region. As will become evident, many of the apparently new developments during this period are actually recurrences, intentional returns to past values, outlooks and practices that had fallen away.

Let's be clear. This is *not* to say that there was an omnipotent God-like creator who created the vibrant Minnesota literary scene in seven days (or some metaphorical equivalent thereof). No, taking the scientific view, the real genesis story is a long period of development, of evolution, of natural processes at work. But those processes were indisputably kickstarted by one forward-thinking poet, who had not a precise vision but an intuition of what might result, of future promise. He only knew that it was the right thing to do, what he was driven to do.

Poetry, despite its undeserved reputation in some quarters as a select or even hermetic art form, does not exist in a vacuum. And, as will become clear, the flowering of this early poetic community in Minnesota coincided with other noteworthy tangential flowerings here—in theater, music, film, radio, socio-political movements, alternative commerce and much more. They all had value and broad impact.

This was a time when "things were…casual, improvisational, free-spirited and ripe with possibilities."[5] It was also a time of awakening, of profound social, political and cultural transformation. The foundation was being laid, or—better—the fields were being prepared to provide a rich yield. Soon the seeds of change were beginning to push upward. Once that work was done, and the philanthropy opportunely fell into place, we attained a sound level of sustainability and abundance that persists to this day.

---

5   Mary Abbe, *Minneapolis StarTribune,* December 9, 2010.

Chapter 1
Introduction: Generativity & Generosity

> What sower walked over earth,
> which hands sowed
> our inward seeds of fire?
> They went out from his fists like rainbow curves
> to frozen earth, young loam, hot sand,
> they will sleep there
> greedily, and drink up our lives
> and explode it into pieces
> for the sake of a sunflower that you haven't seen
> or a thistle head or a chrysanthemum…[1]
> 				–Rolf Jacobsen

In 1958, a young poet from western Minnesota started sowing seeds. He was a poet on the side of the future. His name, Robert Bly, was then virtually unknown.

First, imagine this: At a public poetry reading by Bly in his 1960s and '70s heyday, reciting his own poetry and/or his translations of another's, a witness could not help but notice the incessant movement of Bly's hands—whirling, swirling, not chaotically, but in a sort of counterpoint. They looked like a farmer's hands, "large,

---

[1] "Sunflower," tr. Robert Bly, *Twenty Poems of Rolf Jacobsen* (The Seventies Press, 1977), 21.

veined, capable."² Beyond distracting, one might see it as mere gesticulation, reflex action, habitual body language or even a kind of beckoning. Better yet, call it poetry in motion.

Photo © Gerard Malanga

Still more apt is to see in those characteristic movements the practiced gestures of the sower as he traverses the ground, flinging seeds left and right, up and down, forward and backward, around and around. Bly was a sower sowing words. It sounds positively biblical, parabolic.³ Neither haphazard nor accidental, the seeds are sown, for the most part, in good soil, cleared of rocks and thorns,

---

2   From his poem, "My Father at 85," *Common Ground: A Gathering of Poets from the 1986 Marshall Festival* eds. Mark Vinz and Thom Tammaro (Dacotah Territory Press, 1988), 12-13.

3   I allude to the parable of the sower found in the synoptic gospels (*Matthew* 13.1-23, *Mark* 4.1-20, *Luke* 8.1-15) and in the extra-canonical *Gospel of Thomas* 9. I hasten to add that this is definitely *not* to imply that Bly was Christ-like (!).

loosened and plowed. The sower demonstrates strength, talent, dedication and persistence. Many of the seeds—each one a life-giving miracle—with the requisite rain and sun, will take root and eventually blossom and bear fruit, manifesting in other poets and their poetry, leaving them to repeat the process in turn. Thus, culture is created and sustained. One grateful beneficiary, focusing on the end result, the reaping, dedicates his own book to Bly, "sower of poets."[4]

At the root of the freely used word "culture" is a verb that means, variously, to till, inhabit or worship.[5] As Paul Gruchow, also from western Minnesota, writes: "The idea of culture encompasses not only the arts and inventions of a people, but also the place within which they dwell, all that they strive after, and everything that they find worthy."[6] Bly was engaged in a struggle to bring about positive change in culture, which is always improvable. He was not only focused metaphorically on the growth of the soil, but also on the growth of the soul. And he was zealous about it. A fitting term for Bly's particular work is "poeticulture." Integrating all three root meanings, it involves the cultivating of poets and poetics, being profoundly devoted to poetry, dwelling in its house and feeling at home there.

By the late 1950s, Bly the sower had been gathering seeds and storing them in his own seedbank for a decade, first at Harvard College, next while living the garret life as an autodidact in New York (reading Chinese poetry, the Bible, the Greek Tragedies, Pindar, Horace, Virgil, Dante, Shakespeare, Boehme, Milton, Blake, Wordsworth, Native American history, Whitman, Yeats, Rilke, Eliot, Pound, Lorca, and much else), and then at the Iowa Writers' Work-

---

4   *The Aeneid of Virgil*, tr. Edward McCrorie (Donald M. Grant, 1991), is formally dedicated to Bly with these words in Latin, "*sator vatum*." McCrorie adds in a personal inscription, "You had so much to do with its genesis."

5   Latin, of course: *colo, colere, colui, cultum*. The tilling of a field is primary and explicit in "agriculture" (something Bly knew more than a little about).

6   Paul Gruchow, *Grass Roots: The Universe of Home* (Milkweed Editions, 1995), 47.

shop.⁷ Last, and most decisively, on a 1956-57 Fulbright scholarship in Oslo he happened upon the poetry of Pablo Neruda, Juan Ramón Jiménez, César Vallejo, Antonio Machado, Georg Trakl, Gottfried Benn, Gunnar Ekelöf, René Char and others; exotic plants really, at the time, to North American poets.⁸ That bit of Norwegian serendipity was epoch-making. Its impact on American and Minnesotan poetry would be profound.

Even more surprisingly, in 1957 he returned home for good—that is, to a dilapidated house belonging to an old farm spread that his father had recently bought, adjacent to the farm and the farmhouse where Bly himself grew up—and settled in with his wife, Carol. This was, maybe needless to say, unusual, for he was not a commonplace statistic of the postwar years, part of a process, still accelerating, which had begun soon after the Industrial Revolution, the abandonment of rural areas and small towns by young people of promise. The career opportunities (not to mention the general allure and excitement, and the presence of people of like minds) were in the cities. This applied to aspiring artists as well as anyone else.⁹

For whatever reason, Bly didn't experience the kind of alienation or deracination that led to flight. He was still rooted in Madison, Minnesota (twelve miles from South Dakota). He was, as Wendell Berry would say, a "sticker," one of the "placed people… forever attached to the look of the sky, the smell of native plants, and the vernacular of home."¹⁰ From a heroic perspective, this was his *nostos*, like Odysseus' return to Ithaca, going back to his roots, his landscape, his way of life, his kinship, his heritage, his history, his

---

7   This reading list I have culled from examination of Bly's personal journals and correspondence from the time.

8   For a fuller biographical account of these ten years, see my *Born Under the Sign of Odin: The Life & Times of Robert Bly's Little Magazine & Small Press* (Nodin Press, 2021), 25-40.

9   See Chapter 5 for a good Minnesotan case in point, Bob Dylan.

10   Dorothy Wickenden, "Late Harvest," *The New Yorker* (February 28, 2022), 37.

identity. All of it fraught, naturally. Soon after his homecoming, he was ready to shoulder his seed bag and begin spreading the word(s).

* * *

"Bob will never be a farmer," Carrie (Nelson) Bly had declared to her son Jacob two decades earlier, talking about her younger grandson, Robert. Born in 1926, to children of Norwegian immigrants, he was raised on a wheat and corn farm just outside of town. Carrie, living with Jacob and Alice and their boys after the death of her husband Olai, had a grandmother's keen sense. She was not oblivious to all those times in the summer when Robert, pleading an ailment, told his dad he was not feeling up to doing chores, and then spent the day happily reading in bed. She knew how, during the rest of the year, he excelled in his country school, the one-room schoolhouse that he and his older brother Jim attended.

She saw other signs of young Bly's precocity, including the time in 1937 he entered and won the local 4-H contest for raising lambs—until it was discovered that, at ten, he was two years below the requisite age. As a member of the 4-H Club, an after-school activity with an agricultural emphasis, he had taken this pledge:

> I pledge my Head to clearer thinking
> my Heart to greater loyalty,
> my Hands to larger service,
> and my Health to better living,
> for my club, my community, and my country.

Something tells me he did this with some seriousness, which did not, obviously, extend to bothering with contest entry rules.

Later, as a high school-age member of the Future Farmers of America, another recently-formed organization, he raised his own chickens and sheep, often showing at the Lac qui Parle County

Fair, the Junior Livestock Show in South St. Paul, and even the big one—the Minnesota State Fair. The FFA Creed, adopted during the Great Depression, begins: "I believe in the future of farming, with a faith born not of words but of deeds—achievements won by the present and past generations of farmers; in the promise of better days through better ways, even as the better things we now enjoy have come up to us from the struggles of former years."

Again, in retrospect this seems to have some meaning for Bly's life, for his bountiful, inspirational, challenging, and visionary work, if modified slightly to allow for his altogether unconventional sort of farming and for a faith born of deeds *and* words. After he returned to live in Madison as an adult, he was, consciously or not, adhering to the last part of the creed: "I believe that rural America can and will hold true to the best traditions in our national life and that I can exert an influence in my home and community which will stand solid for my part in that inspiring task."

When Bly started sowing in 1958, he was doing something radical. It was an experiment, but it also was an intervention, a proactive exercise in hope. He took the long view. He was, on his own, bringing new wildness to a poetic landscape that had become depleted, impoverished. American poetry at the time was like a manicured lawn (in a town or city) or tidy rows of cultivated and fenced fields (in the country), where neatness and order were of paramount importance—consider its formalism, its iambic pentameter, caesuras and end rhymes, its tame, fully domesticated approach, its often cool, rational indifference to deep emotion and to the issues of the day, and, in Minnesota, its occasional detachment from the characteristic landscape and real setting of the Upper Midwest.

Bly was not intent on actual, methodical farming, on working the land that had long been terraformed, even by his own ancestors.[11] He sensed that "a neat, orderly landscape seldom enhances

---

11   I use this word not in the science-fictional sense about interplanetary travel, but as Amitav Ghosh does, in *The Nutmeg's Curse: Parables for a Planet*

the ecological function of the landscape."[12] Rather, he was all for prairie restoration. His sowing was a process of wilding, avidly and purposefully introducing new varieties of flowering plants and grasses, both exotic and native.[13] The internationalizing emphasis of poetry from non-anglophone traditions was especially conspicuous in this regard. By means of such borrowing, culture is renewed. Gruchow says:

> There are thousands of species of living things on the prairie, but few of them are natives. The prairie has welcomed strangers of every kind and borrowed ideas from all of its neighboring communities. In doing so, it has discovered how to flourish in a harsh place. The prairie teaches us to see the virtue of ideas not our own and the possibilities that newcomers bring.[14]

Bly was doing this via not only the energy of new translations of world poetry, but also the verve of his critical essays, the provocations of his ideas and suggestions with their source in Jungian psychology, and his own poems and those of others, first as they appeared in his iconoclastic and lionhearted little magazine, *The Fifties, The Sixties and The Seventies*.[15] Following and alongside were

---

in Crisis (University of Chicago Press, 2022), 49 ff., as the substantial alteration of landscapes and ecosystems in North America by Western colonial forces, thereby obliterating almost an entire race and their way of life.

12   Joan Iverson Nassauer, "Messy Ecosystems, Orderly Frames," *Landscape Journal* 14.2 (Fall 1995), 162.

13   See, e.g., Isabella Tree, *Wilding: Returning Nature to our Farm* (New York Review Books, 2019), though my own metaphorical use of this idea involves only flora, not fauna.

14   Gruchow, 79.

15   In *The Fifties* 1, to start with, were translations of the Swedish poet Gunnar Ekelöf, the Danish poet Tom Kristensen, the Belgian-French poet Henri Michaux, plus the critical essay, "Five Decades of American Poetry," which calls for a revolution, internationalism, a new imagination as in the poetry of Neruda, Lorca, Vallejo, Ekelöf, Char, Michaux, Trakl, and Benn, "all of them writing in what we have called, for want of a better word, the new imagination, and mak-

the publications from his Sixties and Seventies Press, and then his own poetry books, *Silence in the Snowy Fields* (1962), *The Light Around the Body* (1967), and *Sleepers Joining Hands* (1973). The new varieties of seeds therein included aspects of the unconscious, the deep/associative image, surrealism, the irrational, politics and a refreshing subjectivity. Bringing to the fore what he called a "new poetry" and a "new imagination" was a radical holistic effort, creating a new habitat, getting down to the root, and thereby repairing the damage done. He was taking a chance, spearheading a new literary movement, seeing what would take hold. But it was a calculated risk, based on a fervent belief. And a marginal undertaking, at least at the outset. As it turned out, his enthusiasm was contagious.

In remaining true to himself and his rural background, Bly the homecomer was a precursor, giving a foretaste of the so-called back-to-the-land movement of the latter 1960s, where place, politics and (in his case) poetry fit into what amounted to a new kind of culture.[16] In encouraging other poets to reconnect with the land, giving them a sense of belonging, the soil was being restored. Never afraid to get his hands dirty, Bly set an example for others. The results would be not only new life, but new liveliness and openness.

Altogether, this transformation was an affront to the status quo. Predictably, some members of the literary establishment thought his efforts quixotic and wrong-headed (see Chapter 3). The new biodiversity and heterogeneity seemed unkempt to those who valued tradition and traditionalism (i.e., the delusion of maintaining "same-as-it-ever-was"). They interpreted the naturalness, including the use of

---

ing contributions to that imagination as enormous as Eliot's or Pound's and with a totally different impact, and on totally different roads." Also, poems by Snyder, Snodgrass, Donald Hall, and Bly himself (with a pseudonym). Plus much more. Seeds were flying out in all directions. See *Born Under, passim*, for all these and more details.

16   As will become clear later, much of the innovation of this turbulent period was actually a throwback to valuable practices of the past, long since discarded or ignored.

a Midwest vernacular (everyday spoken language), as disagreeable wildness, leading to a regressive kind of wilderness. Bly was confronting the sort of opposition that visionaries and prophets usually do, and that signaled success. It was a fight he had asked for.

Bly ultimately changed perceptions, so that the new poetry was seen in a new way. Thus, he and his movement routed their opponents and prevailed over NIMBYism (those who objected with "not in my back yard"), successfully establishing a new literary permaculture; that is, a diverse, sustainable, long-lasting, self-sufficient and resilient ecology modeled on nature, forming the basis for the lively abundance of today (and the last half century).[17] In this way the literary renaissance in Minnesota began.

* * *

To fill in the broader historical background; this was a critical moment in American history. The cataclysm of World War II (1939-45), with its extensive and unprecedented toll of death and devastation, was succeeded by a decades-long Cold War. As Louis Menand writes:

> In 1945 there was widespread skepticism, even among Americans, about the value and sophistication of American art and ideas, and widespread respect for the motives and intentions of the American government. After 1965, those attitudes were reversed. The United States lost political credibility, but it had moved from the periphery to the center of an increasing international artistic and creative life.[18]

The rate of cultural change, specifically of innovation in art and thought, was exceptionally rapid. Soon, "Ideas mattered. Paint-

---

17   This portmanteau word was coined by Bill Mollison and David Holmgren in *Permaculture One: A Perennial Agriculture for Human Settlements* (Transworld Publishers, 1978).

18   Louis Menand, *The Free World: Art and Thought in the Cold War* (Farrar, Straus and Giroux, 2021), xiii.

ing mattered. Movies mattered. Poetry mattered. The way people judged and interpreted paintings, movies, and poems mattered."[19] As will become clear, this was not only the case in the nation's cultural capital, New York City, but also out in the boondocks of the Upper Midwest, in Minnesota. Something was happening here, too, all prelude to our present literary flourishing.

Across the country, after a decade marked (at least in retrospect) by stifling conformity and consumerism, the 1960s (into the early 1970s) was a time of great social and political turmoil, giving rise to a new counterculture in reaction to the stale, outmoded culture of an earlier generation. Political activism replaced political indifference. Early baby boomers were reaching adulthood, and a social revolution was underway, with the clear emergence of identity politics (positively construed). The decade saw: long overdue attention to Civil Rights; the war in Vietnam and growing opposition to it; assassinations; the Black Power movement; the Red Power movement; the Women's Liberation movement; the Gay Liberation movement; environmentalism; the sexual revolution; drug culture/psychedelia; and rock & roll music.

Many young people were tuning in, turning on and dropping out, feeling alienated from the mainstream values and materialism of American life and looking for something better. Restlessness and discontent, idealism and churn, unpredictability. The possibilities of change seemed limitless, as though the world could be remade. Communes, collectives and cooperatives, with their built-in antagonism to hierarchy, once again became commonplace. It was a fascinating if also unsettling time to be alive, and an exciting time to come of age (certainly for some of us).

Great innovation and experimentation came about in the arts, not least in the literary arts. American poetry broke out of its cus-

---

19 Ibid., xii.

tomary insularity to become oral, public, and (from some points of view) shockingly relevant. It was, as Jerome Rothenberg has called it, "the second great awakening of twentieth century poetry."[20] The effects of all this upheaval were also felt in Minnesota, including in the poetic community. Again, in 1958 a young poet from western Minnesota, one remarkably in tune with the big picture, started sowing seeds.

* * *

That sowing was an act of generativity—a term coined by the psychoanalyst Erik Erikson, meaning "a concern for establishing and guiding the next generation."[21] It was future-oriented by definition. But the sowing was also a gift, an act of generosity. Indeed, every seed is a gift that gives life. In his momentous book, *The Gift,* Lewis Hyde lays out the nature of the gift economy, which has much to do with what this book is about.[22] Bly's initial and continued sowing of seeds, a real sort of gift-giving, still—these many years later and after his death—lives in the gifts we in Minnesota share in our literary community, as they move from one person and one generation to the next.

Hyde makes clear that gift-giving establishes an obvious relationship between two parties, the giver and the receiver. As gifts circulate within a group, "their commerce leaves a series of interconnected relationships in its wake, and a kind of decentralized cohesiveness emerges." Most importantly, he says: "The only essential is this: *the gift must always move.*" A connection is made, and the

---

20   "Pre-Face," in Steven Clay and Rodney Phillips, eds., *A Secret History of the Lower East Side: Adventures in Writing, 1960-1980* (The New York Public Library and Granary Books, 1998), 10.

21   Erik H. Erikson, *Childhood and Society* (W.W. Norton & Co., 1950), 266.

22   *The Gift: Imagination and the Erotic Life of Property* (Random House, 1983), the source of the quotations in this and the following three paragraphs. Hyde, not so incidentally, is also a poet and, as a translator, worked closely with Bly. He figures repeatedly in this book.

result is an exchange of energy. "When you give a gift there is momentum, and the weight shifts from body to body."

Gifts also deliver increase. "The increase is the core of the gift, the kernel." That is, exactly like a seed. "When we have fed the gift with our labor and generosity, it grows and feeds us in return. The gift and its bearers share a spirit which is kept alive by its motion among them, and which in turn keeps them both alive."

Apropos the topic of this book, "The spirit of an artist's gifts can wake our own," Hyde says. The gifts of poetry and literature have the power to change lives, as will be evident again and again throughout this book, the power to serve as agents of metamorphosis. "A lively culture will have transformative gifts as a general feature…." Clearly, Bly set out to transform American poetry and, by so doing, to bring poets into a self-sustaining community. That was a matter of looking ahead.[23]

More specifically, Hyde says: "Robert was a very generous person, generous with his time, generous with advice, generous with his books."[24] In 1969, at his public readings Bly routinely handed out to the audience his small self-published booklet of ten tiny poems by the Japanese poet, Issa. Inside the cover are these words: "This booklet is a gift and is not to be sold." Hyde, a recipient, says: "I sometimes wonder if this sentence from this pamphlet wasn't a

---

23 Bly acknowledges as a gift his own fortuitous encounter with many non-English-language poets in the book *Modernistisk Lyrikk fra 8 Land*, (J.W. Cappelens [Oslo], 1955), edited by Paal Brekke, a poet he met in Norway. Years ago, Bly inscribed a copy of that book for me, as follows: "This passion for the writers of 'other lands' is the passion I didn't find in Archibald MacLeish's otherwise valuable class at Harvard. This book is the father and the mother of The Fifties and The Sixties. 'The room was suddenly rich' [quoting Louis MacNeice's poem, "Snow"]. *It was a gift I keep trying to pass on.* [italics = my emphasis]"

24 MG interview with LH, 13 October 2019. Bly's generosity is legendary, as conveyed in personal accounts by too many poets to name.

seed for [my book, *The Gift*]."²⁵ In spreading his versions of Issa's haikus, Bly intended to seed new poems, but sometimes the result of sowing is unpredictable and felicitous.

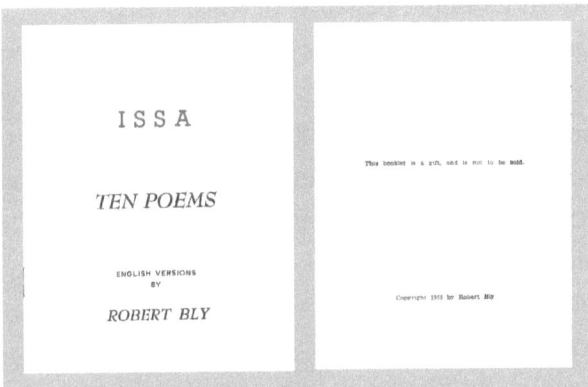

Bly was giving gifts all across the United States, but he was not preoccupied with the nationwide effort and effects. When in Minnesota he, conscious of his connectedness, gave home his full attention, manifesting his "unprecedented generosity toward other, especially younger and unknown, writers."²⁶ It wasn't just the scattering of seeds, it was also his subsequent nurturing and guidance, helping the seedlings and their caretakers to thrive. The surviving plants would then reseed, year after year. And so on. For he was just the first (in this telling) in a long line of sowers and gift-givers.

Poet and memoirist Patricia Hampl recalls, noting that this was before any MFA programs or writing workshops in the area: "It became known...that if you sent a batch of your poems to Robert Bly, he would reply. And he did—thoughtfully, promptly, generously—and with a fiercely honorable candor that alone can extend true respect to a beginning writer. A response like that can keep a young

---

25   Lewis Hyde, "Lessons from Bly's Barn," in *Robert Bly in this World,* ed. Thomas R. Smith with James P. Lenfestey (University of Minnesota Press, 2011), 29.

26   Patricia Hampl, "Midwestern Sublime," in *Robert Bly: 2000 Distinguished Artist* (The McKnight Foundation, 2000), 9.

writer going. There are many of us who will never forget that generosity and the bracing experience of editorial honesty." She then takes the long view: "It may be what's best about the literary life here. That spirit certainly began with Robert Bly."

The instilling of confidence was a gift with abiding momentum. His largesse in encouraging and promoting the work of other poets is a foundational basis for the perpetuation of this ecosystem, making it long-lasting and regenerative. He wanted to create a resilient community reinforced with ongoing mutual support, and with a strong relationship to place.[27] He would sow generously, so as also to reap generously.[28]

As Hampl's remark shows, he was always aiming for young poets especially, for they were the future. To reiterate: Bly first broke ground with his polemics and provocations, prepared the soil with his new ideas, and planted those assorted seeds. Their nutrients filled the heads and expanded the minds of young poets. As Gruchow writes: "in planting we stretch one of the long threads of our culture into tomorrow."[29] More than a sower and encourager, Bly was also a cultivator, a generator, a carrier of life, who equipped, mobilized and motivated young poets to cultivate their own authority. He relied on and expected them to further the effort of revitalization, taking American poetry forward, to keep it healthy and true. They would in turn give rise to more ecological variety, an ideal situation for the growth of the next generation, the aim of which was that all might live healthily and in harmony—a community on the prairie.

Bly continued to be present, available and crucial during these two decades. And he was anything but static—he was continual-

---

27   The literary scene in Minnesota was not what one would call healthy or flourishing. See Robert Hedin, ed., *Where One Voice Ends Another Begins: 150 Years of Minnesota Poetry* (Minnesota Historical Society Press, 2007), especially his fine introduction.

28   Cf. 2 *Corinthians* 9.6.

29   Gruchow, 3.

ly evolving as a poet on his own, innovating, moving more deeply wherever his curiosity and his uncanny sense of salience took him. As his reputation and sway across the nation grew over the years, that personal gain was a public asset for the good of poets in Minnesota, literary culture-makers themselves. He continued to devote huge amounts of time, energy and imagination to learning, sowing, encouraging, generating and advocating. He was looking far into tomorrow, generations ahead, to posterity, to us and beyond.

Hugely influential he was, nationally and on the Minnesota scene. That much is undeniable. He was a true original, a unitary phenomenon, and a transitional figure, "a hinge, someone who represents a moment when one mode of practice swings over to another."[30] That is to say, after Bly, American (not just Minnesotan) poets wrote differently. There is no end to personal testimonials. A few of them follow.

As poet David Wojahn says: "It's hard to overstate his influence. And…that influence was multi-faceted." It came from his poetry (both the introspective Minnesota poems, and the socially conscious ones) and his translations, especially of Spanish language poets. There was also "his theorizing about literature, which always seemed to evolve into theorizing about larger public and psychological matters…. His role was analogous to Pound's in the 'teens and 'twenties." Wojahn concludes: "Sometimes this could seem a little overbearing…. But his energy was pretty amazing."[31]

Another young poet of the Midwest who was energized by Bly's magazine and press, Jim Harrison, says: "Bly pumped an enormous amount of oxygen into the heart of Midwest literature. At least on a regional basis Bly was as seminal as Ezra Pound was in the '20s, and along with his domestic introductions he vigorously introduced so many Spanish poets, from Hernandez to Vallejo, whose nocturnal

---

30   Menand, 125.
31   DW email to.MG, 19 July 2020.

melancholy seemed appropriate to the northern Midwest setting."[32] Hampl says: "We were all hungry for translated work that Robert's publications provided."[33] And Hyde adds: "he was a bit of an agent for world literature."[34]

Another poet (and an early teacher of Wojahn's—see Chapter 7) all over the Twin Cities scene in those days, Jim Moore, says about Bly's role:

> If there was one person who was the most important in that milieu and that time creating a sense of community it was certainly Robert. Especially for young men—but for young women too. He became a kind of a father figure for a lot of us, a sort of literary father that was inspiring and brilliant, and passionate about poetry, kind of outrageous in certain ways… which in the '60s seemed pretty wonderful. So, he was absolutely central.[35]

His influence was everywhere—in the air the poets breathed, in the water they drank, in the soil they were planted in and from which they got their sustenance. They couldn't escape it if they tried.

Through his energy, humor and intensity, Bly inculcated a strong sense of artistic comradeship, of fidelity to the principal of poetry. Cary Waterman says: "Robert's poetry was extraordinarily important to us, to me as a poet and as a human."[36] Which is not to say everyone agreed with him, or even acknowledged his influence. Of course, he was not universally loved, nor were all his interactions with younger poets frictionless (as Hampl's earlier comments hint at) or disinterested. On the drive toward community there were, in-

---

32 Jim Harrison, "A Note on Tom Hennen," introduction to Tom Hennen, *Darkness Sticks to Everything: Collected & New Poems* (Copper Canyon Press, 2013), xvii.
33 PH to MG, 19 February 2020.
34 MG interview with LH, 13 October 2019.
35 MG interview with JM, 7 January 2020.
36 CW email to MG, 26 April 2023.

evitably, bumps—difficulties, irritations and bruised feelings. Such is the cost of progress.

Bly was a figure who represented the crossroads where the mostly rural America of the Upper Midwest and the cosmopolitanism of ideas and poetry intersected. His wilding efforts show his fundamental advocacy of biodiversity, his antagonism to homogeneity in poetry, to monoculture. These exotic seeds were also, in part, a link to the past representing hope for the future. Once domesticated, they would improve nutrition, increase the yield and provide long-lasting nourishment. Gruchow again: "The prairie grows richer as it ages ... The prairie teaches us how to be competitive without being destructive."[37]

Bly did not have a direct hand in everything. An ecosystem, after all, is an organic whole, so everything that happens or appears does so for more than one reason. Although he is here identified as the essential catalyst at the beginning of a long process, ultimately, he was part of a dense cooperative tangle, the "decentralized cohesiveness" that Hyde mentioned above, an interdependent system that he had a hand in creating. The resulting culture is necessarily synergistic. The poets involved do not act merely as individuals, but as a collective, knowing that, as Robin Wall Kimmerer emphasizes, "all flourishing is mutual."[38] They become part of a "web of reciprocity."[39] That involves mutual giving and taking, the sharing and borrowing of ideas, expressions and poems, partaking in the bounty. Minnesota's literary renaissance was ultimately community driven.

The community also becomes self-supporting and self-sustaining, when the individuals involved are not in it for themselves but are rather focused on their shared experience and on the common

---

37   Gruchow, 79.
38   Robin Law Kimmerer, *Braiding Sweetgrass: Indigenous Wisdom, Scientific Knowledge and the Teachings of Plants* (Milkweed Editions, 2015), 15.
39   Ibid., 20.

good. All this symbiosis will become clear later on. "The prairie is a community. It is not just the landscape or the name of an area on the map, but a dynamic alliance of living plants, animals, birds, insects, reptiles and microorganisms all depending on each other. ... The prairie teaches us that our strength is in our neighbors."[40]

This is a book of literary history. It may appear a hybrid, as focus seems to shift back and forth between Bly and others on the Minnesota scene. I mean thereby to show that, in this time period, they are closely related, inextricably intertwined.

All the Chapters examine the various stages and areas of dissemination and the processes of community building, most of which owe something to Bly: the character (literary and otherwise) of the state of Minnesota, and the nature of regionalism; the first germination of Bly's sowing and early resistance to his efforts; the two fundamental books that defined for young poets the "new poetry" that could be homegrown in Minnesota; the settings for the growth of the creative counterculture in Minneapolis; the newly central role of poetry in social/political movements and protest; the countercultural genesis and early growth of the Loft Literary Center; the role of Indigenous culture as manifested locally, in literature and otherwise; the birth and the run of many literary magazines—that came in a torrent—not only in the Twin Cities but also in greater Minnesota and bordering states; the gradual proliferation of public poetry readings and reading programs in Minnesota, both urban and rural, as well as the organizations that gave rise to them; the small press movement as it gained momentum locally; the vital effort to further poetry education among high schoolers and other parts of the populace, while also benefiting young poets themselves, allowing them to continue with their important art.

The subject matter of this book cannot be neatly rolled out in chronological sequence, though each individual Chapter tries

---

40 Gruchow, 78.

to do that, at least roughly. The larger telling is an intentionally discursive omnium-gatherum, noting the ramifying and biodiversity through a profusion of publications, poetry communities, collectives, cooperatives and other organizations and happenings, including the role of bookstores and bookfairs, and the recurring names of the many participants in the larger story.[41] Other mutually beneficial contemporary developments in the arts in Minnesota are noted piecemeal. The overall structure is also recursive, with much inevitable overlap, often returning to the same starting point in 1958. Yet the variegated Chapters are at the same time braided together by anticipation for the next stage, the developments to come after 1980. Glimmers of the future come into view throughout this book.

As we know, all is in flux, nothing stays the same for long. While the wider culture developed in this time frame, so also did literary culture evolve. At first it seems that all those involved were white, cisgender, heterosexual males, but changes soon become apparent. We can observe positive developments on the Minnesota scene in the direction of greater inclusivity, first in the way that women poets organized, and procured for themselves more representation in poetry reading series, in the little magazines and in the small presses. Poetry writing was also being stimulated among a wider range of underrepresented voices—young and old, free and incarcerated, disabled and neurodivergent—than ever before. The inclusion of black poets was happening, slowly but surely. So too with Native Americans and with Latino, Vietnamese, Hmong and East African immigrants. Gradually, BIPOC and LGBTQIA+ poets would be heard and become more visible. Many of the latter developments fall outside this book's time frame, but the winds of change were definite-

---

41 The number of poets' names may seem excessive, even overwhelming, but I feel it part of my mission and responsibility to give every identifiable participant in this renaissance their due attention.

ly beginning to blow, and all for the common good. "Diversity makes the prairie resilient."[42]

The scene today is evidence of the persistent and exponential regeneration of seeds sown a long time ago, evidence of Bly's long-range vision. That much is history, and should not be forgotten; these are not mere relics of a bygone era, but they still function, they live, they teem with endless potential. Despite the fact that he was—by virtue of his gender, sexual orientation, color, ethnicity, religion and education—undeniably a member of the Euro-patriarchal power elite, he was also a disrupter and an agitator. Making a clearing and breaking up the hardened ground of normativity in order to sow seeds and blow past the arbitrarily imposed standards, his work was "a great gift of creative disruption and moral challenge."[43]

He led the way, made it possible to be bold and resistant, to speak out and write courageously. He helped to create an environment where others could thrive. And he was relentless in his efforts, a consequential cultural influencer. While Bly's generosity and generativity were plain to see at the moment, their more significant results have been magnified and have further revealed themselves with the passing of time.

It is not going too far to say that poets in Minnesota today are his heirs across the generations, unwittingly or not. Or that all the participants in the literary scene here and now are indebted and linked creatively to him. He is an ancestor. He was large and complicated. As Whitman says in the last lines of "Song of Myself":

> I bequeath myself to the dirt to grow from the grass I love,
> If you want me again look for me under your boot-soles.

---

42   Gruchow, 77.
43   Gregory Orr email to MG, 29 August 2021.

> You will hardly know who I am or what I mean,
> But I shall be good health to you nevertheless,
> And filter and fibre your blood.
>
> Failing to fetch me at first keep encouraged,
> Missing me one place search another,
> I stop somewhere waiting for you.

There we can find Bly, too. His footprints, signs of his legacy, are all over the place—it would be mendacious to leave them unacknowledged. As a cultural history of an era from a regional standpoint, long ago and not so far away, this book is that acknowledgment and a sort of homage. At the same time, it is hoped that it may serve as a manual of sorts—containing implicit instructions, how-to steps and accounts of exemplary efforts—to empower young poets and writers today and remind them of their responsibility, pointing out the possibilities as they blaze their way into the unknown literary future.

Chapter 2
Sweet Home, Minnesota

> It is good to feel at home. That's what makes me so hopeful about the future—feeling at home.[1]
> –Robert Bly

In 1923, Sinclair Lewis declared that, to the average easterner, "Minnesota is unplaced."[2] That is to say, there seemed little there to merit notice from an outsider. (One might be reminded of Gertrude Stein's oft-quoted and withering remark about her home in Oakland, California: "There's no there there.") To what then did Bly return when he came home from Norway in 1957, after more than a decade mostly away?[3]

By midcentury, for those in the know, Minnesota had a well-earned reputation for its progressive tradition, its history of agrarian populism and grassroots activism, cooperatives, and radical politics (notably the Farmer-Labor Movement of the '20s and '30s,

---

1   Reading in Tucson at the University of Arizona, November 30, 1966: voca.arizona.edu/readings-list/259

2   "Minnesota, the Norse State," in *The Minnesota Stories of Sinclair Lewis,* ed. Sally E. Perry (Minnesota Historical Society Press, 2005), 6 (originally in *The Nation* [May 30, 1923]).

3   At Harvard, in New York, Iowa City, and Oslo. See *Born Under*, 25-40.

and the strong leadership of governors Floyd B. Olson and Elmer Benson, both of the Farmer-Labor Party). In the land of 10,000 (actually 14,380) lakes and of the source of the mighty Mississippi River, roughly evenly divided between prairie (by now mostly given over to farming) and forest (now heavily logged and mined), the populace was predominantly white, the young state having been "settled" by Scandinavian and German immigrants in the latter nineteenth century. Those settlers had forcibly seized the land of and displaced the original Indigenous (Dakota and Anishinaabe) inhabitants who were now scattered in communities and on reservations spread across Minnesota, South and North Dakota or concentrated in an impoverished neighborhood of Minneapolis. This was the original sin of racism in Minnesota. The Twin Cities were also host to the odious practice of racial covenants and redlining that barred people of color from buying homes in certain neighborhoods. And that is not to mention the virulent antisemitism of the 1930s and 40s, especially.

Much more could be said. But, literarily speaking, when Bly began to establish himself on this scene, it is fair to say that Minnesota appeared to have a mixed and minor tradition of self-imposed "exiles"; that is, writers who had left the state voluntarily for different parts of the same nation.[4] The first American to win the Nobel Prize in Literature, Sinclair Lewis, was born in Sauk Centre, in central Minnesota, in 1885, and at age seventeen departed for Oberlin and then Yale. Lewis' most famous novel, *Main Street,* indelibly satirized the smug and stifling small town life of his childhood (in the fictional Gopher Prairie), which belied his actual affection for his hometown and his home state.[5] That is to say, although he re-

---

4   The term "expatriate" connotes self-removal from one's nation and voluntary relocation elsewhere, but not from one's state or region. "Emigrant" is similar in that respect.

5   "Sinclair Lewis: 100 Years of *Main Street,*" the 2021 commemorative exhibition at the Minnesota Historical Society, wonderfully curated by Pat

turned to Minnesota often, the general impression his wandering, his writing and career gave was quite otherwise.

F. Scott Fitzgerald was born in 1896 in St. Paul. He left and returned a number of times before leaving permanently. Not at all a satirist, he was gentler than Lewis in looking back, as when he invokes "the wheat," "the prairies," and "the lost Swede towns" of Minnesota in *The Great Gatsby*. But both writers needed to go and stay elsewhere to feed their muse and make their mark.

Poet Richard Eberhart (Consultant in Poetry to the Library of Congress, 1959-61) was born in Austin in 1904. "When I was young," Eberhart says, "Minnesota was barren of cultural richness and I doubt that I would have matured or progressed as a poet if I had stayed there. There was no nourishment of the soul, the spirit or the mind."[6] After a short time at the University of Minnesota, he left for Dartmouth in 1922.

There were important exceptions to this apparent pattern of untapped potential, of lack of connectedness and commitment to home. The prolific novelist Frederick Manfred for one, who, born in northwestern Iowa in 1912, spent most of his life in Minnesota. The region where the borders of Minnesota, South Dakota, Iowa, and Nebraska meet he dubbed "Siouxland," which long served as the "kingdom of his imagination."[7]

Also, the great poet Thomas McGrath, born in 1916, was raised on a farm in Sheldon, North Dakota, when the Nonpartisan League and the Industrial Workers of the World (Wobblies) were active in the area. Their outlook formed the rock-solid foundation of his political consciousness and his focus on workers. After military service in World War II, and a Rhodes Scholarship, during the 1950s he was

---

Coleman, made amply clear that Lewis did not wholly detest his home state.

    6   Richard Eberhart, "The Writer's Sense of Place," *South Dakota Review* 13.3 (Autumn 1975), 21. He added: "I do not think this is as true today as is shown in the example of Bly and others."

    7   Freya Manfred, *Frederick Manfred: A Daughter Remembers* (Minnesota Historical Society Press, 1999), xi.

living mostly in Los Angeles, trying to both make a living and maintain some sort of literary career (including writing children's books) after having been blacklisted as an unfriendly witness by the House Un-American Activities Committee (HUAC). He called himself a member of "the unaffiliated far left." In 1962 he returned home, to the Fargo-Moorhead area to teach. A brilliant and inspiring teacher, mentor and example, he attracted a loyal and productive community of protégés (see Chapter 12 and elsewhere, below).

An example of his poetry of place, "Beyond the Red River":

> The birds have flown their summer skies to the south,
> And the flower-money is drying in the banks of bent grass
> Which the bumble bee has abandoned. We wait for a winter lion,
> Body of ice-crystals and sombrero of dead leaves.
>
> A month ago, from the salt engines of the sea,
> A machinery of early storms rolled toward the holiday houses
> Where summer still dozed in the pool-side chairs, sipping
> An aging whiskey of distances and departures.
>
> Now the long freight of autumn goes smoking out of the land.
> My possibles are all packed up, but still I do not leave.
> I am happy enough here, where Dakota drifts wild in the universe,

> Where the prairie is starting to shake in the surf of
> the winter dark.[8]

McGrath's reputation rests solidly on his major work, the book-length narrative poem, *Letter to an Imaginary Friend,* with its sprawling Whitmanian lines and sustained attention to historical movements and timelines.

Meridel Le Sueur, radical writer, was born in Iowa in 1900, and gravitated to Minnesota. She was a full generation older than Bly, so her work focused at first on issues from a different era, in tune with the Midwest populist tradition. She paid special attention to working class women beginning in the 1920s, then through the Depression and in the '30s when her reportage and short stories garnered much attention. Like McGrath, she was blacklisted by HUAC as a communist, and, thus sidelined, she also turned to writing books for children (among other things). As the latter 1960s gave rise to a surge in political activism and the second wave of feminism, her writing experienced a revival, her "ripening," and became especially relevant to women activists and writers. She was an inveterate journal keeper. Not primarily a poet, her book of poems, *Rites of Ancient Ripening,* came out in 1975, at an opportune time for this story. She influenced a generation of women, especially.[9]

McGrath and Le Sueur, whose radical politics were so deeply rooted as to seem bred in their bones, will figure steadily in the background of this book. (Manfred, although a good friend of Bly's, was not very invested in poetry, and, as he surely was a positive influence on some young writers, he has a lesser role in this book as more of a lone wolf.[10]) While the three of them (Bly, McGrath, and Le Sueur) had their not insignificant differences, personal and

---

8   *Selected Poems, 1938-1988* (Copper Canyon Press, 1988), 128.

9   Le Sueur notably influenced the founding of the Minneapolis theater companies, In the Heart of the Beast and At the Foot of the Mountain, and she was a guiding star for the Women Poets of the Twin Cities (see Chapter 11).

10 Freya Manfred, op. cit., 52.

otherwise, the trio was remarkably in sync, at least at times, to wit: their highly attuned social, historical, and political consciousness; their thoughtful (though not entirely unproblematic) estimation of Native American culture and history; their regard for the political and poetical example of Pablo Neruda; their experience of farm life and their connection to the land, especially that of home. And their mutual respect was manifest.[11] Jim Moore says:

> All three of them were individualistic in a way, they followed their own paths, and I think at the time, and still today, that was appealing to young poets to see someone like Meridel or Tom or Robert. They were very forceful, they had strong force fields around them, they had big ideas and they were willing to express them and take some risks politically. That was all very attractive and affirming for young poets coming along.[12]

Le Sueur's remarkable poem "Plains Poet," her contribution to a festschrift for Bly at age 65, seems to embrace all three of them, as in these excerpts:

> The struggle of poets on our earth
> Enrich the soil
> Poet of suffering
> You showed me the poet of Dakota plains
> ...
>
> Come to the meadow of bloom you cried
> Abloom together

---

11   McGrath positively reviewed *Silence in the Snowy Fields,* for one thing. And Bly went to great lengths in the early 60s to get McGrath published by Wesleyan University Press, maybe the best poetry series at the time. (McGrath, however, refused the offer.) Le Sueur's following poem seems to convey her respect.

12   MG interview with JM, 7 January 2020.

Sowing Seeds

Gather the seed
You have the bloom of gathered blossoms
Poet abreast the prairie
Appeared to me as a young girl
Out of Dakota
Out of broken soil
…

Oh poet male a light in bloom
Oh meadow bloom from broken fissures
…

We long for you to take the big darkened meadow
Till breaking thundering web
Earth continent splitting
Norwegian poets cry of bringing split into Dakota
   womb space
…

Poet of prairie horizon
Hunger for blooming meadow
Oh tall fresh walker on high horizon
Through broken light
To pit and bloom in Dakota dark
The song is in the earth
Spears, swords of spring
Thrusting up the sword of generation
Poet in the meadow
Come out of split seed
To gather to the earth breast
To spring up bright meadows of lovers and warriors.[13]

---

13   Meridel Le Sueur, "Plains Poet," in *Walking Swiftly: Writings and Images on the Occasion of Robert Bly's 65th Birthday,* ed. Thomas R. Smith (Ally Press, 1992), 60-61.

Did McGrath and Le Sueur also attract, assemble and foster communities of poets? Moore, devoted to both, expresses his outlook, continuing his thought above: "Not to the degree of Robert. Tom was a more solitary, quirky figure, and he was not in the Twin Cities. Robert believed in solitude as a kind of principle, Tom *was* solitude. Meridel was interested in community, but she also was kind of prickly and it was more a theoretical idea for her." Still, it must be emphasized that, like Bly, McGrath and Le Sueur were deeply involved in the life of their respective communities, doing their work and spending time with younger writers, providing both guidance and inspiration as role models. They were literary witnesses. Surely the marks of their influence remain evident in the Minnesota literary ecosystem. But, as this book shall make clear, Bly's sustained and extraordinary efforts at community building had the largest, broadest, and most lasting effect on literary life in the North Country.

Four decades after Lewis' remark, by 1960, Minnesota was less unplaced. But, culturally speaking, the region was still viewed from outside as bland, a backwater, flyover country, although in fact the Twin Cities was a cultural outpost, with art museums, a symphony orchestra, and educational institutions galore. Many new theater companies, a lively music scene, and writers, too.

There were a number of other poets of note: Carl Rakosi (a social worker and head of Jewish Family and Children's Service of Minneapolis), Reed Whittemore (at Carleton College), and Allen Tate, John Berryman, and James Wright (at the University of Minnesota), had all been elsewhere during their earlier formative years. Nevertheless, although it would be wrong to call Minnesota at midcentury a literary wasteland, it definitely was a land of fallow fields.[14] All this was starting to change, however.

---

14 As illustration: *A Selected Bio-Bibliography: Minnesota Authors* compiled by the Minnesota Centennial Literature Group (Minnesota Statehood Centennial Commission, 1958), lists some 700 Minnesota authors, but there are few creative writers of note, other than those just mentioned or mentioned else-

For on the literary front lines starting in 1958 was an agitational and surprisingly fruitful literary magazine called *The Fifties*. Bly, its idiosyncratic editor, was poised to underline (not just exemplify) the desirability of staying put, and to show the way to foster soul, spirit, and mind within one's home (or adoptive home) environment. To reiterate: His exemplary generosity and flair for generativity were plain to see at the time, but the results revealed themselves only gradually. He was betting on a future, not even dimly viewed then, bringing about a remarkable, long-lasting, and self-perpetuating phase of growth.

To be fair and to fill out the picture of Minnesota in those days, there is also the elephant in the room—the state's widespread and well-deserved reputation for frigid and snowy weather. While it may be risky to generalize, "climate, environment and history do affect character" and outlook, as Sir Tyrone Guthrie determined.[15] In the winter of 1959-60, he and others, looking for a site for a new theater, visited Boston, Chicago, Cleveland, Milwaukee, Detroit, and Minneapolis. In Chicago it was windy and the temperature was zero. Then, in Minneapolis, "the temperature was…thirty degrees below zero, and the snow was thrice as deep….it was silent, but you felt that a sharp, bright sword had pierced your bowels through and through."[16]

Against all odds, they decided on Minneapolis. "Why?" he asks. "The weather? The people? The river? We have discussed it often and we simply do not know."[17] But the suggestion is that all three were significant factors. Finally, Guthrie wrote, taking the long view: "it is our hope that the Minnesota Theatre Company may

---

where in this book. Further, the membership roster of the League of Minnesota Poets from August 1958 has (roughly) 250 names, not one of which is found in any of the subsequent publications noted in this book.

15   Tyrone Guthrie, *A New Theatre* (McGraw-Hill Book Company, 1964), 34.
16   Ibid., 49.
17   Ibid., 60.

develop a distinctively Minnesotan style. This cannot come about quickly. It may take ten years or even twenty. The progress will, we hope, be aided by the inclusion in each season's company of a group of graduate students from the University of Minnesota. This is our taproot into the soil."[18]

When the arrival of Guthrie's theater was imminent, David Jones wrote: "The Twin Cities of Minneapolis and St. Paul are not too big to have a sense of community and yet big enough to provide the nucleus of an audience. The new theater should thus be able to draw vitality from communal life and from the peculiar vigor of a provincial locale. There is every chance that what Dr. Guthrie calls a 'solid, cozy family-feeling' will develop, a special kind of solidarity between actors and audience. The most satisfying kind of theatrical experience is that in which the audience feels involved."[19]

Is it possible that another deciding factor in frosty Minneapolis' favor was the famous English theatrical director's awareness of Bly's prominence and presence on the national and local scene? Sir Tyrone contacted him almost immediately after the theater was built, as Bly told Donald Hall: "Guthrie has approached me about doing a Strindberg – play – translation for his theater next year, and of course the royalties would be good on that, but the play unfortunately won't be performed – even if I do it this winter – until the spring and summer of '64."[20] Although the project never came to fruition, at the request of the next artistic director, Douglas Campbell in 1967, Bly wrote an essay on John Lewin's adaptation of Aeschylus' *Oresteia*, "The House of Atreus," intended as part of the Guthrie's play guide, "Setting the Stage."[21]

---

18   Ibid., 177.

19   "A Hope for Theater: Notes on the Tyrone Guthrie Repertory Theater," *Minnesota Review* 1.1 (Fall 1960), 95.

20   RB to DH, 15 July 1963. Bly was still thinking about and learning how to make a living as a poet rather than as an academician.

21   Raymond Bechtel to RB, 12 April 1967. It was published, but not

Sowing Seeds

Back to Minnesota's weather. This excerpt from Mark Vinz's poem, "For the Far Edge," addresses more particularly its extreme version up in the Fargo-Moorhead area and its accordingly unexpected partner, poetry:

> No one will believe the winters,
> the land as flat and broad
> as God's own shinbone,
> where Nordic stormtroops
> wring the manna from the earth
> and build the towns
> whose shadows stretch for miles.
>
> No one will believe the poets—
> poets singing in the sunflowers,
> poets in buffalo robes
> dancing on tiptoe in their own hair,
> Martin Luther and Buddha
> swimming naked in the Red River.
> . . .[22]

Throughout the pages of this book will be found much evidence of the growing sense of community, and, yes, of familial feeling, even among singing, dancing, skinny-dipping poets. Also, the sense of pride in being in or from the region despite its reputation, deserved or not.

* * *

---

in the program notes. Rather it appears in a mass-market paperback edition of *The House of Atreus* by John Lewin (Bantam Books, 1969), as "The Purple Carpet and Contemporary Life," 120-22. Some forty years later, in 2008, Bly's translation and adaptation of Henrik Ibsen's "Peer Gynt" had its premiere at the Guthrie.

22   In Lucien Stryk, ed., *Heartland II: Poets of the Midwest* (Northern Illinois University Press, 1975), 243-4

"Regionalism" is an ambiguous term. Often negatively equated with provincialism, it connotes a constricted local outlook, conservatism, and a lack of sophistication. Furthermore, regionalists in this sense may defensively over-compensate for an inferiority complex about their region with sentimentalized self-aggrandizement, with boosterism. Such geopiety can lead to proclaiming a place "God's country," with the implicit suggestion that God is absent from other places.

The decision to stay where one is planted—in the country or a small town, and maybe especially in the Upper Midwest, roughly equidistant from the coastal hotbeds or "dream coasts" of artistic and literary activity—and to write from and about that place may invite the question: Am I thus consigning myself to never rising above being a local or regional poet, to being marginalized, bush-league, always second-rate?

Not at all. There is the Blakean or Joycean view that "in the particular is contained the universal." And the embrace of regionalism may afford an opportunity for a fresh start, one unencumbered by received or borrowed notions.[23] Thus, the second use of regionalism as a neutral, strictly descriptive term. A unique richness and even diversity may be found in one's own region, if one has the eyes to see and the ears to hear. This then is a kind of dynamic centering, finding a solid place to stand and from which to interpret the world, which can in turn lead to gaining a true sense one's own authentic identity.

Asked how important roots are to an artist, Gary Snyder responds characteristically pithily: "Like roots to a tree."[24] He adds: "The 'nation' is a fiction.... The region is real." Heightened awareness of a particular place's inhabitants, heritage, traditions, history,

---

[23] E.g., from William Blake, *Auguries of Innocence*: "To see a World in a Grain of Sand / And a Heaven in a Wild Flower," or, of course, James Joyce's Dublin in *Ulysses*.

[24] This and much of what follows, from "The Writer's Sense of Place," *South Dakota Review* 13.3 (1975).

language, geology, economy, weather, flora & fauna, and more, and maintaining a love, memory, and deep feeling for the place—these define what it means to be grounded, both physically and spiritually. This may include stories handed down from grandparents and others, local lore, and the words of other poets who have already found a broad and receptive audience; that is, the development of a poetics of place (an intrinsic part of poeticulture).

Some more gobbets on this topic. The Flemish artist Maurice de Vlaminck wrote in the *Dial* magazine: "Intelligence is international, stupidity is national, art is local." Philosopher John Dewey said: "The locality is the only universal." Both were quoted by William Carlos Williams, who felt it was the world that creates the mind, rather than, as Yeats thought, that the mind creates the world. Poet Richard Hugo takes both Yeats and Williams into account when he says: "The place triggers the mind to create the place."[25] Being rooted is essential, but it is not enough. In the preface to his epic poem *Paterson*, Williams speaks of "interpenetration, both ways."

Summarily, William Stafford says:

> All events and experiences are local, somewhere. And all human enhancements of events and experiences—which is to say, all the arts—are regional in the sense that they derive from immediate relation to felt life.
>
> It is this immediacy that distinguishes art. And paradoxically the more local the self that art has, the more all people can share it; for that vivid encounter with the stuff of the world is our common ground.
>
> Artists, knowing the mutual enrichment that extends everywhere, can act, and praise, and criticize, as in-

---

25   Richard Hugo, The Triggering Town: Lectures and Essays on Poetry and Writing (W.W. Norton & Co., 1979).

siders: —the means of their art is the life of their people. And that life grows and improves by being shared. Hence, it is good to welcome any region you live in or come to or think of, for that is where life happens to be—right where you are.[26]

He also says: "any center, any city, any nation, is a place where art begins. Wherever you are, you begin to work with the material, and it tells you where north is."

Wendell Berry, a Kentucky farmer/poet, on this subject: "The regionalism that I adhere to could be defined simply as local life aware of itself. It would tend to substitute for the myths and stereotypes of a region a particular knowledge of the place one lives in and intends to continue to live in."[27] Gruchow, a writer with Minnesota prairie roots, adds to this line of thought: "We are called to lives in particular places."[28] The most concise formulation of all may be McGrath's statement: "Dakota is everywhere."[29]

Place, however important it can be to a poet in terms of physical geography and climate, is also closely tied to ancestry, ethnic and religious backgrounds, and to history (remembered or forgotten). Though change is inexorable, some things persist and can't be erased by time or will. This is the paradox of the "pickled-in-amber" culture of Garrison Keillor's fictional Lake Wobegon, "the town that time forgot and that the decades cannot improve…where all the women are strong, all the men are good-looking, and the children are above average."[30] There's something both negative and positive about that, i.e., regionalist in both senses.

---

26 Tennessee Poetry Journal 1.1 (Fall 1977).
27 *Southern Review* 6, 972-77. (quoted by Vinz in *SDR* 13.3).
28 Gruchow, 146.
29 Thomas McGrath, *Letter to An Imaginary Friend* (Copper Canyon Press, 1997), 136.
30 I found the first phrase in Bill Holm, "Is Minnesota in America Yet?" in *Imagining Home,* eds. Mark Vinz and Thom Tammaro (University of Minnesota Press, 1995), 184.

Suffice it to say that the book in your hands does not mean to be regional in the first sense. Rather in the second, as reflective of reality seen clearly. "It is good to feel at home," Bly said (in the epigraph to this Chapter), "That's what makes me so hopeful about the future—feeling at home." He was taking a larger view of twentieth century American poetry, adding that Eliot and Pound did not feel at home, and thus expatriated themselves.

Returning now to the issue of Bly's return: He had come back, for better or worse, to a shabby house and a landscape "empty of cultural expectation…a place, in his own words, removed from the 'seats of power.'"[31] He had no plans to work the farm, as his older brother Jim was doing. What then did Bly mean to do? What was his purpose?

First, to start sowing seeds, to engage in wilding, to pursue poeticulture via *The Fifties* (later *The Sixties* and *The Seventies*), as we've already seen and as we will see further. To be sure, although standard farming is necessarily a painstaking process of cause and effect, requiring meticulous planning and foresight, often extending years ahead, restoring a prairie to wildness can be other than that. So he continued to pursue his vision on his irregular and merry way, loosening the soil, flinging the seeds, and enjoying the results. He worked very hard, and ceaselessly, if not on a strict schedule.

Second, he also meant to write a new kind of poetry, which so happened to be tied mostly to the land where he chose to remain (see Chapter 4). But there was nothing provincial about Bly's allegiance to this state; he was local, regional, and universal all at once. He said: "I haven't written poems about Minnesota because I think it is the most poetic place in the world, but because if poetry is any good, it can live anywhere; it must be able to live anywhere. Minnesota is

---

31 Patricia Kirkpatrick, "Shadows on the Prairie: Where the Gift Gathers," in *Robert Bly in This World,* ed. Thomas R. Smith, with James P. Lenfestey (University of Minnesota Libraries, 2011), 36.

not better or worse than any other place."[32] It was not that he didn't love Minnesota, it was that he was not a geopietist, a blindered regionalist. His eyes were wide open.

There were two other reasons for his return, as he said: "My cunning involved going out to the Middle West and into a farm place where I didn't have to earn much money and where I could be alone for long periods of time."[33] So it was also partly about finances, third. He was intending to make his living as a poet—not as a teacher in a college or university—and he was keeping his overhead low. Eventually, occasional travel on the poetry reading circuit would supply the bulk of his income (see Chapter 10). He was also demonstrating how it—making a living as a poet—could be done, in part.

Fourth, he was fiercely intent on his own need for solitude. As his influence grew, this was a key component of his oft-repeated advice to young poets. "Intensity can do the work. Put yourself in a position where you can be intense. …when you're alone, or with a person that you truly love, really, really love." Then you can stay in your small town in rural Minnesota. You do need poems about your own land and your own country. "As long as there are great paperbacks everywhere and there are great poets writing, it's possible for the solitary student to find psychic guidance moving just a little ahead of his development. You don't need any place like New York. What you need is a place to work, where you can become transparent, and the unconscious inside you can come forward soberly and guide your growth."[34] The seeds must be allowed the optimal conditions in order to germinate.

---

32   "Going out on the Plain in the Moonlight," An Interview with Cynthia Lofsness and Kathy Otto, with Fred Manfred, in *Talking All Morning* (The University of Michigan Press, 1980) (original date of interview, 1966), 56.

33   "Craft Interview" with Mary Jane Fortunato and Cornelia P. Draves, and with Paul Zweig and Saul Galin, in *Talking All Morning*, 179-80.

34   "The Ascending Energy Arc," Answers to Students' Questions, Suffolk Community College, in *Talking All Morning*, 248.

Jim Moore accentuates the truth of Bly's comments "that attention to place is crucial, but that far from creating a poetry of solely regional concerns, such attention draws the poet inevitably into the larger world in which the region must somehow find its place."[35] That is to say, Minnesota poets were not inevitably regionalists in the pejorative and dismissive sense, incapable of breaking away from their locale or of writing in anything but a "flat" midwestern idiom. Or, for that matter, strictly limited by the mundane stuff of life, such as snow, hockey, ice-fishing, woods, lakes, prairie grass, tornadoes, corn fields, cows, mosquitoes, etc. A link must be found between the particular and the planetary, the local and the worldwide.

Bly was much more than a Minnesotan poet, and more than an American poet; he was a cosmopolitan poet—the world was his city—who had gathered seeds from his travels, mostly literary, some physical, but also psychological and spiritual. His range of reference was international, it circled the globe (in reaction against his formal education at Harvard, with its narrow focus on English language poetry). In this way he was like his modernist forebears, Eliot and Pound, expatriates both.

And yet it just so happened that he lived quite contentedly in his original rural setting.[36] Wallace Stegner has written: "Until it has had a poet, a place is not a place."[37] Bly had put Minnesota on the map. Home, sweet home.

---

35 *Minnesota Writes: Poetry*, eds. Jim Moore and Cary Waterman (Milkweed Editions/Nodin Press, 1987), 10.

36 This decision to stay where he was originally planted—regardless of annual winter stays in New York City for a number of years in the latter 50s and early 60s, plus stays in Europe twice in the 1960s (funded by grants), and a year in California in 1970—was fundamental.

37 *Crossing to Safety* (Random House, 1987), 130.

Chapter 3
Good Soil and Rocky Ground

The germination of a seed is not a quiet event. It is a swelling, a splitting, an eruption.[1]
                      –Ella Duffy

Because something is happening here and you don't know what it is
Do you, Mr. Jones?[2]
                      –Bob Dylan

"I don't want to know James Wright," Bly replied when his friend Donald Hall told him that Wright had joined the English Department faculty at the University of Minnesota in Minneapolis.[3] Wright's first book, *The Green Wall*, had just been given the Yale Younger Poet's Prize and was greeted with widespread acclaim. He had also appeared in the recent anthology, *The New Poets of England and America* (co-edited by Hall), a book that Bly, another contributor, immediately upon publication regretted being a part of. He thought it full of formalist, dull, academic poems, for he had moved on.

---

    1   Ella Duffy, ed., *Seeds & Roots* (Hazel Press, 2022), 5,
    2   "Ballad of a Thin Man," *Highway 61 Revisited* (Columbia Records, 1965).
    3   MG interview with DH, 1 April 2000.

In 1958, without warning, this young poet from Minnesota started sowing the seeds he had gathered and saved over the previous decade. In early summer, the first issue of *The Fifties: A Magazine of Poetry and General Opinion* appeared out of the middle of nowhere.[4] Bly was not aiming at general readers, but primarily at young American poets. And, as its name—which refers to time rather than place—hinted, that intended audience was not regional, but national (at least).

He was interested in utilizing his isolated situation to his advantage—or what he saw as advantage—in opposition to the academic poetry establishment largely based on the east coast. He didn't necessarily want to be part of a literary milieu; rather, a solitary in a hinterland haven, whence he could be as audacious as he wished. (Similarly, he steered clear of an academic position, which he felt would have made him beholden to an institution and thus kept him muzzled.) Still, he sent complimentary copies to a long list of poets (including those in the *New Poets* anthology) across the country; gifts scattered like so many seeds. Success depended on what kind of soil the seed was sown in, whether rich, fertile loam or arid, thorny, rocky ground. Bly found both kinds, both far afield and close to home.

The first germination in Minnesota's emergent literary landscape was fortuitous, though it proved to be tremendous and crucial, because one of those automatic recipients was Wright. He happened at that time to be spiraling downward in a private vortex of despair, dissatisfied with his own poetry, much of which seemed phony to him, and thinking of giving it up entirely. On July 22, he was surprised to find in his Folwell Hall mailbox an unexpected gift, *The Fifties*—with its front-and-center statement: "The editors of this magazine think

---

4   Bly's co-editor for the first three issues, William Duffy, lived in Pine Island, in southeastern Minnesota. Soon the official headquarters of the magazine shifted permanently to Odin House, Madison, in southwestern Minnesota, where Bly lived. See *Born Under*.

that most of the poetry published in America today is too old-fashioned." Ravenously, he devoured it in one sitting, and that same afternoon typed a lengthy letter to Bly, discussing the contents in depth, resonating with nearly everything, and saying in effect, and just a tad hyperbolically, that the magazine had saved his life.

Bly, disarmed and amazed, had to admit the enormous value of Wright's interest. "Thank you immensely for the praise; your concern is the greatest compliment this magazine will ever receive.... I am overjoyed that you feel the phrase 'new imagination' conveys something."[5] He invited Wright out to the farm, and a friendship and key literary partnership was formed that was mutually beneficial from the start. The gift was in motion.

Photo by Carol Bly, courtesy of Bridget Bly

At that moment, Wright's coming on board had nothing consciously to do with Minnesota per se, for he was from Martin's Ferry in eastern Ohio, just across the river from Wheeling, West Virginia,

---

5   RB to JW, 1 August 1958.

hardly the Midwest. But its effect would be felt locally, and very much so. This particular cross-fertilization was not premeditated, rather almost serendipitous, but it changed everything. As it turned out, Bly *did* want to know Wright.

With his many subsequent visits to the farm, riding the bus from Minneapolis, staying and writing in the converted chicken coop, walking the dirt roads, contemplating the landscape and some of its inhabitants (like David, the horse, and Simon, the dog), and talking, laughing, arguing, and collaborating with Bly, Wright took "emotional possession" of his new surroundings.[6] How Wright moved from the stilted formality of *The Green Wall* (1957) and *Saint Judas* (1959, already in press when he met Bly), to the free verse, imagistic poems in his landmark next book, *The Branch Will Not Break* (1963), including "Lying in a Hammock at William Duffy's Farm in Pine Island, Minnesota," "Milkweed," and "A Blessing," is a wondrous tale, and it has everything to do with his relationship with Bly (see Chapter 4). He began to put down roots in Minnesota. He became, in other words, a successful transplant.

Wright enthused in a letter to Hall that Bly is "a propagandist of new ideas."[7] This description is spot-on; it was precisely the purpose of his little magazine to foster a new imagination and persuade poets of the need for a new poetry—to be propagandistic. But we can also connect "propagandist" more directly to its root word, propagate, as in dissemination, that is, the scattering of seeds, diffusion, that is, the spreading of words and ideas, and increase. The magazine was a gift with a now unstoppable momentum and infinite growth potential.

As illustration, an excerpt of Wright's poem, "In Memory of a Spanish Poet," (for Miguel Hernandez [whom Bly had alerted him to]):

---

6   The expression is from Richard Hugo, *The Triggering Town*, 14.

7   JW to DH, 17 September 1958 (in *A Wild Perfection: The Selected Letters of James Wright*, eds. Anne Wright and Saundra Rose Maley [Farrar, Straus and Giroux, 2005], 167).

> I dream of your slow voice, flying,
> Planting the dark waters of the spirit
> With lutes and seeds.
>
> Here, in the American Midwest,
> Those seeds fly out of the field and across the strange
> heaven of my skull.[8]

Again we see Wright's way with words; he couldn't have put the effect of Bly's sowing and propagating any more succinctly.

This is all the more noteworthy given that Wright was miserable in Minneapolis. The English Department at the University was thriving in the 1950s and 60s, in strictly academic terms. Joseph Warren Beach, Robert Penn Warren, and Saul Bellow had all taught there. The poets Allen Tate and John Berryman (in the Humanities Program) were the two literary luminaries currently on the faculty.[9]

Allen Tate had studied with John Crowe Ransom at Vanderbilt University, and later became part of the literary group known as the Fugitives (or Southern Agrarians) that originated from there. He was a formidable man of letters—poet, literary essayist, mentor to Robert Lowell, Randall Jarrell, and Karl Shapiro, and a high priest of the regnant New Criticism. Led by Ransom, this movement was founded on the view that a poem can be studied in isolation from history, psychology, and biography. All well-buttoned up in conventional iambic meter.

Tate and Warren and Leonard Unger had made the University of Minnesota a New Critical hub.[10] Tate was also, needless to say, extremely well-connected to those that mattered in the literary es-

---

8   *The Branch Will Not Break* (Wesleyan University Press, 1963), 31.

9   For a brief recollection of both men as teachers, see Don Olsen, *A Butterfly Sleeps on the Temple Bell: A Reminiscence on the Ox Head Press, 1966-2000* (Cross+Roads Press, 2003), 26-7.

10 As the English Department's website still says: https://cla.umn.edu/english/about/history

tablishment of the day. This helps to explain how it was that T.S. Eliot came to Williams Arena ("The Barn") on campus in 1956 to deliver his lecture, "The Frontiers of Criticism," to an audience of 14,000. Hired in 1951, Tate remained at the University until his retirement in 1968. Patricia Hampl, a student of his in the mid-1960s, remembers his "exquisite hauteur," and that he "reigned frostily."[11]

Note that the department's curriculum did not yet include creative writing; it was solidly based on the study of English and American literature, so that scholars and their scholarship were most admired. (Berryman, although a fine poet, his poetry marked by idiosyncrasy and confessionalism, was also a formidable scholar.) Another sign of the department's emphasis and reputation was the acclaimed series, the *University of Minnesota Pamphlets on American Writers*, begun in 1959 and publishing 103 numbers over the next two decades.

A young staff member, looking back on the days when Tate and his then wife Isabella Gardner hosted great parties, with copious amounts of food and drink, wrote to her, recalling "your home on Irving South, your blazing hearth and groaning board, around which there was formed the one true cosmopolitan center, the one true intellectual exchange (so far as I was ever able to discover) of all the Upper Midwest."[12] Was the University's esteemed English Department thus at that time the core of a literary community in Minnesota, a ground with continuing potential for new growth? Hardly. Any sense of true togetherness created at these well-stocked "salons" likely dissipated along with the next day's hangover.

And then there was the department's ever-present vitriol, with its "often eccentric and always imbibing members" engaging openly in intra-collegiate political warfare, not to mention overt marital

---

11   "Midwestern Sublime," 7.
12   Gordon O'Brien to IG, 29 Dec 1980, quoted in Maria Janssen, *Not at All What One is Used To: The Life and Times of Isabella Gardner* (University of Missouri Press, 2010), 201.

and extra-marital strife. One graduate student, awestruck, remarked: "this must be the hardest drinking English Department in the United States."[13] Tate, Berryman, and Wright were all brilliant and admired teachers but also alcoholics (with the inevitable havoc of missed classes and other erratic behavior).

From Tate's viewpoint, Wright's position was even more precarious than his alcoholism and vexing mental health rendered it. His first book was better than good (i.e., formal and traditional), and he had, like Tate, been a student of Ransom's (at Kenyon College), so he should have been securely in the fold. But he had slipped away, which felt like a betrayal and was unforgivable. Wright's close association with the rebel Bly doomed him, as there was, plainly put, mutual detestation between Tate and Bly. So, Wright was denied tenure and dismissed.

Opposition to the New Critics, together with a nonstop effort to free young poets from their ruinous clutches, was a core tenet of *The Fifties* and *The Sixties*. Bly regularly attacked Ransom, Warren, Cleanth Brooks, and Tate himself. He was promulgating a new poetry, anti-formalist, anti-academic, with a new imagination, all in an effort to reclaim the achievements of the earlier modernist, avant-garde generation (Pound and Williams) that had been suppressed by Tate and others. It is no surprise that Tate wanted absolutely no part of this revolution, and that he mistakenly assumed it was misguided and would prove ineffectual. Bob Dylan, who, of course, if only briefly, was a student at the University at about the same time (see Chapter 5), could have been thinking about Tate when he wrote and sang the words in the epigraph, above.

---

13 Janssen, 212.

A poet of the 'Twenties about to deliver another lecture on the demise of Hart Crane

This image of a penguin in a tuxedo (by Ivar Arosenius) was Bly's transparent dig at Tate (due to the resemblance and the caption), in *The Sixties* 7 (Winter 1964).

Tate, in turn, heaped abuse on Bly often, but he rarely deigned to do so in print—that would be giving Bly too much credit—usually saving it for acerbic comments at parties and other gatherings. His epistolary reaction to the editor of *The Fifties* #1 included this: "It seems to me that the thinking that can describe the iambus as a 'convention' would also describe our walking on two legs as a convention. You are going to have to do better than this if you are going to convince the Old and the Tough."[14] Wright reported a fracas that had erupted at a New Year's Eve department party over *The Fifties* #2 and his appearance in and involvement with it. That second issue also refers to a characteristic of modern poetry as "horrifying to the bourgeois." Bly responded: "It is very interesting that Tate got so mad—by now he will have received the third issue—he subscribes—and be even madder! I like to think of him there, rolling out old Southern curses, as the Union cavalry refuses to obey!"[15] It is clear why Wright found the atmosphere in Minneapolis stifling, and the ground barren.

---

14 AT to CB and RB, 12 February 1959.
15 RB to JW, 3 January 1960.

However widely Tate wielded his considerable clout, he was not at all interested in the local scene. Much unlike Wright, he chose to ignore the land he was standing on. In Minneapolis, he, a resolute southerner and true to his roots, "wore his Confederate [flag] vest proudly and provocatively for special occasions."[16] That was a silent and unambiguous statement. He wouldn't stoop so low as to identify with Minnesota-ness beyond the bounds of the University campus, even had he been conscious of such a thing; his stage was national and Southern.

Nor did he even try to transplant himself. Rather, in keeping with our overarching ecosystem metaphor, Tate was a noxious weed or an invasive species, even a parasite, an organism exploiting the hospitality of his hosts. He could have been anywhere. There was no reciprocity, no meaningful exchange of gifts, no mutual interpenetration, and thus not even a glimmer of community building tied to place. All that would come soon enough, sooner than the imperious Tate could have imagined, thanks to Bly, his young local nemesis.

The Minnesota Review

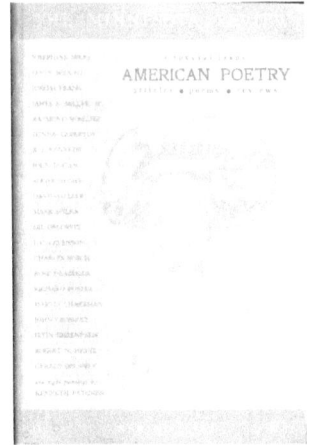

A new literary magazine, *The Minnesota Review,* was first published in fall 1960, edited by Sarah Foster and several others. At the out-

---

16   Janssen, 175.

set, it was not formally affiliated with any public institution, though its contributors were predominantly academicians, several from the University of Minnesota. And, conspicuously, the advisory editor for the first issue was the man with the most leverage—Tate.

That Tate had a lot to do with the sharply defensive and supercilious tenor of this magazine's inaugural editorial statement is all but certain. For it falls just short of an explicit denunciation of *The Fifties* and *The Sixties*:

> Many contemporary little magazines, trying to imitate the spirit of some of their great predecessors of the twenties and thirties, have tortured themselves into artificial poses of truculence when, in fact, they have had very little in view beyond a rather trivial yearning to make the bourgeois beast tremble. But of course the bourgeois beast has learned, since the twenties and thirties, to enjoy its shudders, and as the recent commercial success of the Beats has proven, is willing to pay well for the pleasures of them. We think that such magazines lack a seriousness and integrity that we are hopeful ours will have. And we also think that their a priori ambition to be aggressive puts a crippling limitation on the quality and range of material they may publish.[17]

The editors further state a few principles: they will only print "good" writing; they won't let criticism predominate; and they will "keep our editorial mouths shut after this little initial splurge of self-analysis." In fact, the magazine may have been conceived in the first place as a rebuke of or antidote to *The Fifties/Sixties,* intending to undercut or neutralize its already surprising and subversive power set apart from the academic establishment.

Of course, Bly was far from the only revolutionary poet-leader

---

17   Tate's use of "bourgeois" is plausibly an echo of Bly's comment in *The Fifties* 2, quoted above.

in the country at that time. Others—Charles Olson, Robert Creeley, and the Black Mountain poets, John Ashbery and the New York School poets, and Allen Ginsberg, Gregory Corso, and the Beats—had their own particular visions expressed in other little magazines, and they were uniformly anti-academic. But they were situated on the east and west coasts. In the so-called heartland, Bly was less easily ignored as he was practically in Tate's face.

A year later, Reed Whittemore, a poet at Carleton College in Northfield, secured Tate's help in organizing the first conference of the newly-formed Association of Literary Magazines of America, held in St. Paul in late 1961. Given his eminence and his considerable experience with literary magazines, Tate was made the honorary chair. But then Whittemore, in assembling the rest of the executive committee, including himself (editor of *Carleton Miscellany*) and Henry Rago (*Poetry*), had the nerve to engage the uncouth upstart Bly (*The Sixties*), effectively putting him even more up in Tate's face, which must have rankled.

What is interesting and especially delicious to observe is how, despite having taken this initial anti-Bly stance, the *Minnesota Review* gradually, even inexorably, begins to shed its academic poetry and its old-fashioned outlook. In a satisfying case of poetic justice, the magazine was pulled into Bly's orbit by the powerful force of his gravitational field. It had gotten off on the wrong foot, misreading the zeitgeist. Tate's advisory direction, out of touch, was ditched. The potent seeds Bly had sown were bearing fruit even in this rocky ground.

In subsequent issues, work appears from John Logan, Denise Levertov, E.D. Blodgett, John Knoepfle, Charles Guenther, Dallas Wiebe, Robert Creeley—all poets with friendly ties to *The Fifties* and *The Sixties*—and then even writers in other languages: César Vallejo, Georg Trakl, August Strindberg, and Rainer Maria Rilke, translated by Wright and by Bly himself. After this trend was clear in 1963, *Minnesota Review*'s new editor, Harry Weber, wrote to Bly:

"It's hard to believe that the most influential magazine in the country, at least as far as poetry is concerned, comes from Madison, Minnesota, which somehow makes me believe in God."[18]

The Ivory Tower

We can see Bly further outpacing and sidestepping Tate in the mid-1960s, and also trace some outlines of the future, by looking not to the University's professoriat but to the student-run *Ivory Tower*—a monthly literary supplement (in magazine form) to the *Minnesota Daily* (the student newspaper with a massive circulation to match the student population of more than 42,000). This was arable ground—down in the basement of Murphy Hall—as the young writers on the masthead, who proved to be essential contributors to the literary scene long after, had come into contact with Bly's magazine, books, and activism.

Garrison Keillor, an English major, had poems and fiction published in *Ivory Tower*. Then he became its fiction editor and, in fall 1964, editor of the whole shebang for a year and a half. In this latter

---

18   HW to RB, 25 June 1963. Editors in the latter years of the decade were Roy Arthur Swanson, and Alvin Greenberg, both from Macalester College (when writers from there also appear—Greenberg himself, Roger Blakely, Patricia Kane, C.W. Truesdale, all professors, and Charles Baxter and Roy McBride, both students). Soon the *Minnesota Review* left the state permanently, while retaining its name.

role, Keillor invited Bly to come to Minneapolis for a reading.[19] In the spring of 1966, as a senior in the College of Liberal Arts, Keillor won the poetry contest conducted at the University by the Department of English and sponsored by the Academy of American Poets. Honorable mention in that contest went to Jim Moore, who at the time was associate editor, also contributing reportage, reviews, and poems. Hampl similarly served as associate editor and wrote a few journalistic essays. Their friend Lewis Hyde succeeded Keillor as editor. Three of these four went on to have little magazines of their own (see Chapter 11), the other a long-lived radio show. All of them have had quite successful and disparate writing careers (though all originating in poetry). Other contributors to *Ivory Tower* who will be noted several times again in this book include Franz Richter (art editor), Gregory Bitz, Jonathan Sisson, Sarah and Richard Shaw, Roland Flint, and Edwin Felien.[20]

Ivory Tower gave plenty of attention to related local happenings, including the expanding folk music scene (see Chapter 5). Sarah Shaw conducted "A Conversation with Koerner, Ray, and Glover," in 1964.[21] It is no surprise—except in that this was the *literary* supplement of a newspaper—that there was much on the growing antiwar movement, including photos from the November 27, 1965, March on Washington for Peace in Vietnam (where Bly and Hyde first met), and Francis Galt's essay, "Why I Refuse to Cooperate with the Draft."[22] It was Bly who quickly came to exemplify the necessity for poets to connect with pressing political issues of the day (see Chapter 6).

Hyde says about Bly: "He was the liveliest thing in Minnesota at the time. He had lots to say, and was full of opinions. He seemed to know a lot. We, of course, knew nothing, so anybody who knew

---

19   Hyde, "Lessons from Robert Bly's Barn," 19
20   Also Brian Coyle, Sam Heins, Francis Galt.
21   *Ivory Tower* 65.160 (June 1, 1964).
22   *Ivory Tower* (April 4, 1966).

anything seemed wise to us."[23] Certainly, for young poets in Minnesota and elsewhere in the Upper Midwest it was both surprising and exhilarating that Bly's magazine *The Sixties* even existed. However unlikely its wide circulation and impact might have seemed, it managed to put Minnesota, of all places, on the chart of the new national scene.

Hampl remembers: "I first heard of Robert Bly when I bought a copy of his magazine and discovered there an immediacy and pulse in poetry I had not found in my classes. …a wide world of poetry rushing into my life, spilling over the narrow confines of the *Norton Anthology of English Literature*. I read Bly's magazine, and his good-spirited but deadly attacks on the literary establishment, and I knew I was reading the future."[24] Seeds were being sown.

Other young poets in Minnesota were also affected. Bill Holm wrote: "Here was a magazine with chutzpah, gumption, humor, fine insults, and lively talk—but with neither fear nor pompous respectability to weigh it down. … The magazine became a kind of *Bible* to the young writers of Minnesota. We searched its nooks and crannies for gems of hidden wisdom, poets to read, ideas to use as ammunition on our old-fashioned teachers. … And to think that all this lively international brouhaha was going on in Madison, Minnesota!"[25]

It is invigorating to read these comments, as though we are seeing the seeds germinate and take root in real time. For these lively writers, of a distinct new generation, would reciprocate by making themselves heard long into the future, new sowers sowing seeds in turn, and keeping the gift in motion.[26] They had located ground to stand on and in which to be rooted. They had found their peers—they were learning from, stimulating, and teaching one another, gen-

---

23 MG interview with LH, 13 October 2019.
24 "Midwestern Sublime," 8.
25 BH to MG, 20 August 2000.
26 Indeed, they all have been helpful and inspirational to me in the course of researching and writing this book.

erating tremendous amounts of energy as they read and shared and wrote in a freewheeling manner. Meanwhile, Bly, among other newly established poets, was reinventing American poetry, and these young poets—enjoying their good fortune that he was in Minnesota, and available—wanted to be a part of it.

Chapter 4
Homegrown Poetry
(Two Transformative Books)

> It is said that there are certain spots on the globe where magical lines intersect and wonderful things occur. Southern Minnesota does, after all, include the Bly farm at Madison, where once so many important moments for contemporary poetry were passed, and Pine Island, where the shadow of James Wright's hammock still lies on the grass.[1]
> —Ted Kooser

To repeat: In 1958, a young poet from western Minnesota started sowing seeds. From that beginning in *The Fifties* we can see overt signs of Bly's rootedness in his own Scandinavian heritage—witness the first issue opening with five translations of the Swede Gunnar Ekelöf, for example, not to mention later regard for Tomas Tranströmer and for Rolf Jacobsen and other Norwegian poets—which may have led a few North Country poets of similar background to consider their ancestral lineages. But not until four years

---

[1] As quoted by Philip Dacey in his introductory note, "A Long Road Without Inns," in *Common Ground: A Gathering of Poets from the 1986 Marshall Festival,* eds. Mark Vinz and Thom Tammaro (Dacotah Territory Press, 1988), xviii.

later did Bly's wider impact on literary life in Minnesota begin to become truly obvious.

The first book

Thus, I proffer a provisional amendment to the opening statement above: In 1962, with the publication of his first book, *Silence in the Snowy Fields,* a young poet again started sowing seeds; but, to be clear, this was step two—from then on concurrent with, not simply subsequent to, step one. The sower was now circling closer to home, doing his proximate groundwork. The book's title could hardly be more evocative of Bly's rural home in wintry western Minnesota. Most of the poems therein bear the unmistakable signature of the place and are permanently resonant. (Yet the impact of the book was not at all limited geographically—it was regional and universal at the same time.)

That first book was a long time coming. Bly had initially worked in conventional and melodic iambic pentameter from the English tradition, writing mostly longer poems that incorporated history.² Then, as he began to break loose from formal constraints, manifesting the revolution in himself, and starting his own magazine, he worked on a group called "Poems for the Ascension of J.P. Morgan."³

Bill Holm, of Icelandic heritage, born in 1943, was raised on a farm outside Minneota, a small town some thirty miles southeast of the less-small Madison. He writes: "At the end of the fifties, my high school years, western Minnesota looked to me like a mental wasteland, a psychological bowel obstruction."⁴ He describes finding the aforementioned Morgan poems in *New World Writing,* a magazine in mass-market paperback format. "I read with delight. Here was what I wanted from American poetry, culture, politics, daily life—and hadn't found: cranky attacks on smug Lutherans, respectable Republicans, the 'malefactors of great wealth,' and the killers of joy in the spirit and body." He continues: "This was the dumb world that hovered over Minneota, that no one dared fight, and a Norwegian from Madison had stood up to it in a New York magazine. He was as Lutheran and Scandinavian as I was, and he had said it!"

And on: "Oats! Imagine them in a poem! I had shoveled them in a granary, choking on dust and chaff, and here they were in a poem! There were no oats or Shell stations in T.S. Eliot." Furthermore: "The daily details of a life like my father's were written down with simplicity and dignity...." Holm surely appreciated lines like the following:

---

2   For more on this, see my forthcoming essay, "Haunted in a Landscape of Ghosts: Robert Bly & Little Crow," *Middle West Review* 11.2 (Spring 2025).

3   Intended as a book, it was never published as such, appearing rather in *New World Writing* 15 (1959), 61-77. Many of these poems would finally make their way, in altered form, into *The Light Around the Body* (1967), and one into *Silence in the Snowy Fields* (1962).

4   Bill Holm, "Why I Live in Minneota: A Birthday Essay for Robert Bly," in *Walking Swiftly,* 63.

> "I too am still shocking grain, as I did as a boy, dog-tired, / And my great-grandfather steps on his ship."[5]
> "Each day I live, each day the sea of light / Rises...."
> "the dark tears in the shacks of the oats"
> "On the farm the darkness wins, / And the small ones nestle in their graves of cold...."

These were not stock pastoral poetry props. To this thoughtful, young, rural Minnesotan reader (and others who happened to see them), these images were striking. They leapt off the page.

Both the wide prairie of southwestern Minnesota and the woodland and lake country of the North (where his uncle had a cabin) fixed themselves at an early age in Bly's head, heart, and soul. He thus was not strictly partial to the "horizontal grandeur" of the prairie.[6] Rather, he had, in Holm's terms, both a "prairie eye" and a "woods eye"—as his poetry makes clear. "The prairie eye looks for distance, clarity, and light; the woods eye for closeness, complexity, and darkness." Bly's love for the entire state, its flora and fauna, its landscape, its weather, and its seasons, was deep and abiding. He lived close to the earth and had a mystic's awe of nature. What one might presume would appear peripheral, dull, and unexciting to a "sophisticated" outsider is instead revealed as rich, complicated, and thrilling. That is, it is shown to connect with the inner life, too.

Silence in the Snowy Fields made a big splash in the American poetry sphere—it received more than forty reviews—and it also allowed young Minnesota poets to discover "what they didn't know they knew—about their place, their backgrounds, their imaginations, and the rich heritage and continuing changes of which we are all a part."[7] He was pointing to subtle, important, and profound aware-

---

    5   From "Remembering in Oslo the Old Picture of the Magna Carta," the only one of the "Morgan poems" to appear in *Silence in the Snowy Fields*.

    6   Bill Holm, "Horizontal Grandeur," in *The Music of Failure* (Plains Press, 1985), 16-19.

    7   Vinz & Tammaro, xiv.

ness of our geographical (and climatological) lives, not to mention a particular cultural ethos.[8] Also showing that beneath the mask of the ordinary—in darkness, silence, solitude, and in the attention to minute particulars—was to be found the other world, with a concomitant sense of sacredness, the divine, and the eternal moment.

Consider the first and last stanzas of "Poem in Three Parts":

> Oh, on an early morning I think I shall live forever!
> I am wrapped in my joyful flesh,
> As the grass is wrapped in its clouds of green.
>
> ....
>
> The strong leaves of the box-elder tree,
> Plunging in the wind, call us to disappear
> Into the wilds of the universe,
> Where we shall sit at the foot of a plant,
> And live forever, like the dust.

"I worked in the *Snowy Fields* poems to gain a resonance among the sounds and hidden below that there is a second resonance between the soul and a loved countryside, in this case the countryside of my childhood."[9] The words he used were full of energy, they seemed to rise up from the land and to embody it. There were farms, fields, stones, bones, trees, dust, animals, birds, small towns, woods, lakes, rivers, sky, seasons, sun, and snow, all that he knew intimately. This was pastoral poetry, at least implicitly contrasting the simple life in the country with the more complicated life elsewhere.

Even as Bly's world had been expanding in so many ways (especially after his "discoveries" in Norway), his poems began to narrow their focus when it came to landscape. He was finding his

---

8   The early stage of that white (Norwegian) settler ethos might have been best captured O.E. Rolvaag's novel, *Giants in the Earth* (Harper & Brothers, 1927).

9   Bly, *Selected Poems* (Harper & Row, 1986), 27.

true center, using more of what was most immediate to his senses. At the same time, he was decisively throwing off the straitjacket of the academic poetry of that era, with all its formal and psychological restrictions—meter, rhyme, the usual rhetoric and metaphors, and intellectualism. Since 1958, signs of this realignment had been gradually revealed in his own critical essays, translations, and the few poems of his that had appeared in his magazine and in others.[10] Now those signs were on full display.

The poems in *Silence* are mostly about the inward world, the poet's feelings. Confident in his own imagination, he follows wherever it leads, as energy flows between the natural world and the human. With subtle historical references, he uses straightforward, colloquial language. The poetry is subjective and personal (neither autobiographical nor confessional), intuitive/non-rational, and quiet. Unorthodox and quietly revolutionary.

Here is "Watering the Horse":

> How strange to think of giving up all ambition!
> Suddenly I see with such clear eyes
> The white flake of snow
> That has just fallen in the horse's mane!

Bly himself says of these poems: "The rhythm of the lines is… adapted from Waley's translations of Chinese poems, Frank O'Connor's translations of Celtic poems, and my own translations of Machado…."[11] Elsewhere he cites John Millington Synge, the Irish playwright and poet, whose work focused on the lives of Irish peasants, the rural working class. He also adds about Antonio Machado: "He is the father of that book."[12] In other words,

---

10   See *Born Under, passim.*
11   *Selected Poems,* 26. O'Connor's translations in *The Fountain of Magic* (1939) that he liked particularly were "Winter," "Autumn," "Hugh Maguire," "County Mayo," and "How Well for the Birds."
12   "Robert Bly: Interview," in Ekbert Faas, *Towards a New American*

these poems did not rise up spontaneously, fully formed, out of the Minnesota ground.

Rather, Bly was hewing to and borrowing from some eclectic traditions, thereby bringing a new internationalism, a kind of cross-cultural collaboration, all informed now by Jungian psychological emphases. They were the means of wilding, an alternative to the relatively narrow and conservative literary education he had received.[13] And, maybe most remarkably, he was finding a way for it all to co-exist, to live beautifully in harmony with his own Midwestern demotic language, and his experiences in that particular place, climate, and culture. The poems, simple on their face, wore their learning lightly; these traditions were only implicit in the mix. Almost as if by a kind of strange magic.

These loco-descriptive poems were thus authentic, genuine, also introspective, limpid, fresh, direct. Dream life took on importance. And solitude was shown to be a high value. Consider in this context Ralph Waldo Emerson's transcendentalist viewpoint: "In the woods…. Standing on the bare ground,—my head bathed by the blithe air, and uplifted into infinite space,—all mean egotism vanishes. I become a transparent eyeball; I am nothing; I see all; the currents of the Universal Being circulate through me; I am part or particle of God."[14] Such is the value of paying attention, being wide open to what is all around.

Bly was using images of the objective world of Minnesota to—by means of imaginative leaps—reflect his own subjective inner state, the landscape of the unconscious mind, inviting readers to experience both the mystical revery of living in harmony and reciprocity with nature and a cosmic vision, and to make journeys to their own inward worlds. Elemental rural images did not confine his poetry to one place but opened the world up to pervasive spiritual

---

Poetics: Essays & Interviews (Black Sparrow Press, 1979), 223.

13   Details in *Born Under*, 25-40

14   "Nature," in *Ralph Waldo Emerson: Essays & Lectures* (The Library of America, 1983), 10 (originally written in 1836).

and psychological concerns. They were a source of energy for amazing creativity and intensity, unlimited by place and time.

For young poets also from or in the countryside of Minnesota and the Upper Midwest, the recognition/familiarity factor made this influence even greater. With his notable use of the first-person singular pronoun "I" in this book, Bly surely helped all those young poets, writing poems solitarily, to feel affirmed as they assumed the same manner of representing their own outer and inner lives. Two examples, the first being the first two stanzas of what we may call a woods or lake poem:

> These pines, these fall oaks, these rocks,
> This water dark and touched by wind—
> I am like you, you dark boat,
> Drifting over water fed by cool springs
>
> Beneath the waters, since I was a boy,
> I have dreamt of strange and dark treasures,
> Not of gold, or strange stones, but the true
> Gift, beneath the pale lakes of Minnesota. [15]

Or this, the first stanza of "Driving Toward the Lac Qui Parle River," a prairie poem:

> I am driving; it is dusk; Minnesota.
> The stubble field catches the last growth of sun.
> The soybeans are breathing on all sides.
> Old men are sitting before their houses on carseats
> In the small towns. I am happy,
> The moon rising above the turkey sheds.

The particulars were so obvious and meaningful to some. The uni-

---

15 "After Drinking All Night with a Friend, We Go Out in a Boat at Dawn to See Who Can Write the Best Poem." (William Duffy and Bly were up north on Kabekona Lake, preparing the third issue of *The Fifties*. For details on Duffy's involvement in the first three issues of *The Fifties,* see Chapter 4 of *Born Under.*)

versals were revelatory, reassuring, and freeing to all poets who had ears to hear. It was earth-shaking, really. The subject wasn't far away—in urban cultural centers on the coasts—but close by, just out the door or down the road. The extraordinary—the sometimes elusive spiritual dimension—could be located in the apparently modest bits of one's own, not someone else's, life. All it required was acute awareness and engagement.

Enough from me. Converging testimonials from young poets, on their initial encounters with his book, follow. Patricia Kirkpatrick: "Robert Bly's gifts have awakened many readers and writers. The Minnesota landscape of his childhood awakened him, and that gift—the spirit of a particular land—has been given to many, whether the land was…a birthright the writer was born to or a heritage the writer sought." She adds, "I received Bly's poetry of an essential if undervalued American landscape as a gift…."[16] She also notes that many of the poems are in "plain, colloquial language," and show "the subtle but steady interplay between literal physical description and metaphorical suggestion. Sometimes it's hard to tell the difference between those last two…."[17] No more sense of placelessness, or spiritual homelessness. Rather, one can confidently situate oneself.

Jim Moore says, remembering the socio-historical context of the mid-1960s: "in *Silence*…he really focused on this Midwestern landscape, and that was wonderful for a lot of us who were young and trying to figure out what our heritage was and what it was worth writing about at a time of great national turmoil. Things were very unsettled, and to have this book come along with poems about the snow falling and so on was really quite wonderful."[18]

Even for a poet from elsewhere in Middle America, *Silence* exerted a pull. Louis Jenkins, born in Oklahoma, then living in Colorado and Kansas, found the book to be "electrifying. I thought

---

16   Kirkpatrick, "Shadows on the Prairie," 43.
17   Ibid., 33.
18   MG interview with JM, 7 January 2020.

poets all lived in England or New York, someplace far away. This was the landscape I knew and the language I knew, only more, it was poetry. ... I puzzled over the poems. So simple, yet they contained so much. The poems were full of things I knew, barns, farmhouses, fields... ordinary midwestern landscape, dull as dirt, suddenly transformed, their mystery lighted up like the gas in a neon tube."[19]

Bill Holm writes: "*Silence in the Snowy Fields*...seems to me one of the great formative books of American literature in the twentieth century. It brings into consciousness parts of our lives and places we had never seen clearly before. My own western Minnesota that I simultaneously hated and loved proved more full of metaphor and mystery than I (or anyone else) imagined."[20]

One did not have to be from a small prairie town to appreciate these poems. St. Paulite Patricia Hampl says: "The book was a revelation...for me, as a Minnesota kid, a stunning proof that you could write about this place, and it counted in the larger world. The book was about a rural landscape, and I was a city girl, but Minnesota snow is Minnesota snow."[21]

Kirkpatrick, again, says Bly "used the imagery of that landscape to show that the place itself is not only a source of literal nourishment and spiritual sustenance but also a playing field for historic events and their political consequences."[22] It may be that, as Garrison Keillor left serious poetry behind in the latter 1960s, he did not entirely leave behind his encounter with Bly and *Silence*. That is, captivated by the name of the Prairie Home Cemetery in Moorhead, he started a radio program, "The Prairie Home Morning Show," which soon blossomed into a full-blown variety show, "A Prairie Home Companion," centered on the not-quite-fictional town of Lake Wobegon, populated

---

19   "How I Discovered Robert Bly," in *Walking Swiftly*, 35-6.
20   Holm, "Why I Live in Minneota," 69.
21   PH email to MG, 19 February 2020.
22   Kirkpatrick, "Shadows on the Prairie," 37.

primarily by Scandinavian and Lutheran residents. He learned that a splendid career could be made spinning such tales, writing monologues, stories, and novels—all of them getting below the surface—around the people in such a place.[23]

* * *

Suffice it to say that the book's effect was phenomenal. With language often characterized as flat, plain, minimalist, and imagistic, it served as the primary example of what was becoming known as the Deep Image school of poetry. In a nutshell, that meant deploying images arising from the unconscious depths to connect the inner world of the psyche with the outer world of the cosmos. He was expressing what was otherwise ineffable.

Back to Hampl, who says that as an English major at the University of Minnesota she studied mostly "British, not American, writers, and especially writers of the past. … Whitman…was considered at best an eccentric, at worst a barbarian."[24] (This mirrors almost exactly Bly's experience twenty years earlier at Harvard. Remarkable, how little had changed.) But this new book, she continues, "opened my eyes and ears to the lyric possibilities of the contemporary American vernacular—and an unapologetic Midwestern vernacular at that—the very voice I had been taught to disdain in my classes. … When I read *Silence*…I experienced one of those galvanizing moments that change everything. I simply understood…that everything that had been dismissed about the world around me and which, unwittingly, I was being educated to dismiss was in fact the material of a life's work, the reason to be a poet at all. … The voice of our life right-here-right-now had not been rendered, and Robert Bly…was refusing to turn himself into a faux English poet in order to win the prizes that came with that bargain."

---

23   The first radio broadcast was on July 6, 1974, from the campus of Macalester College and before an audience of fewer than twenty.

24   Hampl, "Midwestern Sublime," 7.

The second book

James Wright, in contrast to Bly, *had* made that bargain with the devil, and then repented of it (see Chapter 3). But his third book, *The Branch Will Not Break*, which represents a sea change in his poetry—largely due to their fast friendship, their discussions, their co-translating of Georg Trakl and César Vallejo, and Bly's editing of Wright's poems—stands as the twin of *Silence*.[25] That is, these two books together were the *ur*-texts of the new Deep Image poetry, poems that "value and celebrate solitude, the earth, elemental presences, and the inner life."[26]

Wright had been looking for nourishing ground in which to put down roots and create. Since he had been going out to the farm, starting in September 1958, and staying overnight in the revamped

---

[25] See my essay, "Bringing Blood to Trakl's Ghost," *Antioch Review* 72.4 (Fall 2014), 636-54; and *Born Under,* esp. 21ff., and 48ff.

[26] Thomas R. Smith, "A Poet with no Business Sense: In Praise of Tom Hennen," afterword in Tom Hennen, *Darkness Sticks to Everything: Collected & New Poems* (Copper Canyon Press, 2013), 167.

Sowing Seeds

chicken house, many of his poems were written or started there, with clear reference to the landscape. (So also at Duffy's farm, less often and always in tandem with Bly.)

And in his quest to find the spirit of the place, he took root. Lawrence Durrell writes: "Everyone finds his own 'correspondences' in this way—landscapes where you suddenly feel bounding with ideas."[27] Wright plainly had found rapport with the place, a "triggering town," so to speak. Bly had liberated Wright from his early "old-fashioned" influences. Both of their poems now "bore the indelible mark of Minnesota, making the land and their new aesthetic inseparable and teaching an entire generation of readers that one could write about the state in a way that was not stale and anachronistic—that Minnesota was capable of sustaining a viable poetry."[28]

The Branch was another book full of dreams, moons, stones, bones, horses, and dust. And Wright had learned at last really to pay attention, to be patient, as exemplified by the remarkable "Lying in a Hammock at William Duffy's Farm in Pine Island, Minnesota," a litany of sensory images that ends with the stunning, revelatory, rueful, but also joyful statement: "I have wasted my life." He had a rebirth and a new life concentrated on the new poetry. As another of the famous poems from this book, "The Blessing," ends: "Suddenly I realize / That if I stepped out of my body I would break / Into blossom." That germination noted above (in Chapter 3) now had its happy and intended, if not exactly foreseen, result.

Wright expresses his new-found satisfaction in "Today I Was Happy, So I Made This Poem":

> As the plump squirrel scampers
> Across the roof of the corncrib,
> The moon suddenly stands up in the darkness,

---

27 Lawrence Durrell, "Landscape and Character," *Spirit of Place: Letters and Essays on Travel* (E.P. Dutton, 1969), 160.

28 Robert Hedin, ed., *Where One Voice Ends*, xxv.

> And I see that it is impossible to die.
> Each moment of time is a mountain.
> An eagle rejoices in the oak trees of heaven,
> Crying
> *This is what I wanted.*

He had not left his troubles behind, not at all, but he found some respite and, as in *Silence in the Snowy Fields*, he was making the mystical connection between the outer world and the inner. Consider at the last this poem full of attention and mystery, "Milkweed":

> While I stood here, in the open, lost in myself,
> I must have looked a long time
> Down the corn rows, beyond grass,
> The small house,
> White walls, animals lumbering toward the barn.
> I look down now. It is all changed.
> Whatever it was I lost, whatever I wept for
> Was a wild, gentle thing, the small dark eyes
> Loving me in secret.
> It is here. At the touch of my hand,
> The air fills with delicate creatures
> From the other world.

It is noteworthy that, shortly before both books were published, Bly's own Sixties Press published *The Lion's Tail and Eyes,* an anthology of ten poems each by Bly, Wright, and Duffy. A primer of deep-image poetry, its purpose was, as Bly says, "to show a poetry without direct statement."[29] He was presenting a poetry of images to describe "the fundamental world of poetry…the inward world. The poem expresses what we are just beginning to think, thoughts we have not yet thought. The poems must catch these thoughts alive, holding them in language that is also alive, flexible and animal-like

---

29   RB to DH, 27 September 1962.

as they."[30] The local connection was so plain that Bly initially tossed around the following tentative book titles with connections to Minnesota history and geography: *Past the Days of Ramsey*, *Past Pillsbury and Ramsey*, and *The Source of the Mississippi*.[31]

About the combined liberating effect that *Silence* and *The Branch* had on local aspiring poets, Hampl recalls:

> It may be hard now to capture the provincial self-consciousness—and its attendant feeling of worthless-

---

    30   Robert Bly, "Note," in James Wright, William Duffy, and Robert Bly, *The Lions' Tail and Eyes: Poems Written out of Laziness and Silence* (The Sixties Press, 1962), 6. Duffy is left out of this chapter's discussion as his poetry career, such as it was, always urged on by Bly, stalled permanently after this book.

    31   RB Journal, 29 December 1959. Minnesota's nineteenth-century history, especially in regard to its Dakota inhabitants, weighed much on his mind in the 1950s. See Chapter 8 and, again, my forthcoming "Haunted in a Landscape of Ghosts."

ness—of that era. … I don't mean that we felt personally worthless, but that there was this bulwark of legitimacy that made everything from New York—and better yet, from London—what really counted. We *received* culture and literature; we didn't make it. Or we made it but were "regional." *Silence in the Snowy Fields* and *The Branch Will Not Break* shifted that in a stroke.[32]

In the literary world, at least, Minnesota would no longer be unplaced.

Other writers reiterate Hampl's remarks. Michael Dennis Browne, then a young professor at the University of Minnesota, recalls: "*Silence* was a key book for many of us, as was *The Branch*."[33] David Wojahn, one of his many students, says: "Reading early Bly, and James Wright's breakthrough work done at the same time thanks in no small measure to Bly's influence, changed my life. The discovery that literature of the first order could arise from the places where I came from, and not from New York or San Francisco or Boston, was a revelation, and that got me going on the path."[34] Kirkpatrick remembers being given these two books. "For me these poems were the revelation of an inner life that took place in a landscape I knew from my childhood in Iowa. They showed me what poetry could be in contemporary life."[35]

Michael Moos recalls walking into a bookstore in Moorhead, "by chance" taking *The Branch* off the shelf and, "by chance" opening it to "A Blessing." He writes, "by the time I arrived at the poem's closing lines, I was hooked. I knew I wanted to use words that way. … That one poem changed my life. [It] ignited my giving

---

32 PH email to MG, 19 February 2020.
33 MDB email to MG, 13 June 2020.
34 DW email to MG, 19 July 2020.
35 Kirkpatrick, "Shadows on the Prairie," 41.

my life to writing poetry."[36] Wright's own transformation/blossoming led in turn to his.

* * *

Books like these did not make Allen Tate happy. But, entirely unanticipated by him, he and his kind were soon to be left behind. Jonathan Mayhew writes: "By all accounts the proliferation of creative writing programs in U.S. universities in the 1970s brought with it an institutionalization of the deep image school." He adds: "Very few literary modes in the history of the world have been so successful in purely *quantitative* terms as the poetry of deep image, given the expansion of writing programs during this period."[37] The irony here is thick, as Bly himself famously and repeatedly deplored the ubiquity and doubted the utility of such programs (even though he was an early participant and beneficiary).

This new Minnesota poetry, sown first by Bly and then Wright, came into the fore over the next two decades, both in Minneapolis and St. Paul and all over the state. There was a sudden genuineness and self-consciousness in it, especially vis-à-vis the Minnesota landscape. An entire generation of poets in the region was directly inspired and influenced by those two.

Tom Hennen remembers, when he was twenty years of age in 1962, driving with a friend to nearby Madison:

> We had been told he was a real, live poet and that he lived …in a tree house a few miles out of town. That did not seem unlikely to us—for a poet. … Uninvited as we were, we were nevertheless welcomed enthusiastically by both Robert and Carol and offered food and yak dung tea (that is what Robert called it…). Later in the afternoon, James Wright, who had been

---

36   Michael Moos email to MG, 28 May 2024.
37   Jonathan Mayhew, *Apocryphal Lorca: Translation, Parody, Kitsch* (The University of Chicago Press, 2009), 99.

> napping in the chicken coop/writing shack, came into the house and made the afternoon as complete as could be. We were overwhelmed in a wonderful way by all the talk of poems and poets and the humor and the literary gossip. In the evening, we left with our hands full of books given to read and to keep. Our heads were full of poetry, and we now knew real live poets could be anywhere.[38]

And those poets were not only real and alive in Minnesota, but also approachable and generous.

Wojahn says that while Bly was always "the loudest voice in the room.... he never seemed interested in molding followers and disciples. The Minnesota writing community of that era was small, but there were a good many voices in it who differed in important ways from Bly. And it was a *community*: I was mentored, formally and informally, by Michael Dennis Browne, Jim Moore, Trish Hampl, and especially James L. White." Bly was not meaning to create poets in his own image. Nevertheless, while the fluid, diffuse, and ubiquitous influence of Bly's example was good as an initial prod, prompt, and inspiration, it was also dangerous if hung on to too tightly.

As he became the dominant poetic figure in Minnesota, there were hazards for young poets who had put themselves under his sway. Bly's friend David Ray foresaw this early on: "That's the terrible impact of you & Wright. It will result in so much imitation, even on the part of people who don't want to be derivative in any way."[39] Louis Jenkins admits that as he first entered Bly's orbit in the latter 1960s, "I wrote bad imitations of Robert Bly (and James Wright and others."[40] Garrison Keillor, out of the University and just

---

38 Tom Hennen, "A Thick Skin and a Job You Can Stand." http://www.shiningrockpoetry.com/retrospective-essay-by-tom-hennen/

39 DR to RB, 13 May 1963.

40 "How I Discovered Robert Bly," in *Walking Swiftly*, 38.

getting into radio, wrote to Bly about waking up early at a mutual friend's house in New York: "I put together laboriously some pieces of that morning into a poem which I've been afraid to read anyplace lest somebody accuse me of imitating you. I mention this by way of saying a few poets can re-order our consciousness so that from time to time we live inside their poems, and that you are one of them."[41]

It is unsurprising that an aspiring young poet, open to such a powerful influence, would imitate or write in an imitative or highly derivative manner. The same applies to artists of all kinds. The point was to learn from such apprenticeship and to then grow into one's unique, individual style.[42] A decade or so later, Bill Holm had sent some poems for Carol Bly to read; she reacted: "Objections to the poems are just the old ones, of echoing Robert's work… It'd be one thing if you were short of talent and so you gained a little overtone and undertone by twanging Bly's string, but you aren't."[43] Surely many other young poets were in the same boat. The Minneapolis critic and editor James Naiden (see Chapters 9 and 10) derisively referred to such epigones, dependent and imitative poets, as "Blylings."

Many fine poems have been written in Minnesota in the decades since, even as Bly's and Wright's marks are still discernible. Bly's message was not that a poet from Minnesota had to stay in Minnesota, but that one could and still be a poet, with an endless abundance of material to draw on. The example of these two poets' work was inspiring to rising poets as it opened their minds to what

---

41 GK to RB, 9 April 1969.

42 See my essay, "Captain Robert Bly, Ortega y Gasset, and the Buddha on the Road," *Kenyon Review* 35.4 (Fall 2013), 203-24.

43 CB to BH, n.d. (later 1970s?). She perceptively details the problems: "Any sentence beginning with 'It is…' is swiped from Neruda, Vallejo and Robert and I'm afraid we all should tell ourselves we just have to give up the 3rd person present tense impersonal structure because those guys sewed it up." Also, "the Bly type of surreal," "the combination of anapest and iamb that Robert works out, with that kind of caesura that he uses a lot," and "that philosophical, deliberate weary tone that is his."

regional poetry could be and as they started their own careers, writing their own poems, and setting new examples for other poets in turn. Thus, their crucial role in the development of literary life here.

A fitting end to this Chapter is a poem from a student of Wright's at Macalester College (where he taught after the University of Minnesota had let him go). We get from it a strong sense of how poems do their work of propagation and transformation, and of how the lineage of the poetry of place from Bly and Wright would continue. "On a Night When Poetry on Paper Gets Us Nowhere," written in the mid-1960s, is the first poem in the first book by Freya Manfred:

> I am going to let the leaves of my poems flicker in
> the wind
> Until they are scooped and swung
> And left to lie fluttering between the rocks.
> Grasshoppers can make prints across them
> Until they turn green and brown like the prairie;
> Until the pink rocks crumble loose over them,
> I will let them lie.
> And the next month in an evening
> When near clouds melt off into south coming rain,
> A heavy water drop ahead of the pack
> Will soak the last words to dirt.
> A week later, rain gone by,
> There I hope a goldenrod will grow.[44]

---

[44] Freya Manfred, *A Goldenrod Will Grow* (James D. Thueson, Publisher, 1971), 9. In this context I am also reminded of Richard Brautigan's *Please Plant This Book* (self-published, 1968), consisting of eight seed packets (for flowers and vegetables), each imprinted with a poem.

Chapter 5
A River Runs Through It:
Dinkytown & the West Bank

> All around us were good people, old-fashioned grassroots intellectuals and artists who made a sort of ramshackle paradise...[1]
> –Garrison Keillor

"Now at last I was in Minneapolis where I felt liberated and gone, never meaning to go back."[2] After graduating from Hibbing High School, way up on the Mesabi Iron Range, in 1959, young Robert Zimmerman had boarded a Greyhound bus, ostensibly to attend the University of Minnesota. He adds: "I suppose what I was looking for was what I read about in *On the Road*—looking for the great city, looking for the speed, the sound of it, looking for what Allen Ginsberg had called the 'hydrogen jukebox world.'"[3]

Bob Dylan wanted much more—and less—than a college education. "Folk music was all I needed to exist."[4] He first stayed

---

1 Garrison Keillor, "Foreword," in Cyn Collins, *West Bank Boogie: Forty Years of Music, Mayhem and Memories* (Triangle Park Creative, 2006), 6.
2 Bob Dylan, *Chronicles, Volume One* (Simon & Schuster, 2004), 234.
3 Ibid., 235. The phrase is from "Howl."
4 Ibid., 236.

at the Jewish fraternity house, Sigma Alpha Mu (one brother, a "Sammy," was the future bookseller, Bill Savran), gravitating to Dinkytown, the largely student-occupied neighborhood anchored at the intersection of 4th St. and 14th Ave. S.E., on the northern edge of campus; then a hatchery for the barely nascent Minneapolis counterculture, a microcosm of the spirit of the time across the country.[5] In its bohemian atmosphere he at once found the record store, where he discovered the music of Odetta.

Soon, with a new used guitar in hand and some of her songs and Leadbelly's in his head, he dropped in at a coffeehouse, the Ten O'Clock Scholar, "looking for players with kindred pursuits."[6] He was wanting to collaborate. At 418 14th Ave. S.E., the Scholar (a.k.a. The Squalor, to some) was a hangout where avowed philosophers, graduate students, ABDs, misfits, activists, artists, writers, poets and wannabes, drank coffee or tea (no liquor license—imbibing only back in the alley), smoked, played chess, talked, read, and wrote.[7] Also, musicians—in the evening there was live music on the four-inch-high stage. Dylan met guitarist/singer John Koerner and other players there as his tuition in folk music began in earnest.

---

[5] This was a much different place than it had been in the 1930s and 40s, as described by Frederick Manfred in *Dinkytown* (Dinkytown Antiquarian Bookstore, 1984).

[6] Dylan, 237.

[7] "The Squalor" from Eric Fraser Storlie's memoir, *Go Deep & Take Plenty of Root* (CreateSpace Publishing, 2013). ABD is the unofficial designation (All But Dissertation) for graduate students stuck, sometimes permanently, in the limbo of having completed the required coursework for a PhD but not the doctoral thesis itself.

Photo courtesy Hennepin County Library

One journalist a few years later quoted owner Dave Lee, who said that he regularly kicked Dylan out. "Dylan would come in and sing, and for a while it was all right, but that monotone would go on and Muriel [his wife] would say to me 'They're beginning to leave. You'd better get rid of him.'" Clepper writes: "But he kept coming back, singing as if only for himself."[8]

Quickly overshadowing his university classes, Dylan's informal, peripheral education soon included the blues, music with black roots. He saw the connection to the place where he was from:

> Highway 61, the main thoroughfare of the country blues, begins about where I came from . . . Duluth to be exact. I always felt like I'd started on it, always had been on it and could go anywhere from it, even down into the deep Delta country. It was the

---

8   P.M. Clepper, "Dylan's Fortune," *This Week* [Sunday magazine of *Minneapolis Tribune*] (March, 27, 1966), 8.

> same road, full of the same contradictions, the same one-horse towns, the same spiritual ancestors. The Mississippi River, the bloodstream of the blues, also starts up from my neck of the woods. I was never too far away from any of it. It was my place in the universe, always felt like it was in my blood.[9]

This acknowledgment of his Minnesota roots and their pull may stand as this boy from the North Country's pledge of allegiance of to his home on the range, to his neck of the woods, "where the winds hit heavy on the borderline," even as he wanted so badly to be gone.

Soon he became mesmerized by Woody Guthrie, "head over heels in singing nothing but Guthrie songs—at house parties, in the coffeehouses, street singing, with Koerner, not Koerner...."[10] The experience changed his life. "The sun had swung my way. I felt like I'd crossed the threshold and there was nothing in sight."[11] Then Jon Pankake, "a folk music purist, enthusiast … authoritative and a hard guy to get past"—mainly because he had, with Paul Nelson, just launched the important and trailblazing folk music fanzine, *Little Sandy Review*— told him that he had to quit singing Guthrie only, and introduced him to the music of Ramblin' Jack Elliott. Pankake was renting a room upstairs in the house (on 5th St. and 14th Ave.) owned by a character named McCosh, who had a used bookstore one block south at 1404 4th St. S.E.

Bob Spitz describes this bookman's prominent place on the scene: "During the day, the Scholar attracted an in-group of Dinkytown's self-styled heads, presided over by Melvin McCosh, the Scholar's resident radical. A parlor anarchist who was a good ten years older than the rest of the crowd, McCosh ran an alternative bookstore a few doors away where fellow sympathizers gathered to play cards or chess, philosophize, and rail against America's Real-

---

9   Dylan, 240-1.
10 Ibid., 247.
11 Ibid., 248.

politik and the pretentious creeps who fed the system."[12] Garrison Keillor remembers the anarchist sayings posted around the shop, including: "The last capitalist we hang will be the one who sold us the rope."[13]

McCosh was an eccentric for sure, an intelligent, knowledgeable, and highly opinionated bookseller who considered his bookstore "an oasis of sanity."[14] It was a good spot to feed one's head, find one's comrades, and a critical component of "the intellectual infrastructure" of the time and place.[15] Although sui generis, he also had an eye to community. Each spring he sponsored a "Festival" in his yard, with—by his own report—booze, a pot of stew, and musicians playing.

Photo retrieved from preservehistoricdinkytown.org

---

12 Bob Spitz, *Dylan: A Biography* (Norton, 1989), 80.

13 November 1, 2021. https://garrisonkeillor.substack.com/p/post-to-the-host-694

14 Melvin McCosh, "Life from Inside Bookstore Windows," *Minneapolis Star,* March 10, 1979.

15 This term from Kristen Eide-Tollefson, long-time bookseller at the Bookhouse in Dinkytown, herself McCosh's successor (in the good important ways).

Now this account of urban topography and human geography, of the setting for later developments, begins to directly impinge on our larger story. Just after James Wright's life was changed in 1958 by the first issue of *The Fifties,* that packet of wild and powerful seeds (see Chapter 3), he told Bly that it was important to supply McCosh with copies to sell at his store: "He is the non-academic, and also non-pasteurized, non-supermarketish kind of bookseller who nevertheless has a certain kind of influence around this place."[16] Bly visited McCosh's on his next visit to the city, in an effort to keep spreading the word.

Dylan traces his view of the scene, including a trio that was key in the revival of folk music and blues, before his departure for the bigger world of New York: "As far as other singers around town, there were some but not many. There was Dave Ray, a high school kid who sang Leadbelly and Bo Diddley on a twelve-string guitar… and then there was Tony Glover, a harp player who played with me and Koerner sometimes."[17] Dave Morton, whom Dylan fails to mention, was another important musical, hipster friend and presence at the Scholar.

Morton, also one of the "radicals, freethinkers, and psychopaths"[18] boarding at McCosh's house, was far out. Like most folk musicians, he played the old standards, but also began writing his

---

16 JW to RB, 16 September 1958. There were other Dinkytown booksellers. Perine's Campus Book Store mostly (but not exclusively) sold textbooks for courses at the University. Nearby, Heddan's also had used books, but its owner apparently did not have McCosh's charisma or quirky panache. Jim and Kristen Eide Cummings' the Book House in Dinkytown did not start until 1976, but it rapidly became absolutely essential and filled the gap left by McCosh's departure from the scene.

17 Dylan, 256. In a few years, Koerner, Ray & Glover put out an album, *Blues, Rags and Hollers* (Audiophile, 1963), a cornerstone of the folk and blues revival.

18 These were McCosh's words, quoted in Carol Masters and Marv Davidov, *You Can't Do That! Marv Davidov, Nonviolent Revolutionary* (Nodin Press, 2009), 30

own songs. "These were topical songs about humanitarian issues and civil rights. The struggle for desegregation in the South was becoming a bloody business."[19] In 1961, Morton, together with Marv Davidov (see Chapter 6) and four other Minnesotans, went to Jackson, Mississippi as Freedom Riders (civil rights activists challenging the segregation practices in the Deep South). All six were arrested and sentenced to four months' imprisonment at the notorious state penitentiary, Parchman Farm—subject of Bukka White's "Parchman Farm Blues," which Dylan and Morton likely already knew of (unless they were listening instead to Mose Allison's recently recorded "Parchman Farm").

Two years later, Morton, whom his friend Davidov calls "the first hippie in Minnesota,"[20] put out *Region,* "a new magazine of the arts & social analysis" (likely an unintentional echo of *The Fifties'* prominent subtitle, "a magazine of poetry and general opinion," but which Morton had undoubtedly seen). It was the first evidence in Minnesota of the "mimeograph revolution," producing a literary magazine on the cheap, thereby undercutting the usual profit-driven paradigm.[21] Morton was the primary editor, with the collaboration of Davidov, Carl Klein, and Hugh Brown (another Dylan friend, subject of his song, "Talkin' Hugh Brown"). As stated in the back: "The money for the magazine came from two poetry reading benefits & several donations (the largest was $20)."

---

19   Howard Sounes, *Down the Highway: The Life of Bob Dylan* (Grove Press, 2001), 58.

20   Masters and Davidov, 36.

21   Surely the *Little Sandy Review,* mentioned earlier in this chapter, owed its existence to the mimeograph machine, but it wasn't a literary mag. For more on this phenomenon, see "A Little History of the Mimeograph Revolution," in *A Secret History of the Lower East Side: Adventures in Writing, 1960-1980,* eds. Steven Clay and Rodney Phillips (The New York Public Library and Granary Books, 1998), 12-54.

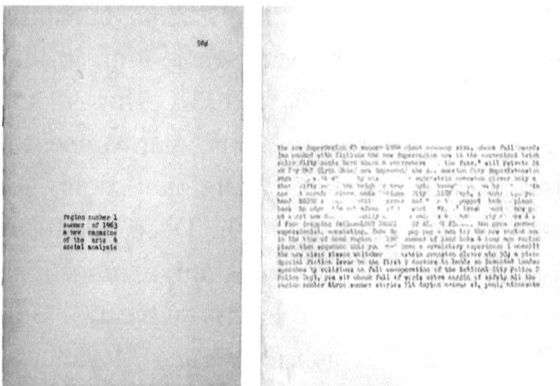

Despite its name, *Region* both was and wasn't a regional magazine. But three issues in two years—with its mix of politics (mostly anarchist), sex, drugs, music, poetry, fiction, and criticism—made plain that its writers and readers were on the rolling edge of the counterculture that would soon engulf America's youth. Contents included: poems by Jonathan Sisson, Richard Shaw, and Roland Flint (all at the University and contributors to the campus literary mag, the *Ivory Tower*); nonfiction, "Big Joe Blues," by local blues harp wizard Tony Glover (in which he mentions Dave Ray); short reviews of the novels *Catch-22, Naked Lunch* and *One Flew Over the Cuckoo's Nest,* by Irwin Klein (then a grad student in English, later a famous photographer); fiction, a raunchy short story by Tom Olson; and various other bits—a defense of Lenny Bruce and free speech, reports of visits to the Museum of Modern Art and the Guggenheim in New York, notices for SNCC (the Student Nonviolent Coordinating Committee, in the forefront of the Civil Rights Movement), plus the tongue-in-cheek suggestion to "smoke page seventeen" of the second issue, etc.—all of which conjointly communicate the rich and disparate flavor of the times, surely one thing that a wide-ranging arts magazine should do.

And, as usual in those days, members of the establishment (like Dylan's Mr. Jones) just didn't get it. Bob Lundegaard in the

Minneapolis Star, apparently shocked or disgusted by and unable to see beyond Tom Olson's short story (among other things), called *Region* "a largely pornographic, mimeographed magazine started by some University of Minnesota dropouts. Its last issue was fall 1965 [the reporter was mistaken, it was summer 1964], whereupon its editors dispersed."[22] His relief at its demise is apparent. Each issue advertised McCosh's bookstore, a key distribution point that *Region* shared with Bly's *The Sixties,* and where they would likely have appeared side by side.[23]

* * *

In 1962, the Minneapolis campus of the University of Minnesota, based on the east bank of the Mississippi, began gradually to extend its physical plant across the river gorge, via the Washington Ave. bridge, to the West Bank, also called Cedar-Riverside (the neighborhood's main intersection).[24] Cedar Avenue, known as Snoose Boulevard from the late 1800s when it was heavily populated by Swedes (putative *snus* [or moist snuff] users), was home to Dania Hall, an important cultural center for Danes, Swedes, and Norwegians. Founded in 1886, it had early on presented lectures from Knut Hamsun and others, plays by Anton Chekov, August Strindberg, and Henrik Ibsen, Swedish vaudeville, and

---

22   "Sizing up the Little Magazine: Is it the Voice of Professor or Protester?" *Minneapolis Star,* April 17, 1966.

23   Then Morton moved to California with his band, the Jook Savages, and *Region* was no more. He returned a few years later, and established the All-American City Super Extension Gallery upstairs from McCosh in the old firehouse on the West Bank. In those years his musical groups, the Vipers, Group X, and the Even Worse Jug Band performed on the West Bank at the Triangle Bar.

24   After World War II and the G.I. Bill, the number of students at the University grew exponentially. And the Baby Boomers were soon to reach college age. The first buildings were the Social Sciences Building, Blegen Hall, and what became known as Heller Hall, followed by Wilson Library.

traditional Scandinavian music and dance.[25] Cedar Ave. was also renowned for its many bars.

A year or two after the University's river-crossing, the folk and blues music scene followed. One of the owners of the Scholar, Dave Lee and his wife Muriel, opened Caesar's Bar in 1965 at 320 Cedar Ave.[26] Even the Scholar itself moved in 1966 to a defunct bar at 247 Cedar Ave. (on the site occupied by Theater in the Round since 1969). However, most of the musical stalwarts, including Maury Bernstein, Koerner, Ray, & Glover, Willie Murphy and the Bumblebees, the Sorry Muthas (with Bill Hinkley, Judy Larson, and Papa John Kolstad), and others, dug in at the Triangle Bar.[27] Gradually, they were also playing routinely at the Viking Bar, the 400 Bar, Palmer's, and the Five Corners Saloon, all in the immediate vicinity.[28] Soon, in 1970, the West Bank School of Music was founded, providing education in folk, blues, jazz, rock, country, and world music. This was, as Garrison Keillor (who was living on the West Bank then) put it: "a sweet time when everybody was an artist of some sort and stayed up late and talked with fervor and moral clarity and had tremendous metabolism."[29]

The literary scene, as measured in bookstores, shifted locations too. Having been evicted by a Bridgeman's restaurant expansion from his space in Dinkytown in 1964, McCosh moved his books into an abandoned firehouse at 1501 S. 4th St. on the West Bank, "a signal event," as Keillor says. He stayed there until 1971. And in 1965, Bill Savran, the son of a department store owner in Bismarck, North Dakota, a U of M graduate, opened Savran's Paperback Shop

---

25   Coincidentally, Bly by this time had translated Hamsun, Strindberg, and Ibsen.

26   It so happens that I was a bartender here eighteen years later.

27   An excellent source for this is Cyn Collins, op. cit. Leo Kottke recorded his first album, "12-String Blues" (Oblivion, 1969), at the West Bank iteration of the Scholar.

28   Another popular bar was the Mixers, on Washington Ave. (then Minneapolis' skid row), connected to Cedar via Seven Corners. See Storlie.

29   Keillor, "Foreword," 5.

nearby at 301 Cedar Ave. Employee Carolyn Zniewksi remembers: "The bookstore carried a huge inventory. Many titles were difficult to find elsewhere. We had a large occult section, and a large 'commie' section both of which were notable."[30] It became the go to place not just for its vast and eclectic array of new books including much poetry, but also for the latest issues of all kinds of literary and alternative magazines, papers, other publications, and community news. Indeed, as Tom Rusch remembers, one of the criteria for hiring at the bookstore was the applicant's sun sign.[31]

1974 photo by Linda Gammell

A key part of the all-important infrastructure supporting poets, writers, and their writing, bookstores had always been there, of course. There were the national and some local chains. But with the societal changes wrought by the political and countercultural currents of the 1960s, together with the accompanying growth of poetry writing, the mimeograph revolution, and the small press movement, soon a new kind of bookstore began to appear, of which Savran's was the prime

---

30   CZ email to MG, 1 May 2024.
31   So he says in the short TPT film on Savran's. https://www.facebook.com/watch/?v=1160280745406053

example in the region. It was, therefore, a gathering point for the leftist intellectual and countercultural community in the Twin Cities.

Back row, l. to r.: Carolyn Zniewksi, Bill Savran, Marly Rusoff, Diana Lynn. Front (and middle): Kris Johnson, Laurie Savran (daughter Deborah on her lap), Tom Ott (Photo from the *Minnesota Daily*, January 1971)

Regular patrons included Keillor, Tony Glover (who brought in Patti Smith after her performance at the Walker Art Center in 1972), Robert Bly, and many others. It was also another important organ of social cohesion. Marly Rusoff, a full-time employee with a grand future (see Chapter 7), said: "The bookstore ran like a family. People came through the door and were treated like family."[32] Several sites around the neighborhood began to be used for

---

32   Miguel Otárola, "His West Bank Bookstore Was a Literary Hub and Springboard" (Bill Savran obituary), *Minneapolis StarTribune* (October 2,

poetry readings, many including Bly (see Chapter 10), likely with customer overflow into Savran's.

By the latter 1960s, the West Bank welcomed the then burgeoning counterculture in Minneapolis and became a hotbed of anti-war and other political and anti-establishment activity. At this point, "Dinkytown was pretty collegiate. The West Bank…was where you'd go if you wanted to score some pot."[33] The street level of Dania Hall housed Richter's Drugs, a store/pharmacy that had become a hippie hangout, sometimes called "the heart of the West Bank." Bands like the Paisleys, the Litter, and Jokers Wild played up on the third floor in the auditorium/dance hall. In 1970, a benefit for the Black Panther Party defense fund was staged there. A site of some controversy, it was occasionally raided by the Minneapolis Police. So too the Electric Fetus, the nearby record store and head shop—both for displaying a poster depicting President Nixon and his wife naked, and for having a nude record sale (customers who showed up unclothed received a free album or hash pipe).

The Coffeehouse Extemporé, from 1965, and the New Riverside Café, started by a collective in 1970, were new places to meet and hang out, minus the alcohol. Utopian ideals of freedom, emancipation, and participation—approached by but not always matching with lived reality—were pervasive. And rent was cheap. Also, a spirit of revolt, led by youth; everywhere, or so it seemed, was anti-establishment movement, radical, grassroots activism, collective activity, with open and alternative social forms and efforts, like the phenomenon of the Free University, and putting together a food cooperative—not to mention the new poetics.

* * *

2020), B4. Zniewski adds (another sign of the times): "If you wanted to mail books to anyone in prison…they had to be new and mailed by a bookstore. Bill paid the postage and charged no handling fee on any books mailed to prisons."

33   David Wojahn email to MG, 19 July 2020.

An aside: While the street scene on the West Bank and in its vicinity was a perpetual theater—given how people looked, dressed, acted, spoke, and thought—it was also fertile ground for theater companies. First, on Seven Corners (the busy intersection where Cedar Ave. begins), in a side room of Mama Rosa's restaurant, Beth Linnerson, a waitress there, started the Moppet Players. Dedicated full-time to presenting theatrical shows for children, she soon was joined by Martha Boesing. After a few years and personnel changes, it became the Children's Theatre Company (still going).

At the same time, the '60s saw the rise of radical and experimental theater. On the periphery of the Seward neighborhood in south Minneapolis, which was closely linked to the West Bank (physically and in spirit), the Firehouse Theatre Company opened in a renovated firehouse on Minnehaha Avenue. Avant-garde drama was its purpose, and staff members included Paul and Martha Boesing. It put on premiers of plays by Megan Terry (some notorious for nudity) and Sam Shepard, plus older ones by Ionesco, Brecht, and Beckett. In 1969, their lease lost, the company moved to San Francisco.

The same year, the Theatre in the Round, a community theater of long standing, moved to a new space on Seven Corners, renovated after a fire at Bimbo's Pizza Parlor and Emporium, and the razing of the entire building, including the relocated Ten O'Clock Scholar. Many poetry readings would also be held there (see Chapter 10).

Sowing Seeds

Photo courtesy Hennepin County Library

The Powderhorn Puppet Theatre was founded by David O'Fallon and Ray St. Louis in 1973, named after the nearby Powderhorn Park neighborhood in South Minneapolis. On May 1, 1975, two weeks after the end of the Vietnam War, they, having been joined by Sandy Spieler, put on the first Mayday Parade and Festival, an annual community event now regularly involving tens of thousands of people. Known for its large-scale puppets and political activism, in 1979 it adopted a new name, In the Heart of the Beast Puppet and Mask Theatre.[34]

---

34 Note: Spieler, another visionary, became the long-time Artistic Director of HOBT in 1976. See *Sandy Spieler: 2014 Distinguished Artist* (The McKnight Foundation, 2014).

At the Foot of the Mountain was launched as an experimental theater in 1974 by Paul and Martha Boesing, Jan Magrane and three others who consulted the I Ching: "responding to the hexagram 'The Spring at the Foot of the Mountain'" whence came their name and inspiration. ... "Collectivity, community, and political commitment were essential elements of the theater company from the beginning, but by the end of the first summer season [1974]...the group had shifted toward a focus on women's experience."[35] After Paul and other men left the company, it "began to identify as feminist theater." Martha then taught an early class at the newborn Loft (see Chapter 7). It eventually moved into the Cedar-Riverside Peoples' Center on the West Bank (also a site for poetry readings).

Meanwhile, when Jack Reuler, twenty-two, a recent graduate of Macalester College, was dismayed by the absence of people of color in the Theatre in the Round's production of "The Great White Hope," in 1975, he decided to found a multiracial theater company, Mixed Blood, which then occupied the firehouse on the West Bank (which had also served as the second location of McCosh's Books and was the site of the first Loft benefit readings [see Chapter 7]).

* * *

In the neighborhood, many large, old houses were now communes, with communards working the vegetable gardens just out the door; soon the People's Pantry was set up (eventually becoming the North Country Co-op); so also the offices of the Twin Cities Draft Information Center and the Honeywell Project (founded in 1968 and led by Davidov—see Chapter 6) at 529 Cedar Ave. Next door in "Liberty House" was the office of *Hundred Flowers*, the underground newspaper collectively run by *Ivory Tower* alumnus Edwin Felien, Marly Rusoff, and friends, which, along with its attention to nation-

---

35 Lynne Greeley, "At the Foot of the Mountain: Historical Overview," in *Restaging the Sixties: Radical Theaters and Their Legacies,* eds. James M. Harding and Cindy Rosenthal (The University of Michigan Press, 2006), 130.

al and international news, had its fingers on the pulse of the local scene. But more on that ahead (see Chapter 7), when Dinkytown comes back into play and Rusoff takes on a major role in one of the most consequential Chapters in the history of the Minnesota literary renaissance.

To close this Chapter about two University neighborhoods important to this history, consider this cheeky parodic advertisement for "West Bank/Dinkytown, The Other Minneapolis" from the staff at *Ivory Tower*:

> "Darling," she says, "the neighbors are going to the Bahamas." But when your wife asks "Where are we going for our vacation?" look her in the eye and say "Minneapolis?" *That* should give her something to think about. She knows that Minneapolis is the City of Lakes and the home of the Billy Graham Evangelistic Association. But does she know about Dinkytown and the West Bank, where life is lived like it really is? On the fun-filled West Bank, which many have called "reminiscent of Hemingway's Paris," you can mix at the Mixers with disgruntled socialists and young executives. You can whistle at prostitutes, watch construction projects, hear the music of a thousand car radios during rush hour, or just relax in your rooming house and smoke pot. In colorful Dinkytown, which many have called "reminiscent," you can hear the new sound and style of student life today, while your wife gets in a little shoplifting. Tell your wife that *this* summer you're going to inter-act. Ask your travel agent for further details.[36]

---

36   *Ivory Tower* 14.7 (April 3, 1967), 5. No name attached, but the guest editor for this issue is Garrison Keillor, and the editor is Sam Heins. The Mixers by, the way, was a popular and gritty bar on Washington Ave., just a block or so west of Seven Corners. For more on it and its denizens, including poet James Wright, see Storlie, 135ff.

There were big changes in store for the neighborhood. In 1971 the construction of a huge housing complex, intended to be a "city within a city," began. Cedar Square West opened in 1973, with over a thousand apartments initially, dominated by a 39-storey concrete tower. It was designed by Ralph Rapson, head of the Architecture School at the University of Minnesota, and also the architect of the Guthrie Theater.

Chapter 6
Bread & Roses:
Minnesota Radical/Radical Minnesota

> Artists are the antennae of the [human] race.[1]
> –Ezra Pound

> Art as radar acts as 'an early alarm system,' as it were, enabling us to discover social and psychic targets in lots of time to prepare to cope with them. This concept of the arts as prophetic, contrasts with the popular idea of them as mere self-expression.[2]
> –Marshall McLuhan

As I was saying: In 1958, a young poet from western Minnesota started sowing seeds, seeds of different varieties. *The Fifties*, we might remember, was presented not only as "A Magazine of Poetry" but also of "General Opinion." Those last words were intended, in part, to give license to young poets to use their poems to engage with politics—widely construed to include public affairs, socio-political issues, current events, history, government, economics, lies,

---

    1   "The Teacher's Mission," reprinted in *Literary Essays of Ezra Pound* (New Directions, 1954), 58. I surmise that Pound was thinking of "antennae" in the zoological sense, not the technological one.
    2   *Understanding Media* (McGraw-Hill, 1964).

class, inequality, civil rights, human rights, ecology, peace and war, activism and protest. Bly the sower, social critic, and showman, was one of those responsible for leading poets out of the complacent, conformist 1950s with its false consciousness, and on into the tumultuous, countercultural 60s, radicalizing them. His leadership in that revolution had major, long-lasting, still detectable impact, across the nation and here in Minnesota.

He asked in that first issue: "Why do so few poets write now of business experience, of despair, or the Second World War?" Because they write in the "old tradition," Bly says:

> A new style is invented to deal with new subject matter, and...the most important experiences of our time. There is an imagination which realizes the sudden new change in the life of humanity, of which the Nazi camps, the terror of modern wars, the sanctification of the viciousness of advertising, the turning of everyone into workers, the profundity of associations, is all a part, and the relationships unexplained... There is an imagination which assembles the three kingdoms within one poem: the dark figures of politics, the world of streetcars, and the ocean world... We need poets now who can carry on a sustained raid into modern life, and in work after work, carry on the green and vigorous waters of this profound life.[3]

This was, in essence, his manifesto. Poets all over and in Minnesota heard this call.

In the same issue, James McCormick's facetiously titled report, "Good News from Chicago," tells of racism, collusion, corruption, anti-union activity, in Mayor Daley's "stormy, husky, brawling,

---

3 "Five Decades of Modern American Poetry," *The Fifties* 1 (1958), 38-9.

/ City of the Big Shoulders."[4] And Bly himself, using the pseudonym Charles Reynolds, has two poems, "England: The Nation in the Sea," and "Voyage of the Hungarian Dead After Death," both working examples of what his essay above called for.

Bly received a lot of pushback. In the third issue he stated his credo: "We believe that artists above all are not exempt from fighting in national issues. The greatest poets, Yeats among them, have opposed their government, or any organ of it, which was harmful to the people. Americans as a whole have been trained too much toward *tolerance*; when a false shepherd calls, they follow along like sheep."[5] As often, he was looking back and looking ahead simultaneously.

In 1959 was published his group of "Poems for the Ascension of J.P. Morgan" (see Chapter 4). Some must have thought: How dare he criticize the long-dead, great financier? And why? Well, Morgan's influence was still ascendant and pervasive.[6] The title of one of the poems, "None of Us Is Innocent," foreshadows the gist of some of Bly's later antiwar poems. Bill Holm describes his excited discovery of these as a high school student (see Chapter 4): "cranky attacks on…respectable Republicans, the 'malefactors of great wealth,' and the killers of joy in the spirit and body."[7] Many young Americans, feeling stifled in the conformist postwar and Cold War years, were ready for this.

In spring 1962, *The Sixties* #6 began with "Some Poems Touching on Recent American History." They include three poems by Wright, from his forthcoming third book, including "Eisenhower's Visit to Franco, 1959." Bly's four poems mention Henry Cabot Lodge, the cane fields in Cuba, and the United Fruit Company in

---

4 Carl Sandburg, "Chicago," 1914.
5 "A Note on Hydrogen Bomb Testing," *The Fifties* 3 (1959), 51.
6 Not to mention the fact that, today, JP Morgan Chase & Co. is the largest bank in the U.S. and also the world.
7 "Why I Live in Minneota."

Guatemala. "Condition of the Working Classes: 1960" is full of surrealistic changes, including: "the extricated [car] axles change to missiles with warheads / Climbing up, and the stages change into the aisles of a church..." Like a bellwether, he seemed to sense what was just around the bend.

In the same issue's essay, "On the Necessary Aestheticism of Modern Poetry," Bly takes on the poetic establishment of the New Critics, and John Crowe Ransom directly, who "presents modern poetry...as a poetry in which there is nothing public, no moral stand, no interest in public life."[8] Although ancient Greek and Elizabethan poets took an interest in public issues, now poets like Allen Tate "are praised for *avoiding* moral issues." Bly points out the untruth of Ransom's characterization of "the modern poet as one whose poetry, unlike the poetry of the past, takes no interest in moral questions or in the great issues of public life." That is, poetry that is purely aesthetic.

The reason for Ransom's misapprehension is his "disgraceful...elegant isolationism," his omitting from consideration all poets not writing in the English language, including Unamuno, Machado, Benn, Brecht, Apollinaire, Éluard, Mayakovsky, Pasternak, Neruda, and Vallejo. This view, Bly wrote, "which is now accepted as a truism in the universities, in the workshops, must be rejected..." Thus, Bly's revolution, his internationalizing, his wilding push for a renaissance.

A few early poems in *Silence in the Snowy Fields* (1962), part two of his sowing operation, seemed ominous, such as "Unrest" ("A strange unrest hovers over the nation: / This is the last dance..."), "Awakening" ("The storm is coming...") and "Poem Against the Rich" ("I hear the sad rustle of the darkened armies..."). Kirkpatrick calls this "a visionary dread toward the 'weather ahead' in America."[9] Bly, his antennae at work, was becoming restive, warning of

---

8 *The Sixties* 6 (Spring 1962), 22-4.
9 Kirkpatrick, 34.

the direction in which the United States was heading. As was another Minnesotan at the same time, whose voice was even more widely heard. In 1962 Bob Dylan first performed "A Hard Rain's a-Gonna Fall," a surrealistic song that, with its implicit sense of the social and political upheaval (the ongoing Cold War, and the struggle for Civil Rights) gaining energy, shows that he was in tune with the nation, that he, too, had a touch of prophetic power. It was recorded along with the equally pungent "Masters of War," and "Blowin' in the Wind"[10]

Bly was not a political or ideological poet in the same way as Thomas McGrath (see Chapter 2, from whom he learned much), but he felt it his responsibility and believed in the power of protest. And he was willing to shoulder a leading role, using his gift for sincere showmanship. There was always in those days an activist dimension to much of his poetry (even when not so obvious), and a polemical tone (also in his criticism, of course). As we shall see (Chapters 9, 12 and 14), even the act of publishing a little magazine and a small press was in itself political, in that it was autonomous, anti-institutional, anti-commercial, etc. Bly the sower was truly radical, "going to the root or origin; touching or acting upon what is essential and fundamental...characterized by independence of, or departure from, what is usual or traditional; progressive, unorthodox, or revolutionary (in outlook, conception, design, etc.)."[11] This definition also conveniently includes not just the poetical sense but also the political. And it was part of the larger process of wilding.

Bly met much resistance to his political poems and he gave it much thought. He wondered why so few American poets had written poems that dealt with political realities. "I think one reason is that political concerns and inward concerns have always been regarded

---

10   All three were recorded on *The Freewheelin' Bob Dylan* (Columbia Records, 1963). This album was followed by *The Times They Are a-Changin'* (Columbia Records, 1964).

11   The Oxford English Dictionary, s.v. "radical."

in our tradition as opposites, even incompatibles."[12] He continued with a brief look back at the 1950s from a psychological perspective:

> It's clear that many of the events that create our foreign relations come from more or less hidden impulses in the American psyche. It's also clear I think that some sort of husk has grown around that psyche, so that in the Fifties we could not look into it or did not. The Negroes and the Vietnam War have worn the husk thin in a couple of places now. But if that is so, then the poet's main job is to penetrate that husk around the American psyche, and since that psyche is inside *him* too, the writing of political poetry is like the writing of personal poetry, a sudden drive by the poet inward… Once inside the psyche, he can speak of inward and political things with the same assurance.

Finally, Bly (once a farm boy running through wheat and corn fields) writes not of husks but of the seeds themselves:

> The life of the nation can be imagined also not as something deep inside our psyche, but as a psyche larger than the psyche of anyone living, a larger sphere, floating above everyone. In order for the poet to write a true political poem, he has to be able to have such a grasp of his own concerns that he can leave them for a while, and then leap up into this other psyche. He wanders about there a while, and as he returns he brings back plant seeds that have stuck to his clothes, some inhabitants of this curious sphere, which he then tries to keep alive with his own body.

---

12   Robert Bly, "Leaping up Into Political Poetry," foreword to *Forty Poems Touching on Recent American History,* ed. Bly (Beacon Press, 1970), 9. This essay had originally been written several years earlier.

This may seem unconscious sowing, sowing by happenstance, but it all follows from choosing to leap up into the psyche of the nation or to penetrate the husk, from choosing to write a true political poem. "The true political poem...like the personal poem, moves to deepen awareness."

His passion for poetry, for matters spiritual and literary, psychological and political, plus the tremendous energy he gave to antiwar work, was a powerful combination. Especially in a time when a young person, particularly male, had to be engaged in some way with the Vietnam War. Those young men also stood in need of exemplars and inspiration.

To start, Bly participated with tens of thousands of others in a student-led antiwar demonstration in Washington, D.C., on November 27, 1965.[13] The FBI file on Bly notes both that soon after, on December 2, "the subject had donated $40 to the Minnesota Committee to End the War in Vietnam (MCEWV)," and that the sponsoring organization of this committee was the Socialist Workers Party.[14] (J. Edgar Hoover was probably salivating.) Walking where his talk would soon be, Bly was intent on national and local involvement as an antiwar activist.

In early March, 1966, Bly, along with poet David Ray at Reed College, formed on short notice a group called American Writers Against the Vietnam War for a series of readings in the Northwest (beginning in Portland, Oregon). Soon they embarked on a nationwide campaign, barnstorming college campuses, enlisting other prominent poets and writers, mostly local, to join the cause.[15] When they got to the University of Minnesota, on May 14, Bly was joined

---

13   And he wrote a poem about it: "At a March Against the Vietnam War (Washington, November 27, 1965)," published in *The Light Around the Body* (Harper & Row, 1967), 34.

14   U.S. Department of Justice, Federal Bureau of Investigation, Nw#: 58622, DocId: 34274190

15   Details in *Born Under,* 192-217.

by Karl Shapiro, Galway Kinnell, and three poet-instructors from the Poetry Workshop in Iowa City—George Starbuck, Marvin Bell, and Donald Justice. The one other local participant was Ann Casson, an accomplished actor and the wife of Douglas Campbell, Tyrone Guthrie's successor as artistic director of the young Guthrie Theater. (Bly had asked John Berryman to participate, but he refused.) They also brought the fresh-off-the-press anthology, *A Poetry Reading Against the Vietnam War*, one more means of sowing seeds.[16]

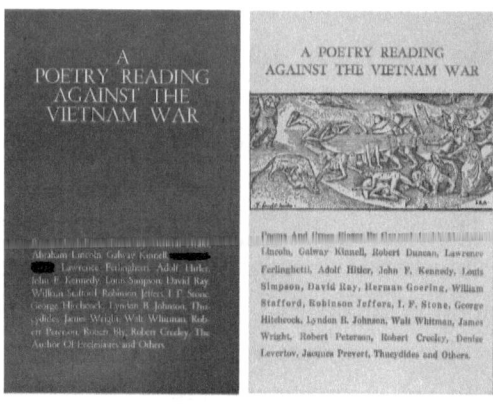

Left, 1st edition (expurgated); right, 2nd edition

This read-in was a watershed event for young poets in Minnesota who were among the more than 500 in attendance, including students Hyde, Moore, Hampl, Keillor, Galt, Sisson, Richter (i.e, the *Ivory Tower* crew, see Chapter 3), and professors Keith Gunderson (Philosophy) and Mulford Q. Sibley (Political Science), among others. For them (except the last), this may have been their first real taste of impassioned poetry dealing with an urgent and relevant issue of the day—in this case, the primary issue facing young men of draftable age (and the persons who loved them)—and getting broad media coverage. Call it part three of sowing seeds, still concurrent and conjoint with parts one and two in a triple-pronged effort. It was a whole new world, and new or renewed understanding of the

---

16 Its main purpose was to provide material for similar read-ins.

value and purpose of poetry was a piece of that. It was probably not a possibility that many of them had foreseen. But its effect was galvanizing.[17]

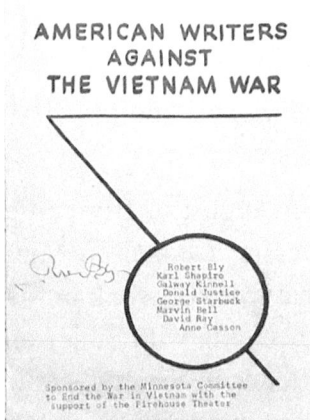

Hampl indicates that, in fact, this was the first poetry reading she had ever attended, and that it was "an eye-opener." Understandably. The audience was anxious, wondering: Would Bly and the other participants be arrested and jailed? She continues: "They were actively encouraging draft-age young men to refuse to serve; they were writing and reading poetry that was telling the political truth against their own government. It was scary, and it was courageous. And it made poetry absolutely essential and as real as the bread and roses we sang about."[18]

Bread, sustenance for the physical body, and roses, sustenance for the heart, the psyche, and the imagination; or, put another way, the intersection of poetry and politics. The second verse of that song (from a 1911 poem by James Oppenheim), arising from suffragist Helen Todd's statement, "Bread for all, and roses, too," had immediate application:

---

17 Note the sponsorship of MCEWV and of the avant-garde Firehouse Theater.

18 Hampl, "Midwestern Sublime," 8.

> As we come marching, marching, we battle, too, for men—
> For they are women's children and we mother them again.
> Our days shall not be sweated from birth until life closes—
> Hearts starve as well as bodies: Give us Bread, but give us Roses.

Three months later, on August 6, Bly participated in an antiwar march from the University campus in Minneapolis to the State Capitol in St. Paul. That evening, back in Mayo Auditorium, a capacity crowd heard Bly, along with Sibley and a few others.[19] Bly subsequently wrote a letter to the city's newspaper editor: "Your editorial, 'About Picking the Right War' (Sept 24), declares that a man must either object to all wars, or to none. Only the pacifist, you say, has the right to object to the Viet Nam War. There is no middle ground... Your position is ridiculous."[20] He then brought up the Nuremberg trials. Minnesotans who read the newspaper were getting a taste of this poet.

The next spring, for a local audience at the First Universalist Church in south Minneapolis, Bly reprised "The Angry Arts – a Napalm Poetry Reading," which he had been part of in New York earlier that year.[21] Again, Ann Casson participated, and Herbert Burke, an English professor from St. John's University in Collegeville. Poet Carl Rakosi, then living in Minneapolis, says: "I still remember the little thrill I felt when Robert Bly introduced me years ago at an anti-Vietnam war reading..."[22] Bly also was reading antiwar poems (primarily) on KUOM, the University's radio station (1967).

---

19   Again, as noted in Bly's FBI file.
20   *Minneapolis Tribune,* September 30, 1966.
21   For more on the New York event, see *Born Under,* 201-2.
22   "Carl Rakosi, in Conversation with Tom Devaney," *American Poetry Review* 32.4 (July-August 2003)..

And he kept moving around the state. Poet Cary Waterman and her then husband, Charles, also a poet who had recently taken a job at Mankato State College, first had contact with Bly via his antiwar activities, when he came to campus to read. Such a positive connection was made many times over as Bly went from place to place.

He had all along been putting together what would be his next book of poetry, *The Light Around the Body*. While to many readers it seemed dramatically different from his first book, on closer examination it was perfectly in line with the way he had long been moving. Bly's debt to Neruda figures the largest here, as he fuses Neruda's surrealist style with political poetry (much as Neruda did himself). The Vietnam War added a new dimension, new details, including merchants, executives, bankers, generals and presidents. One poem that merges the "country poems" of *Silence* with these new "political poems" is "Driving through Minnesota During the Hanoi Bombings," which begins:

> We drive between lakes just turning green;
> Late June. The white turkeys have been moved
> To new grass.
> How long the seconds are in great pain!
> Terror just before death,
> Shoulders torn, shot
> From helicopters, the boy
> Tortured with the telephone generator,
> "I felt sorry for him,
> And blew his head off with a shotgun."

The shocking juxtaposition was one way of reminding us Americans of our complacency and our complicity.

As the war was grinding on, Bly, ever outspoken, was getting more and more widespread attention, not for himself but for the cause. He turned his draft card in to the Department of Justice in Washington, D.C. At the awards ceremony when *The Light* won the National Book Award in 1968, Bly's speech lambasted the U.S. government for its policies in Vietnam, and even his own publisher, Harper & Row, for its collusion. He handed over his check to a young draft resister, planted in the audience, encouraging him to use the $1,000 to encourage others to resist the draft.[23] (This was, according to his FBI file, a seditious violation of the Selective Service Act of 1948.) An uproar ensued, and it made national news.

How did it play back home in Minnesota? The *Minneapolis Tribune*'s headline read: "Poet Robert Bly Charges HHH 'Famous for his Lies.'"[24] Picking up on his hardly central attack on Hubert Horatio Humphrey, a favorite son, former mayor of Minneapolis, U.S. Senator, and current Vice President, the article shows that he had struck a local mainstream nerve. And what business did a poet have doing this? Barbara Flanagan, newspaper columnist, later that year, in a piece entitled, "Suddenly It's the Poets Who Make Headlines," wrote: "Eugene McCarthy runs for president. Allen Ginsberg is profiled in the *New Yorker*. Robert Lowell marches on the Pentagon. Robert Bly refuses a White House invitation."[25] I'll say it again: something was happening here, and many of those in the older generation, the Mr. and Mrs. Joneses, didn't know what it was. To those who did, this was heartening.

Bly would do benefit readings for the Twin Cities Draft Information Center, a basically illegal, *sub rosa* operation on the West Bank, founded by David Gutknecht in 1967. Here is a contemporary account of TCDIC, written by a wet-behind-the-ears high school newspaper reporter (i.e., me) anxiously approaching draft age:

> Housed in a rickety two-story building on Sixth St. and Cedar Ave., TCDIC employs about seven full-time paid workers, as well as forty-nine or fifty part-time volunteers. The seven counselors advise up to

---

23 Again, the details are in *Born Under,* 209-12.
24 *Minneapolis Tribune*, March 7, 1968.
25 *Minneapolis Star,* September 6, 1968.

eighty draft-age men a week. Most of the counselors have either turned in their draft cards, refused induction, are conscientious objectors, or are non-registrants waiting to be imprisoned. Almost all of them admittedly have tendencies toward anarchy. …

The movements of draft resistance, women's liberation, gay liberation, and tax resistance are all getting together to oppose the war in Vietnam. …the resistance is gaining such momentum that if the draft is not soon abolished it might be done away with by revolutionary tactics.[26]

Photo by the author

---

26   Mark Gustafson, "Draft Center Counsels Resisters," *The Viewer* (Mounds View High School) 16.13 (April 24, 1970), 6

In April 1969, Bly led a poetry reading in the main ballroom of Coffman Union at the University, "in benefit of national and local Chapters of Resist, a group that opposes the draft and the Vietnam War." This was part of a ten-city tour, and included other nationally known poets Robert Creeley, Galway Kinnell, Ed Sanders, and Diane Wakoski. A month later, on Memorial Day, an anti-Vietnam War march from Northrup Auditorium at the University to the Federal Building in downtown Minneapolis, organized by the Minnesota New Mobilization Committee, took place and was followed by a gathering and picnic at Loring Park, at which Bly read poems.

Bly's poetry kept the attention of the University's newspaper, the *Minnesota Daily*. October 15, 1969, was the first nationwide Moratorium Day, and that day's issue printed Bly's "Counting Small-Boned Bodies," from *The Light*. On January 6, 1970, the entire front page was given over to an excerpt from "Unrest," a poem (cited above) from *Silence in the Snowy Fields,* way back in 1962, that prefigured U.S. involvement in Vietnam and the tensions in American society" This, too, was a way of seeding in a vast field of student readers.

Beginning in early 1966, Bly had learned the value of publicity in getting the message of the antiwar movement across. Involvement in local politics was another way in which he demonstrated to young poets what poetry could do and be. In 1970, thirty-one-year-old Earl Craig, U of M instructor, civil rights activist, a Black man, and (in the words of the newspaper) "an avowed radical," was running as an independent candidate for the U.S. Senate (he was seeking the DFL nomination in the primary against Humphrey). In his first campaign swing outside the Twin Cities, he went to western Minnesota and visited not only former governor Elmer Benson (of the Farmer-Labor Party) in his home town, Appleton, but also Bly, in his home town, Madison.[27] He knew how visible and impactful this poet had become.

---

27 *Minneapolis Star* (April 22, 1970).

Bly participated often in Honeywell Project events and actions. The Honeywell Project was founded in December 1968 by Marv Davidov. An early Freedom Rider (see Chapter 4), Davidov was a fervent believer in nonviolent revolution, and an instrumental figure in this time of antiwar activism.[28] Honeywell, Inc., originally a maker of thermostats, was Minnesota's largest industry, largest private employer, and largest military contractor. The focus of the Project in those days was antiwar, specifically concerned with Honeywell's manufacture of antipersonnel (i.e., categorically inhumane) fragmentation bombs widely used by U.S. forces in Vietnam. Regular demonstrations were held locally, with a broad array of participants, and efforts were made to get inside the stockholders' meetings as legitimate shareowners.

On April 27, 1970, the eve of Honeywell's annual meeting, a rally was held at the Macalester College fieldhouse in St. Paul. Molly Ivins, near the beginning of her storied journalistic career, reported for the *Minneapolis Tribune*: "More than 3,500 people roared to their feet and cheered last night after Jerry Rubin screamed, 'We're gonna make Honeywell stop making bombs and go back to makin' honey!'" Rubin was famous as a defendant in the trial of the Chicago Seven (Abbie Hoffman, Tom Hayden, and others) held in the wake of the protests and the "police riot" at the Democratic National Convention in August 1968.[29] Ivins continues: "The audience was equally enthusiastic about poet Robert Bly, who read 'The Teeth Mother Naked at Last.' The long antiwar poem bitterly contrasts the war in Vietnam to some of the odder 'normal' features of American life and children, alive and dead." One more indication how poetry had gained a central place in antiwar efforts.[30]

---

28 See Carol Masters and Marv Davidov You Can't Do That! Marv Davidov, Nonviolent Revolutionary (Nodin Press, 2009), passim.

29 The term from the findings of the Walker Report of the National Commission on the Causes and Prevention of Violence, as released on December 1, 1968.

30 Molly Ivins, "Rubin, Crowd Zero in on Honeywell," *Minneapolis*

While he was traveling around the nation, Bly also continued doing poetry readings on college campuses around the state—Augsburg, Hamline, Macalester, Carleton, St. Olaf, Gustavus Adolphus, St. John's, and the rest. These were not always specifically antiwar events, but those also continued as necessary. For example: On April 30, 1970, President Nixon announced that he was expanding the war into Cambodia. A student strike (i.e., a boycott of college classes) ensued across the country. On May 4, four students were gunned down by National Guardsmen at Kent State University in Ohio. On May 5, at Hamline University in St. Paul, Bly read at a campus rally.

It should be recognized that the poetry community in Minnesota was not completely in step or in unison with Bly and his comrades. James Naiden was writing for the Minneapolis newspaper as he was preparing to launch the first issue of his magazine, the *North Stone Review* (see Chapter 9). He referred to Bly as a "pietistic moralizer...who gets a big, orgasmic kick out of accusing everyone, especially those who are the least responsible, for the folly of Vietnam." This is in obvious reference to Bly's "Teeth Mother" poem, in which he links the everyday behaviors and expectations of average Americans with the horrific deaths of children in Vietnam. Naiden continues: "Bly's pontifications about the guilt of all mankind because of Vietnam...[are] a bloody bore as a continual source of both poetic inspiration and critical criteria."[31] Apparently, Naiden resented how Bly had shown that all of us—including him—were spiritually sick, complicit, with blood on our hands, that none of us were innocent. As Jacqueline Rose recently put it: "We are all accountable for the ills of the world in which we live."[32]

Tribune, April 28, 1970, 20. Other speakers that night, non-poets, were Staughton Lynd, Stewart Meacham, and Barbara Deming.

31   This was in a review of John Berryman's *Love & Fame, Minneapolis Tribune,* (January 12, 1971).

32   Jacqueline Rose, *The Plague: Living Death in Our Times* Farrar, Straus and Giroux, 2023), 34.

Bly was remarkably prescient about the fracturing of truth during this period, the startling disconnect between official pronouncements and what was actually going on. In short, the president's lies. This had started with the much earlier-composed "Listening to President Kennedy Lie About the Cuban Invasion" in *The Light*. He was able, and directed others, to connect the dots. He drew on his early deep connections with the land, his place, his people, his heritage, and his awareness of the ways in which processes like the industrial revolution brought about disintegration and alienation. He showed the close link between the mundanities of our everyday lives as Americans and the terror/horror we were wreaking in Vietnam. That is to say, the banality of evil.

What effect did Bly's activism and political poetry have on the local literary community? Rather than attempting to identify specific links, it is safe to say that he had set an example and created an environment inclined to further developments. The Smith Park Poetry Series (see Chapter 10) ended its first season on June 1, 1974, with "Poetry and Protest." The influence of Le Sueur, McGrath, and Bly is clear. The program lists general issues—the subject matter of poems and subjects for discussion—as follows: Linda Pucci (welfare), Lowell Gomsrud (war), Alphonse McGee (prison); also minority perspectives: Nic Puente (Chicano), Muriel Tate (Blacks), Gerald Vizenor (Indians). "If poets have the special, clear consciousness and gift of skill with language they are supposed to have, and if they as a result can speak for the 'people,' what are they saying about society? And what are they doing to make change happen? Please come and read and rap about Poetry of Protest."[33]

The next year, in 1975, Davidov, with the help of another radical organizer, Carl Voss, planned to start a new Minnesota Chautauqua circuit, another throwback to the old days. "We will be bringing a variety of people in who have energy and confidence, who are reaching for

---

33 Found in the Caroline Marshall papers, Minnesota Historical Society.

the roots, who can inspire audiences to have faith in their capacities to change things. We want to be a catalyst to bring people together, and not just for performance."[34] The first (and last) was held on January 31 at the U of M's West Bank auditorium in Willey Hall. Participants included the Apprentice Dance Group, musician John Koerner, David Dellinger, a longtime radical pacifist and member of the Chicago Seven (with Jerry Rubin, above), and, it almost goes without saying, Bly.

We have seen in the preceding Chapter the political content of the serial publication *Region*. There would be more to come in *Hundred Flowers, Black Flag, North Country Anvil,* and much else (see Chapters 7, 9, 12). After the Vietnam War had ended, there remained many big and important steps to take against classism and racism in American society.

* * *

As this Chapter comes to a close, I wish to draw attention to one unsung visionary in this literary social justice movement. In 1978, Jim Dochniak, Minneapolis poet, guest-edited a special "Midwest People's Culture Anthology Issue" of John Crawford's *West End* magazine.[35] He wrote, as an introduction, meaning to be all-inclusive:

What you will find is, hopefully, a beautiful, single—communal—voice, the voice of a people telling of our communal history and struggle… A people's culture is a history of the struggle to survive, to remain human—the struggle to remember our past, to take control of our present, to mold our future, and to recognize our strength and joy—our health—our communal selves.

On a facing page, Crawford regretted "the scarcity of Native American, Black and other national minority writing in this issue." Despite Dochniak's best and tireless efforts "it takes more than a

---

34   Minnesota Literature Newsletter (December 1974).

35   *West End* 5.1 (Summer 1978). Contributors include, Le Sueur, McGrath, Linda Hasselstrom, Jane Dickerson, Earl Nurmi, Cary Waterman, and Mary McAnally-Knight.

few months' cooperation to undo years of racist editorial practices on the part of other, white-dominated publications."[36]

Dochniak, undaunted, at the same time was working to put together his own Midwestern magazine, *Sez: A Multi-Racial Journal of Poetry & People's Culture,* in winter 1978. Poet Margaret Hasse was one of four contributing editors, along with Earl "Pete" Nurmi, Mary McAnally (Etheridge Knight's ex-wife, see Chapter 11), and Craig Volk. Dochniak had recently quit the Loft's board, in part frustrated by that organization's apparent exclusivity and whiteness (see Chapter 7). As he says about that first issue: "We wanted to put together a magazine which did more than to reflect visible and accessible literary 'scenes' in Minnesota and the Midwest; we felt this was already being done by the many existing literary journals in our area." Instead of that "limited view… we wanted to focus our attention on literature and artwork which came… from communities which, for one reason or another, were cut off from mainstream America."[37]

---

36   John Crawford's West End Press, with its emphasis on working-class and women poets, briefly set up shop in the Twin Cities in the latter 70s. It then published several prose works by Meridel Le Sueur and poems by Earl "Pete" Nurmi, but moved on to Cambridge, Massachusetts.

37   "Introduction," *Sez* 1 (Winter 1978), i. This is also the source of the

Another way to put it, he felt that the local literary scene had become something of a monoculture in terms of its contributors. The natural balance had been upset, robbing the scene of the nutrients necessary to maintain the essential fertility of the soil. Duchniak noted: "In our area, since the mid-1800s, there has been a literary and artistic tradition which has not only celebrated Midwestern ground, but has also reflected people's struggles to survive ethnically as well as economically. This tradition has had its roots in the working class, and has received little or no recognition from the academic and leisure classes."

But times had changed. "With the largest urban Native American population in the country here in Minneapolis, and quickly growing Spanish speaking, Asian, and Black populations statewide, we felt special attention should also be given to non-white writers; their work was just not finding print." Also, "there were other communities which…deserved more exposure: the incarcerated, the handicapped, the aging, the economically disadvantaged, communities with a shared experience different than, say, the 'average' Midwesterner."

While, as we will see, there had been in the region increased attention to Native Americans (Chapter 8), and COMPAS had been reaching out to some of those other communities (Chapter 15), *Sez*

---

following quotations.

intended to go deeper, to push harder, to "continue trying to uncover and publish literature and artwork which is rooted in racial and ethnic traditions, as well as work which reflects the experiences and themes of our more 'submerged' communities." Also, "to provide exposure for literature and artwork which has arisen from people's struggles for self-determination and a more humanitarian society."

Its geographical focus would be strictly midwestern, especially Minnesota and the Twin Cities. Dochniak gives thanks to, among others: Le Sueur, McGrath, *The North Country Anvil*, Jim Perlman, Mary Ellen Shaw, KFAI Community Radio, and John Minczeski. The contents included "Five Twin Cities Black Poets" (including Roy McBride—see Chapter 10), "Prison Poetry" (twelve poets write from five midwestern prisons, most students of McAnally, Hasse, and Volk in the Arts in Corrections program, see Chapter 15), and "On Mental Illness" (ten poets who "are or were mentally ill," including Nurmi).

This work was the result of seeds sown by LeSueur and McGrath, most obviously. But surely for the purposes of this book, Bly's front page activities, his gift as a leader for attracting attention and building community, is still the predominant framework in which Dochniak's important advances may be seen. Dochniak serves as the most obvious bridge, I think, both between Bly's political consciousness and his emphasis on poetry from other cultures, especially Spanish language poetry, and greater attention to multicultural influences and those from other marginalized people. Soon after this issue, Dochniak and Nurmi participated with McGrath and Jerri Alexander, in a program called "Poetry and Social Change,", part of St. Paul's Poetry Downtown Series, sponsored by COMPAS and the Landmark Center.

The Northland Cultural Workers Conference, put on at Metropolitan Community College in April 1979, was focused on regional issues. 200+ progressive artists from the region attended. *Sez* was one of the sponsors. One upshot of the conference was the formation of the long-lived Northland Poster Collective (on East Lake Street), using art as a means of organizing, filling gaps in cultural representation, forming community by telling stories, and pursuing social and political justice.

That autumn, in November 1979, together with the African American Cultural Center of Minneapolis, *Sez* co-sponsored a three-day "Black Market Book Fair" downtown with over thirty Minnesota small press publishers, some from the Black community, book and magazine exhibits, workshops for teachers, librarians, readers and writers, focusing on job and publishing opportunities for writers, on grants, on how to self-publish and sell books, and how to use small press in schools and libraries. The great Gwendolyn Brooks read her poetry, and over forty Twin Cities Black poets, dancers, musicians, and storytellers also performed. The fair reportedly attracted over 700 attendees.[38]

Sez 2/3, the next (and last) issue, came in 1980. (Martha Knapp had replaced Volk as a contributing editor.) Dochniak's "Report to the Stockholders" includes a sweeping critique of the entire literary landscape and a list of ambitious objectives. First, "to provide support, encouragement, and vehicles of exposure for Minnesota's Third World literary talent." Second, to do the same "for…writers such as prison poets, poets incarcerated in mental institutions, street poets, gays and lesbians, 'ethnic' writers, etc. …. with the goal of bringing about a greater awareness of the region's cultural diversity." Third, "to seek out, support, and encourage writers whose work focused on current social and political issues." And finally, "to support and encourage writers whose work focused on current class concerns and to develop new, more immediate mechanisms for the delivery and presentation of that work with the goal of making poetry and literature more accessible to wider audiences."

---

38 Jim Dochniak, "Black Market Book Fair," in *More than a Gathering of Dreamers: A Guide to Organizing & Exhibiting at Book Fairs,* ed. Ed Hogan (Coordinating Council of Literary Magazines, 1980), 16-21.

Sowing Seeds 121

The new issue includes an interview with McGrath, plus a new section of his *Letter to an Imaginary Friend*. There is also recent poetry from the Nicaraguan struggle for liberation. A section "On Aging" includes Hasse and her mother's correspondence with Emilie Mellenthin, a ninety-ish woman in a nursing home out in Marshall (Hasse's mother's home town): "The Memorable Past: Letters from a Nursing Home."

Under the title "Remembering Vietnam" are poems by longtime peace and antiwar activist, Polly Mann, including "Testimony from the Vietnam Winter Soldier's Hearings / Detroit, 1979":

"WE BLEW THEM AWAY," you say,
Cloudy eyes shooting right and left.

Dandelions, I muse,
Fluff of gray on a bright spring day.

. . .

"THEY WERE LITTLE KIDS…
…SPOTTED BY THE CAPTAIN WHO SHOUTED LOUD:

'STOP. GET OUT.
AIM AND FIRE.'"

"WE DID," you whisper.

"WE DID. WE DID. WE BLEW THEM AWAY."

Like dandelion fluff.
Like candle flame.

This horrific poem cannot help but recall Bly's "Driving through Minnesota During the Hanoi Bombings," quoted earlier in this Chapter. Inevitably, Mann had heard Bly read numerous times in Marshall (fifty miles from Madison), where she was living, in the 1960s and 70s. (Looking to the future, we might add that in 1982, in Minneapolis, Mann was one of the founding members of the still very active and highly visible [e.g., demonstrating every Wednesday on the Lake Street Bridge] feminist antiwar organization, Women Against Military Madness/WAMM.)

More poems are by Charles Waterman, McGrath protégé, Dale Jacobson, and by Jane Dickerson. Excerpts of her "I read your poems" speak subtly to the issue of this Chapter. It begins:

> every month I read your poems
> in the small books and magazines,
> but none of them
> tell me how to live
> in the city
> ...

and it ends:

> each day sees another face,
> another free verse published
>
> the word's a crime
> if the poet cannot speak
> or will not.

Other moves similar to those that Dochniak was spearheading were in the air: In 1976, Jack Reuler founded the Mixed Blood Theatre on the West Bank, a multiracial theater company meaning to explore issues around race within the theater framework (see Chapter 5). The same year, Lou Bellamy founded Penumbra Theatre, Minnesota's only Black professional theater company. And they both still thrive.[39]

---

39 Mixed Blood has evolved. "Programming has grown to include disability communities, immigrant and refugee populations, Minnesota Latinx, Transgender and biracial Twin Citians, and the East African Muslims that reside in proximity to Mixed Blood's converted firehouse home." www.mixedblood.com. As has Penumbra. "Our space will center the Black experience, learn from and support people of color who are not Black, and welcome white individuals interested in building resiliency and competency for racial equity and racial healing work. Penumbra will stand in solidarity with and support indigenous communities upon whose land the work is located." www.penumbratheatre.org.

The matter of politically conscious poetry cannot be dismissed as politically naïve, as some have tried to do. Nor, in this case, as a sign of times that are past, as ancient history, or as a nostalgic Boomer fixation on our glory days. Jim Moore, thinking of the role poetry played in the antiwar movement, says: "today I think poetry is a very big factor for young people in terms of what's happening at the national level politically, and also just in terms of racism and the environment. There are thousands of young readers of poetry by young poets, and they are leading the way."[40] Many examples are found in the publishing lists of the four major independent literary presses currently operating in Minnesota.

---

40   MG interview with JM, 7 January 2000 .

Chapter 7
Stirring the Air, Shattering the Glass, and a Sudden Feeling: The Loft

We didn't even know we were young,
we just ran around with all the energy of the young,
filled with ideas….
                –Michael Dennis Browne

"Each year the Loft Literary Center engages more than 5,000 beginning, intermediate, and advanced writers in learning opportunities, hosts more than 250 authors in readings and dialogues that draw more than 15,000 people, connects with more than 200,000 unique visitors through digital resources on our website, collaborates with at least thirty local and national organizations to enrich the literary environment and, through contracts, awards, and grants, pays writers more than $400,000."[1] Impressive, but how did it all begin? Well, modestly, and fortuitously, as follows.

In 1968, Marly Rusoff, an erstwhile student at the University of Minnesota, shared a house on the West Bank with Lewis Hyde and his girlfriend, Betsy. With a small proofing press from her late father's bindery, she was helping Hyde put out his literary magazine, the *Nickel & Dime Quarterly* (see Chapter 9). As Rusoff tells it, one day she was sitting in the kitchen with her housemates, when

---

1   https://loft.org/about/about-us

> ...all of a sudden, the back door flew open and literally slammed against the wall. There was a glass jar on the window that went crashing to the floor. And in walked Robert Bly—that was how I first saw him. He walks in, the glass shatters, the air is stirred, you know, this force enters the room. He doesn't say hello, he says "Pablo Neruda is the greatest poet that's ever lived!" That was my introduction to him. It made a tremendous impact on me.[2]

It was a foretelling. The jolt of that dramatic entrance (and the invocation of Neruda) would continue to reverberate and resonate in her life in the ensuing years.

Laurie Savran, who worked at Savran's Paperback Shop (owned by her husband, Bill) on Cedar Avenue, a few blocks away, was a friend of Rusoff's from back in Sunday school at Aduth Jeshurun synagogue in South Minneapolis. With her help, Rusoff got a job at the bookstore. She later met Edwin Felien, a U of M graduate (and, like Hyde, a former staffer of the *Ivory Tower*), who had been part of the Georgeville commune in Stearns County, Minnesota. He would cut a wide swath as an agitator and a peace activist (years later a Minneapolis City Council member). They soon married.

In April 1970, a new underground weekly newspaper, *Hundred Flowers,* appeared in Minneapolis. It came together through the efforts of Felien and a collective on the West Bank, including Rusoff, Warren Hanson, Dickie Dworkin, Tom Utne, Brian Coyle (another eventual Minneapolis City Council member and gay activist), and numerous others. Dworkin, from Chicago, functioned as editor. He had been radicalized by the "police riot" at the Democratic National Convention in 1968 and Days of Rage organized by the Weathermen faction of the SDS (Students for a Democratic Society) in 1969. In a workshop at Saul Alinsky's Industrial Areas Foundation, Dworkin

---

[2] MG interview with MR, 31 October 2019. All of Rusoff's remarks in this chapter are from this.

met Marv Davidov, who suggested he come up to Minneapolis and put his high school and college newspaper experience to use. Davidov found Dworkin a place to stay and a few like-minded contacts.³

Warren Hanson, the art director, had taken part in an earlier meeting, hoping to start an underground, antiwar, poetry and music-oriented newspaper. But he deferred to the "older, wiser" Felien, the one with the "vision and action agenda," who had been moving in a more radical direction with comrades from the commune.⁴ After his recent time out in the Bay Area, Felien said it "absolutely had to be political." He adds: "We agreed there would always be something countercultural in the paper. There would be at least two or three music reviews. We would try to be as local as we could be, and our politics would be heavy."⁵

---

3   Richard Dworkin, "So Here's What I Recall About What Brought Me to Minneapolis," *Southside Pride* 34.2 (February 2024), 17.

4   Warren Hanson, "Another Flower Speaks," *Southside Pride* 34.2 (February 2024), 8.

5   This quotation and those in the next two paragraphs are from Felien, "Confessions of an Unrepentant Maoist: *Hundred Flowers,* 1970," *Southside Pride* (December 19, 2016). Felien soon bought a house in the Powderhorn neighborhood, and the effort became communal, as they all moved in and put together the issues there.

In one sense it picked up where *Region* had left off (see Chapter 5), but it went much further and was without a literary focus. Like Minneapolis' own version of *The East Village Other* and *The Berkeley Barb,* the paper was very much concerned—on a national and local level—with antiwar and civil rights activism, ecology, women's and gay liberation, the Black Panthers, the Honeywell Project, Timothy Leary, sex & drugs & rock 'n' roll, as well as the hippie counterculture focused on communal living and the start of the food co-op movement.[6] As Felien says, "I suggested the name... with the slogan under the masthead: 'Let a Hundred Flowers Blossom, Let a Hundred Schools of Thought Contend.' ... It sounded countercultural enough to satisfy flower children, and it was Maoist enough to satisfy me."

Given the regional emphasis of this study, the following report stands out, as Felien continues:

> One of our first issues [May 22, 1970] was our North Country issue where we called for secession...we published an update on the Declaration of Independence in which we talked about how the Vietnam War was illegal and unconstitutional and how it was no longer possible to reason with such tyranny. We argued that Minnesota and parts of North Dakota (the watershed areas of the Mississippi, Minnesota, and Red Rivers) should unite with parts of Canada and form a new North Country.

This also is a foretelling of the near future, when a new magazine, *The North Country Anvil,* would spring to life (see Chapter 12). Root-and-branch identification with and pride in place was strong in Minnesota. This also comports with the rag's emphasis on local resistance, including the Red Barn uprising in Dinkytown, and the

---

6   This was not the first underground newspaper locally. But the *Minneapolis Free Press* and *Raisin Bread* did not have nearly the impact and repercussions.

Moratorium at the U of M, Augsburg College, and Gustavus Adolphus College in St. Peter.

Soon Rusoff, busy with the newspaper, heard about an empty storefront in Dinkytown. Working at Savran's had strengthened her determination to have a life involving books, and now the idea of opening a small new bookstore seized her. Wishing to avoid competition with her employer, she and he decided on a business partnership, each of them putting up an initial financial stake. In 1970 they opened Savran-Rusoff Bookdealers at 1302 4th St. S.E., next to the Varsity Theater.

Dinkytown was not finished, by any means, even if now overshadowed by the West Bank (see Chapter 5). The spring of 1970 saw a forty-day uprising that, on the face of it, was in opposition to the fast-food chain Red Barn's effort to establish a corporate foothold in the community by ousting five small businesses and demolishing several buildings. But the protest, occupation, and resistance were fully in sync with the antiwar movement—they were "bringing the war home"—and matters came to a head a couple of days after the National Guard's killing of four students who were protesting President Nixon's just announced bombing of Cambodia at Kent State. Subsequently, the "law and order" mayor of Minneapolis, ex-cop Charles Stenvig backed down, and the police withdrew.[7]

Rusoff says: "That area had interested me from early on. And, of course, there was still the mythos of Bob Dylan in Dinkytown. When I was in high school, I went to the Ten O'Clock Scholar. It was a walk on the wild side to have an espresso, really." But that was then, this was now (and the Scholar was gone). "I wanted to create a space for my friends, who were poets and writers, Jim Moore and Trish Hampl, and others."

---

7   See the 2015 documentary film, "The Dinkytown Uprising," directed by Al Milgrom, director of the Minneapolis Film Society (another important new presence on the cultural scene in the 1960s), and Daniel J. Geiger: https://www.youtube.com/watch?v=KhpofvQnCT0&list=PLvT4xODe2Ibwdgm-5VRK208ODMnVdu_TwM

Savran's involvement, beyond monetary, was to offer the recognition of his already established name, his advice, and his help in supplying the store's inventory. Otherwise, the day-to-day operations were entirely Rusoff's. Hers was a multi-dimensional book store, but focused on and reflecting her own interests. For one, the poetry section was outsized, with a lot of small press books and little literary magazines. The store quickly attracted local poets (and poets visiting from elsewhere in Minnesota, such as Louis Jenkins from Duluth and Mark Vinz and Michael Moos from Moorhead), pretty much all of them. Like bees to honey, they naturally gathered and there met others on the same wavelength. Bly often stopped by when in Minneapolis.

Rusoff says: "I taught myself through my own bookstore. I became interested in Jung, as everyone did. So I set up a big section on Jung." She continues: "Suddenly I had Jungians around me all the time and I would talk to them." That included Bly, of course, who had been reading Jung since the 1950s, and had regularly incorporated Jungian ideas in his critical essays in *The Fifties* and *The Sixties* as well as in his poetry. Rusoff says: "Bly would come in and talk about Jung, and he told me I was a *hetaira* [companion, friend]. I think it was in the Great Mother books there were four different feminine archetypes. He sort of dubbed me that type of woman, which was interesting to me, because I didn't know what I was, exactly."[8] But she would know soon.

Another young poet from rural Minnesota, Joe Paddock, was living in Dinkytown and struggling with the "ego-dreams" of his literary ambitions, when he, without forethought, wandered into the bookstore. "I entered and, to use the Jungian term, 'synchronistically' came upon the book *Man and His Symbols,* conceived and edited by Carl G. Jung. ... This book triggered a psychic opening in me beyond the realm of surface rational

---

8   Rusoff attended Bly's second Great Mother Conference in 1976, up on Burntside Lake (near Ely).

consciousness in which I had been living... A new world yawned open for me as I turned the pages of this book..."[9] Another life changed by a bookstore and a book found by happenstance. Poet Michael Dennis Browne, since 1971 a professor at the University, was frequenting the store. He added the same book to the reading list for his writing classes.

Rusoff also stocked many books on radical politics. Thus, much as *Hundred Flowers* had been, the bookstore was, as she says, "absolutely" a by-product of leftist politics and counterculturalism. "We were questioning everything. ... It was question everything, question the government, they're lying to us, question the identity roles." And, "there was a sense of a revolution happening." During the massive and violent eight-day antiwar demonstrations in 1972, the so-called "Dinkytown riots," with thousands of people in the streets, she would field telephone calls asking if she could see the armored police or National Guard bus parked in their nearby staging area.[10]

Meanwhile, literary life raced ahead and broadened. One December, Browne offered to do a reading of Dylan Thomas's "A Child's Christmas in Wales," as he says, "with my fake Welsh accent."[11] It proved popular and became a tradition. Rusoff also started a program for children on Saturday mornings. "Everybody (including Garrison Keillor) came to read at my children's story hour. They did it to help support the store." There was a lot of excitement around the place, and it kept buzzing.

Jim Moore has written about that time: "there wasn't so much a community of poets as a group of friends and acquaintances who lived throughout the state and whose paths occasionally crossed at poetry readings and other such gatherings...the appropriate meta-

---

9   Joe Paddock, *Infinity's Edge: Jung, Tao, & the Poet's Way* (Red Dragonfly Press, 2020), 14.
10 See Ed Felien, *Take the Streets!* (Southside Pride, 2008), 40ff.
11 MDB email to MG, 13 June 2020.

phor for 1971 was that of an extended family—with relatives scattered all over the state and the usual squabbles and joys, rituals and traditions, black sheep and patriarchs and matriarchs associated with a family…" And there were "the close family ties—shared values and assumptions—that united poets…"[12]

When asked if she had a sense at the time that a new literary movement was underway, Hampl answered:

> When you're young and trying to make your way, I don't think you see such trends, not really. The one big game-changer, though, was Marly's bookstore (we went there almost daily) and her idea of starting what became the Loft. The store was an absolute magnet for writers and serious readers. She was our Sylvia Beach. It wasn't Paris, but Rusoff & Co. was as close to James Joyce and Hemingway's Shakespeare & Co. as we got—and it was very close. A cultural center well before Marly formally hatched the Loft.[13]

Crowding was a growing problem, for both the books and the customers. When a space above the store, half of what had originally been a small apartment, became available to rent in 1973, Rusoff took the chance and expanded her square footage. "The book loft," as she called it, had a generous selection of poetry, and children's books in an adjoining room. There were also a few chairs, a comfortable couch, and a coffee pot. It was a good spot for hanging out, chatting, and reading silently—with no other purpose originally envisioned. The other half of the upstairs space, across the hall, was occupied by an insurance agency.

---

12   Minnesota Writes: Poetry, 9.
13   PH email to MG, 19 February 2020.

Photo courtesy of the Loft Literary Center

After a couple of years of intense work, Savran's accountant told Rusoff that, since the store had shown little or no profit and in light of her admittedly shoddy paperwork, Savran was now the owner. Rusoff dissented. She felt it was her store, she had created it, formed its character, fostered its clientele. She found a way to return to Savran his original outlay of $2000 and his inventory of books, and they amicably ended the partnership. The store gained a new name: Rusoff & Co. She forged ahead, walking a tightrope, with many rooting for her success—readers, poets, and business associates like Norton Stillman of The Bookmen, Inc., the wholesale book distributor, who offered forbearance, at times allowing her up to 120 days to pay her bills.[14]

In late September 1973, Neruda died. The reported cause was prostate cancer, but given his past affiliation with the Communist party and his more recent connection with Chile's Socialist presi-

---

14   MR email to MG, 25 April 2023. Stillman was also the owner/publisher of Nodin Press.

dent Salvador Allende (whom *Hundred Flowers* had praised), compounded by the fact that Allende had just been removed from power by a U.S.-supported *coup d'état* led by Augusto Pinochet, the strong suspicion was that this was another lie, that Neruda had been assassinated/poisoned.[15]

Felien then told Rusoff that the neighboring insurance agency upstairs was owned by a financial organization somehow affiliated with the exploitative, neocolonialist, U.S.-owned, multinational corporation, the United Fruit Company. Neruda's famous poem, "The United Fruit Co.," translated by Bly, begins:

> When the trumpet sounded, it was
> all prepared on the earth,
> and Jehovah parceled out the earth
> to Coca-Cola, Inc., Anaconda,
> Ford Motors, and other entities:
> The Fruit Company, Inc.
> reserved for itself the most succulent,
> the central coast of my own land,
> the delicate waist of America.
> It rechristened its territories
> as the "Banana Republics"
> ...[16]

Rusoff says: "I was horrified that I was sharing a staircase with an organization that might have been involved somehow in the assassination of Neruda."

The next step would prove to be an especially momentous one in Minnesota's literary history. And it involved Bly, naturally. Rusoff, no doubt recollecting their first encounter, describes how it happened:

---

[15] The CIA was involved, under President Richard Nixon and his national security advisor (and Bly's Harvard classmate!) Henry Kissinger.

[16] In *The Sixties* 7 and in *Twenty Poems of Pablo Neruda* tr. James Wright and Robert Bly (Sixties Press, 1967), 63.

One day Bly came upstairs to look around and I said: "I need to sanctify this space. Because I think they are bad people across the hall. Would you read some Neruda for us today?" I pulled a book off the shelf and handed it to him. There were maybe five people in the store, and Bly read Neruda. We had a séance, sort of. It was important to me that he had come up and done that. Then, when he left, I had this sudden feeling that that's what this space should be for—this space, off the street, we could do things here. It was really a moment that I saw, by poems being spoken out loud, in a small space, in an intimate atmosphere, that this was important, these words needed to be articulated.

Bly was the medium, in this view, helping the group to make contact with the recently dead poet. And he had given a gift, planted a seed, leading to a "sudden feeling," a revelation that gave birth to an idea. Soon, through a grassroots effort, the book loft was being used as a site for poetry classes and readings.

Moore and Hampl (also former *Ivory Tower* staffers), still putting out their magazine, *The Lamp in the Spine* (see Chapter 9), had recently moved back to the Twin Cities from Iowa City. Rusoff recalls: "Somehow we just came up with the idea that when the store was closed at night, they could use the upstairs for classes." Moore, who may have been the instigator, began so doing that next spring. As he wrote offhandedly to their mutual friend, Lewis Hyde: "I'm teaching a poetry class now. I put up signs and charge $1 per class. I'm doing it at Marly's store. 15 people are coming, about half students, half janitors, etc. Bring a big bottle of wine and everybody gets drunk. It's fun!"[17] In retrospect, Moore says: "It was an exciting moment… We were a community waiting to come together, a community that was

---

17   JM to LH, 7 April 1974.

suddenly very much there."[18] Another turning point.

Wojahn says: "it was the first writing class I ever took."[19] Wendy Knox recalls some of these meetings: "He was a very good teacher, and a firm, reliable but gentle workshopper. I specifically remember one…where he made the astonishing confession that he unplugged his telephone when he was writing. I was amazed…I had never conceived that I could make myself unavailable to the outside world like that…"[20] Then Hampl taught a class on women's literature, the kind of subject matter as yet unheard of at the University's English Department just a few blocks away (and where she would eventually earn the highest distinction as a Regents Professor). Hampl says: "People were hungry for this, and they came in good numbers, paid a little something, and it was a start." Other early classes were taught by poet John Minczeski and playwright Martha Boesing (see Chapter 5).

These classes may have been of some minor financial benefit to the teachers themselves. And there was no shortage of enthusiasm and optimism. But it was becoming distressingly clear to Rusoff that she could not afford to pay rent on both the ground floor and upstairs spaces. She shared her concerns with Browne:

> I said to him, "I don't feel this is mine to close. I think it belongs to the community now. But I can't afford to continue doing this. What do you think about setting up a guild or an association of people who care about literature, poetry, and the arts, and we keep the place open? I think we could do it if we get everyone to pay a $15 a year membership. Then I think I could manage it. What do you think?"

---

18   Jim Moore, "The Loft: Then and Now," *Views from the Loft*, ed. Daniel Slager (Milkweed Editions, 2010), 329.

19   DW email to MG, 19 July 2020. The other Wojahn quotations in this chapter are from the same communication.

20   WKC (Wyndy Knox Carr, aka Wendy Knox) email to MG, 16 November 2021.

Browne was encouraging, as were Hampl and Moore. Rusoff then asked Jenny, the manager of Sammy D's, the Italian restaurant just across the street, if they might put on a fundraising spaghetti dinner in her big basement space. She agreed, and so Rusoff planned a gathering.

Garrison Keillor served as the moderator, the "lowly emcee," as he says in a characteristic deflection.[21] Gregory Bitz (yet another *Ivory Tower* compadre), always the jokester, "was fantastically funny," reading his poems and wearing a silly baseball cap with hands on top that clapped after each one, which added to the merriment. Several other poets with a connection to the store read their own poetry, and there was music (including Bill Hinkley and Judy Larson) overseen by Keillor (whose variety show, "A Prairie Home Companion," was just getting rolling; see Chapter 10).[22] Amid all the fun, Rusoff was urging attendees to sign up and contribute. "People would ask me what it was, and I would say 'I'm not sure yet, but it's going to be a place where we can continue doing the things we're doing.'" Browne says, "the sense of community was palpable."[23] By the end of the evening she had, as she estimates, 170 or 200 memberships.

Around the same time, at Marshall-University High School, one block north, the evening adult/continuing education program was having some difficulty filling its poetry classes. The person in charge, Melissa Marks, asked Rusoff if they could collaborate. Rusoff agreed, and says, "there was a need for a non-judgmental, non-juried entry into literature. We were the counterculture to the University. I'm not going to tell someone that they can't become a writer." A judicious and far-sighted outlook, indeed. She, too, was on the side of the future.

---

21 GK email to MG, 8 June 2022.
22 Keillor, Bitz, et al., did something very similar in April 1974 on behalf of the Cedar Riverside Environmental Defense Fund. See Chapter 10.
23 MDB email to MG, 13 June 2020.

At first this co-sponsorship was done under the name of the bookstore. Early courses in late 1974 and spring 1975 included "Poetry Writing" with Minczeski, "Writing for Children" with Diane Amussen, "The Private Journal" with Christina Baldwin, "Erotic Novel Writing" with Dan Brennan, "A Feminist Poetry Workshop" with Coco Weber, "Writing for Publication: Nonfiction" with Paul Gruchow, and "The Eternal Feminine" taught by Nor Hall ("looking at literature, fairy tales, mythology, and religion from a Jungian perspective"). They were covering the waterfront and auguring the illustrious prospects of a major and comprehensive literary organization.

And so it began. Soon "The Loft: A Place for Poetry" was officially underway, even as it was a relatively informal operation—they were figuring things out as they went along. Next, they incorporated and filed for non-profit, 501(c)(3) status, and a board of directors was assembled, including Moore, Hampl, and Phebe Hanson. Quickly that board expanded, to include Wojahn, Dochniak, Minczeski, Jim Perlman, Sue Ann Martinson, and others. Wojahn says "I believe I was The Loft's first treasurer… I know the board's principal task was to vote on proposals for classes, and from the very start the Loft offered a pretty extensive variety of them." With a subsequent grant from the Minnesota State Arts Board, Martinson was hired as part-time coordinator.[24] In the summer of 1975, this formal notice appeared:

> The Loft is a gathering space for writers, artists, and people who care about the arts. Some of the activities that will be taking place there are: candlelight storytelling, poetry readings, art shows, including fine printing, small group music performances, children's story hour on Saturday mornings, and children's book

---

24 Peter Mladinic succeeded her in 1977, followed by Jill Breckenridge-Haldeman in 1979, and Margot Kriel in 1980.

> fair, special seasonal readings (Christmas, equinoxes, Halloween, etc.), play readings, evening classes (co-sponsored by Southeast Alternatives Community Education), projects and workshops suggested by members.
>
> The Loft also provides an extensive library of small press books and magazines.
>
> Writers, artists, readers—all interested persons—are invited to become members of the Loft. In addition to activities, it offers a place to sit around, to write or sketch, to read magazines or books, or to talk over a cup of coffee. The Loft is a unique place for people to come together—a focus for growing energies in the arts and in the community.[25]

This early self-description and mission statement sounds both idyllic and visionary. As Moore has put it, "I felt then, and I continue to feel, that an organization like the Loft can serve as inspiration, goad, and gathering place for those who believe that political change, cultural change, and artistic innovation are not only all of a piece, but also feed each other in unexpected and crucial ways."[26] A steady course of poetry readings at the Loft began to appear on the schedule (see Chapter 10). Earliest readers included Browne, Jenkins, Moore, and Hampl. There were also invitations to participate in open readings. The Loft was becoming a center of literary life in Minnesota.

Now that it was operational, the Loft's next fundraiser was held on Buddha's birthday in May, 1975, at the old firehouse on the West Bank (which McCosh's Books had vacated; it was now a community center leased to the Cedar-Riverside Arts Council, and the Mixed Blood Theater would occupy it soon). Many young poets participated, all seated on the floor (as usual in those days), includ-

---
25 Minnesota Literature Newsletter (July-August 1975).
26 "The Loft: Then and Now," 329.

ing Bly, Hanson, Browne, Hampl, Moore, Jenkins, Ellen Kennedy, Hasse, Caroline Vogel, and a mime, Rick Shope. Not surprisingly, Bly was the center of attention. He had suggested the "Sufi style" associative format, that every poem had to connect somehow with the theme or an image in the previous reader's poem, based on an audience member's request.[27]

More benefits for the Loft (by then renamed "A Place for Literature and the Arts," with a new Dinkytown location, 406 13th Ave. S.E.) followed at the Firehouse: in January 1977, with McGrath (who broke his leg while dancing), Judith Guest, and others; on April 29 with a major outside attraction (and friend of Bly's), Allen Ginsberg; and in November 1977, with Le Sueur (who suffered a heart attack), Roy McBride, John Calvin Rezmerski, Kate Green, and Carol Connolly.[28] Another was held in March 1978, at the Whole Coffeehouse (in the basement of the University's Coffman Union on the East Bank) with jazz from MotherChild and poetry from McBride, Green, Minczeski, Dochniak, and others. Two months later, Bly and Eugene McCarthy, former U.S. Senator and presidential candidate, were scheduled to read in Coffman Union's Great Hall as a benefit for the Loft's move from Dinkytown to a new site above the former Modern Times Dry Cleaners in the Powder-

---

27   See Mike Hazard's video, "A Sampler of Minnesota Poets," https://www.youtube.com/watch?v=k97IyaylAJw It was presented by the Museroom, a service of CIE, the Center for Internationalizing English, "a tax exempt and non-profit organization which brings the media and the arts together in ways which damage neither and benefit both." There are other shorter videos of individual poets (and the mime) from the same reading.

28   This reading is invoked in McBride's poem, "Monsters on the Horizon": "I remember the night well. / I remember that night so well. / Loft benefit at the Firehouse. / Night of Meridel's heart attack. / I was local color / rounding out the program. … Monsters on the horizon. / I remember that night well. / Cedar Square looming. / New Riv. barricading / behind cases of bean sprouts. / New Town – In Town. / Old Town – Downtown. / Portents – Signs / Blueprints – Rhymes / and poetry / trying to contend / with monsters on the horizon…." *Secret Traffic: Selected Poems* (Nodin Press, 2013), 30-2.

horn neighborhood at 3200 Chicago Ave. S. (McCarthy had to cancel at the last minute, so Bly induced Etheridge Knight [see Chapter 11] to come in his place.)

As the plethora of fundraising benefits make obvious, the Loft needed a steady stream of money to stay afloat. The organization started experiencing sharp growing pains in 1977-78. Tension arose in trying to stay true to the Loft's countercultural and politically progressive/leftist origins as a place founded by poets for poets to hang out and to foster community, while, at the same time, developing and expanding as a professional outreach organization that aimed to do the most good and thus needed to seek institutional funding. As Moore says: "We assumed that there was a strong connection between what was happening politically in the country and what was happening in the artistic world. It made perfect sense to us…that if we saw policies or institutions that were inimical to artistic and literary freedom, we would oppose them."[29] In 1977 they began to apply for grant money from private institutions. Moore adds: "There were interminable conversations/arguments about which foundations and organizations we should take money from…and which must be avoided at all costs."

The mid-70s was when more and more sources of funding to support literary enterprises in Minnesota began to be available. There was the National Endowment for the Arts, of course, but also the Minnesota State Arts Council (later the Minnesota State Arts Board), the St. Paul Council of Arts & Sciences, and the Southwest Minnesota Arts and Humanities Council. Private funding came from the Bush Foundation, the Hill Family Foundation, the Jerome Foundation, and the McKnight Foundation.

A near breaking-point was reached when the Loft was awarded a grant of $1,500 from the Dayton-Hudson Foundation, which stipulated that all promotional material for Loft events acknowl-

---

29   Moore, "The Loft: Then and Now," 329.

edge the foundation's corporate-owned chain, B. Dalton Booksellers, just about to open a branch two blocks away from Rusoff & Co. (Ouch!) It was painful enough for Rusoff and the others to imagine accepting corporate money that they felt would ultimately taint and have power over their work. (This was in line with Bly's own adamant and repeated refusal to accept any government money—however needy he was—while the Vietnam War was going on.[30]) The board initially rejected the grant, though chiefly due to the conditions imposed.[31]

But soon the board voted again, 6-4, with some bruised feelings, in favor of accepting. It was a matching grant, requiring that they solicit money from other sources, too. Wojahn says: "That meeting I remember well. Jim [Dochniak] thought that taking the money…was a sellout, a matter of aesthetic, moral, and ideological purity. One of those classic rifts between the party-liners and the pragmatists." Asked if it felt like the beginning of the end, he says: "Well, maybe the end of a particular countercultural conviction that can't be upheld if you want a non-profit to actually be successful at its mission. It's a far cry from today, when the first thing you see when you open a Graywolf or Milkweed title are all the logos of the corporate sponsors."[32] From a purely pragmatic perspective, it was, however distasteful it seemed, time to let go—at least partially—of youthful ideals that were no longer realistic given the trajectory the Loft was now clearly on, on its way to becoming an institution.

---

30 See, e.g., *Born Under*, 203-11. Even after the war, in 1978, he said "When the government gives money, it results in the domestication of the poet. I think that the NEA is an even worse catastrophe, in the long run, to the ecology of poetry than the universities." *Talking All Morning*, 286.

31 For more details, see Rebecca Weaver, "The Urgency of Community: The Suturing of Poetic Ideology During the Early Years of the Loft and the Jack Kerouac School of Disembodied Poetics" (Ph.D. dissertation, University of Minnesota, 2011), 149-164.

32 DW email to MG, 19 July 2020.

Sowing Seeds

At the end of this book's time frame, Bly is still involved with the Loft. In September 1979 he participated in yet another benefit for the organization, together with Browne, McGrath, and Jill Breckenridge-Haldeman; with music and poetry by MotherChild/ PoetryJazz; and with rock music by the 5th Avenue Band; all held at the Cedar-Riverside People's Center. And then, as 1980 began, in late January, Bly delivered three lectures at the Southern Theater on Seven Corners (West Bank)—on Rilke's *Poems for the Hours of Prayer*, on Rilke's "Seeing Poems," and on Rilke's *Sonnets to Orpheus*—all sponsored by the Loft.

A month later, still in the depths of winter, came another two events that further signal Bly's broad reach in these years. On February 22, The Loft sponsored an Evening with Local Magazines, with statements by editors of *Sez, Machete, Lake Street Review, North Stone Review, Sing, Heavenly Muse!* and *Moons and Lion Tailes* (see Chapter 9). And one week after that, on February 29, co-sponsored by the Minneapolis Park Board, the Loft presented "A Night of Leaping in Honor of Leap Year," including leaping lessons, a pogo stick contest, an open reading of leaping poetry, and potluck dinner at Nokomis Park Center, 2401 E. Minnehaha Parkway. The cost: $1.00 or free with pogo stick. The far-reaching influence of the sensational "Leaping Poetry" issue of Bly's magazine, *The Seventies* 1, in 1972, also published by Beacon Press as a book, was still advancing.[33] This playful event was another, practically inevitable, indication of the original leaper's legacy of throwing and sowing seeds. Also offered to attendees was an essay from that issue, "Looking for Dragon Smoke," reprinted on a large folded sheet by Ally Press (see Chapter 14).

---

33 In the first essay therein, "Looking for Dragon Smoke," Bly writes of "leap from the conscious to the unconscious and back again," which epitomized the basis for the poetics he was pushing. For details, see *Born Under*, 265-85.

One more event, an especially fitting conclusion for this era, brings us back to the impact of Rusoff's first fateful meeting with Bly, and to her epiphany from his impromptu Neruda reading that was the seed/germ of the Loft Literary Center. On April 11, 1980, together with various University of Minnesota groups and community sponsors, the Loft put on a "Celebration of Pablo Neruda" at Willey Hall on the West Bank. Readers were Bly and Le Sueur, with music from the Chilean folk group, Inti-Illimani (still playing their song, "Venceremos" ["We Shall Win"] dating from Allende's time). This was a benefit for the Chilean resistance that was persisting during the long and brutal regime of the dictator Pinochet. The Loft kept in touch with its origins and its original political ideals, even as it was on the cusp of a new era.

* * *

Many years later, in 2015, at a party for the Loft's 40th anniversary, Browne, who seems to have determined that Rusoff's Jungian archetype was Mother (i.e., not *hetaira*), presented this poem for the "Great Loft Mother," as he called her, looking to both the past and the future:

Sowing Seeds

Here's a toast to Marly, the Mother of Us All,
who brilliantly began,
who lit the lamps, laid down the paths,
primed the pumps, hauled the water,
welcomed the writers, the writings, the readers, the
   readings;
come in, come in,
be sure to dream,
said Marly, the Mother of Us All.

And here's to those who came after
into the house that Marly built,
to the grace of their labor,
the thousands of hours,
some known about, so many others
sewn unseen into the growing fabric.

Back then, how could we have guessed what would be?
We didn't even know we were young,
we just ran around with all the energy of the young,
filled with ideas, some of them—
I hope I'm remembering right—
just a little bit crazy.

And here's to the here, to the now of the Loft,
and whatever's to come,
to whoever you are who will make the changes;
let's raise our glasses to you,
to the dream made real,
to the spirit of all that's been done, and done so well,
Brava, Bravo, Brava, Bravo,
and everything beginning with you,
O Marly, Mother of Us All.[34]

---

34   Thanks to MDB for sharing this with me.

Chapter 8
Indigenous Culture in the North Country

> Before the white man can relate to others he must forgo the pleasure of defining them. The white man must learn to stop viewing history as a plot against himself.[1]
>
> –Vine Deloria, Jr.

> We are killing men with black hair [in Vietnam] because the Minnesota Historical Society owns the scalp of Little Crow.[2]
>
> –Robert Bly

Although the term Native American Renaissance may be problematic—for one thing, despite almost five centuries of conquest, plunder, and disease, the persistent exertions of European settlers and the U.S. Government, Native culture and traditions had not been eradicated and therefore, arguably, did not need to be reborn; and for another, Native America was not monolithic, but com-

---

1 *Custer Died for Your Sins: An Indian Manifesto* (Macmillan, 1969).

2 A statement "inscribed in my memory" from "one of the many public events around the Vietnam war protests," says Hyde, "Lessons from Robert Bly's Barn," 23. See also my essay, "Haunted in a Landscape of Ghosts: Robert Bly & Little Crow," forthcoming in the *Middle West Review* 11.2 (Spring 2025).

posed of many nations—it is surely true that, in the ferment of the mid-1960s and the '70s, among Indigenous communities at large there arose increasing political activism and more open resistance to unremitting colonialism. These new beginnings included a resurgence in ethnic pride and fresh literary and artistic production in those communities.

This Chapter intends to represent a broad picture as seen mainly in the territory of Minnesota and the surrounding region, an important piece of the specific literary renaissance described in this book.[3] At the same time, among some white poets, writers, and readers, interest in and acknowledgment of Indigenous culture was growing. Some of it quite positive, some not so much, but still a necessary part of the entire picture.

Poet Thomas McGrath launched his little magazine *Crazy Horse* in 1962 (see Chapter 12), using the name of the Oglala Lakota leader who had fought in the Black Hills and elsewhere against the U.S. Government's westward expansion, and whose most famous success was the defeat of General Custer at the battle of the Little Big Horn in 1876. Soon McGrath landed at Moorhead State College in Moorhead, Minnesota, just across the Red River from Fargo. That eastern edge of North Dakota was the region in which he, the son of homesteaders, had been born and raised.

---

3   In this chapter different terms are used somewhat interchangeably to describe the same peoples (usually corresponding to the usage in a primary source). Broadly speaking: Native American, Native, Indigenous, American Indian or Indian; more specifically: Ojibwe, Chippewa, Anishinabe or Anishinaabe, and Sioux, Dakota or Dacotah.

Sowing Seeds

The masthead reads: "*Crazy Horse* is an irregular publication edited by a dead Sioux chief who is presently reincarnated in a group of Western Poets." This might seem perilously close to (if not outright) white appropriation of Indigenous history. Still, McGrath's unusually deep respect for Native American peoples and lore in the western territories—as becomes clear in his magnificent book-length poem, *Letter to an Imaginary Friend*—was intrinsic to his language of revolution and communism, and his attacks on American capitalism and imperialism/colonialism.

In glaring contrast to *Crazy Horse* is the first appearance, the next year, of *South Dakota Review,* edited by John R. Milton at the University of South Dakota in Vermillion (on the state's eastern edge, midway between Sioux Falls and Sioux City).[4] At its start, this magazine ran no risk whatsoever of cultural appropriation. Rather, the first issue manages almost entirely to ignore the central presence of Native Americans in the history of the area and the American West, the region with which it purports to be explicitly concerned. It reads as nothing less than an egregious and ignoble act of erasure. (Eventually, as shown below, Milton would see at least glimmers of light.)

The poet and scholar Gerald Vizenor, from the White Earth Band of Ojibwe, had been teaching at the University of Minnesota during those years. In 1964 he started Nodin (Ojibwe for "wind") Press in Minneapolis. Initially, this was in order to publish his own poetry, *Seventeen Chirps,* Haiku in English, but also *Summer in the Spring: Lyric Poems of the Ojibway,* (1965), his interpretations and re-expressions of traditional songs and poems (reissued in 1970 as *Anishinabe Nagamon: Songs of the People*). After Vizenor sold it to Norton Stillman in 1967, Nodin Press was to become an important and long-lived fixture of the independent and small press movement in Minnesota (see Chapter 14).

---

4   The South Dakota Review 1.1 (December 1963).

Another contemporary glimpse of Native America in a white literary context, however minimal (and therefore ultimately disappointing), may be had in the second issue of Franklin Brainard's magazine *Plainsong* (Spring 1967) (see Chapter 9), with its front cover image of Black Elk by Duane Noblett (then at Minneapolis College of Art and Design). On the rear cover is a poem by Ray Smith, "Black Elk on Harney Peak," which acknowledges John G. Neihardt's *Black Elk Speaks,* a 1932 book that was reprinted as a mass-market paperback in the 1960s, when it became quite well-known.[5]

A tremendous legacy of oral tradition, of stories, songs, and chants, not to mention of visual art—ignored or misrepresented and marginalized in the wider and dominant white culture—was there to be reasserted and rediscovered. Recognition was long overdue. It is also apparent, as in the example of Vizenor, above, that more Native writers were beginning not only to bring that legacy to the fore, but also to compose new poems and prose in the English language and in contemporary forms.

The publication of N. Scott Momaday's novel, *House Made of Dawn,* in 1968, was a significant step in this nationwide literary

---

5   Though also controversial, later, as some saw the non-Native Neihardt as misrepresenting the words of the Oglala Lakota holy man.

flowering, lifting Native concerns and outlooks into the mainstream, so to speak. Momaday was Kiowa, and his book inspired sparked "an unabated explosion of Native American novel, short story, poetry, autobiography, and drama."[6] In 1969 came *Custer Died for Your Sins: An Indian Manifesto* from Vine Deloria, Jr., Standing Rock Lakota. A non-fiction work more in line with the growing Red Power movement, it exploded some myths about Native culture, and, partly within the context of the Civil Rights Movement, called for a re-examination of the treatment of Native Americans by the U.S. Government, the Church, anthropologists, and other social scientists. The publication of each book was a watershed event.

This renaissance did not follow the usual course of some other literary, political, social, and cultural movements of the time, which often gathered momentum in the Upper Midwest only after their development on the east and west coasts. For, given the high concentration of Indigenous, especially Anishinaabe and Dakota, persons in the state, much of this renewal originated and took shape here on the land that had been stolen from them. Dennis Banks, of the Leech Lake Band of Ojibwe, was in the Minnesota State Prison in Stillwater when, as he writes, "I began to read about Indian history and became politicized in the process. I would read the papers and see that demonstrations about civil rights and the Vietnam war were going on all over the country. … we had no organization to address social reform, human rights, or treaty rights. …there was no movement specifically addressing the police brutality that was an everyday fact for Indian people or the discrimination in housing and employment in Minneapolis."[7]

Subsequently, Banks, Clyde Bellecourt, George Mitchell, Harold Good Sky, "and a number of determined women—among them

---

6 Sean Teuton, *Native American Literature: A Very Short Introduction* (Oxford University Press, 2018), 2.

7 Dennis Banks with Richard Erdoes, *Ojibwa Warrior: Dennis Banks and the Rise of the American Indian Movement* (University of Oklahoma Press, 2004), 60.

Francis Fairbanks and 'Girlie' Brown," founded the radical American Indian Movement in Minneapolis in the summer of 1968.[8] AIM "immediately established an Indian patrol to prevent the police from further harassing our people. We patterned it after the patrol created by the Black Panthers in Oakland."[9] But it was soon to be a force nationally, first in its participation in the nineteen-month Occupation of Alcatraz (an island offshore from San Francisco) from 1969-1971, which some see as the de facto start of the Red Power Movement.

* * *

Ten years after he first began sowing seeds in 1958, Bly was still at it. In fact, he was more intentional than ever, as he knew the importance of utilizing his notoriety as an antiwar activist, then at its peak, in order to help organize resistance and to spread the word; the future depended on such efforts. At the ceremony for the National Book Awards in March 1968, with the war in Vietnam still raging, in front of New York City mayor John Lindsay and other assembled dignitaries, Bly's acceptance speech made the same link as several poems in his award-winning book, *The Light Around the Body*: "Something has happened to me lately. Every time I have glanced at a bookcase in the last few weeks, the books on killing of the Indians leap out into my hand. Reading a speech of Andrew Jackson's on the Indian question the other day—his Second Annual Message—I realized that he was the General Westmoreland of 1830. His speech was like an Administration speech today. It was another speech recommending murder of a race as a prudent policy, requiring stamina."[10]

The most striking difference between Bly's second book and his first, *Silence in the Snowy Fields,* is its obvious attention to

---

8 Ibid., 62.
9 Ibid., 63.
10 The speech has been printed several times, but see: *Walking Swiftly*, 269-70.

American history, especially with relevance to the ongoing war in Vietnam (see Chapter 6). That and political anger, plus a stronger component of surreal imagery and surrealist juxtapositions, together comprised a book of heightened and "fierce moral vision."[11] Bly's ever-deepening exploration of Jungian thought had further sharpened his own awareness of the link between the willful forgetting of the historical mistreatment of Indigenous populations and current U.S. military policy in Vietnam.

A prominent example is the poem, "Hatred of Men with Black Hair," which opens by referring to some of the recent convulsions of decolonization in Africa, then moves quickly to the aftermath of the Dakota-U.S. War of 1862 (in Minnesota):

> I hear voices praising Tshombe and the Portuguese
> In Angola, these are the men who skinned Little Crow!
> We are all their sons, skulking
> In back rooms, selling nails with trembling hands!
>
> We distrust every person on earth with black hair.

Note that Bly implicates himself, and white Minnesotans. The poem ends:

> Underneath all the cement of the Pentagon
> There is a drop of Indian blood preserved in snow:
> Preserved from a trail of blood that once led away
> From the stockade, over the snow, the trail now lost.[12]

The last reference plainly is to the "Trail of Tears" (the forced removal of tens of thousands of natives—Cherokee, Muscogee, Sem-

---

11   Kirkpatrick. On Bly's work and the war in Vietnam, see *Born Under*, 192-217.

12   *The Light*, 36. For one striking image, Bly may have also been remembering "Beneath all the statistics, / there is a drop of duck's blood. / Beneath all the columns / there is a drop of a sailor's blood," the first four lines from Federico García Lorca's poem "New York (Office and Attack)."

inole, Chickasaw, and Choctaw—from their ancestral lands to the Oklahoma territory, a bald and barbarous attempt at ethnic cleansing) following the Indian Removal Act of 1830, when Andrew Jackson was President. Its relevance to the Vietnam War is clear, but the example of Little Crow, and his importance in Minnesota history, was especially meaningful to Bly.

In 1862, after decades of mistreatment and humiliation, of pressure to become farmers and to abandon their traditions and beliefs, and of other grievances, the Dakota were on the verge of starvation. Soon came the uprising, and the Dakota-U.S. war began. Eventually led by Ta Oyate Duta (Little Crow in a mistranslation), the Dakota began a desperate effort to survive and to drive the settlers out, ultimately unsuccessful. The most horrific consequence was the vindictive hanging of thirty-eight Dakota men in Mankato on December 26, 1862, at the order of President Lincoln—the largest mass execution in U.S. history.

A year later, near Hutchinson, a farmer shot Little Crow as he was returning home and scalped him (to collect a bounty).[13] Little Crow's scalp and skull went to the Minnesota Historical Society, where they remained, ignominiously!—the retention a potent sign of the continuing prevalence of barbaric and racist attitudes toward our Indigenous neighbors—for more than a century, until 1971 (when finally returned to Little Crow's descendants for burial).

Lewis Hyde, who has many roles in this present literary study, writes in a recent book:

> If, in the psychology of individuals, unresolved traumatic memories present themselves symptomatically (as obsessions, acting out, self-mutilation, nightmares, flashbacks, fainting spells . . .), does something similar hold for the psychology of nations? Does unexamined history reappear in some

---

13   Details in Gary Clayton Anderson, *Little Crow: Spokesman for the Sioux* (Minnesota Historical Society Press, 1986), 8.

> form of collective acting out, nightmare, flashback, and so on? If so, then forced forgetting doesn't resolve or transcend a violent past but obliges it to live on by displacement.[14]

That is to say, "violence denied and repressed doesn't disappear; it repeats." Bly certainly recognized the psychological and spiritual hazards of such repression for white descendants of European immigrants, as the epigraph to this Chapter indicates.

A year after *The Light* won its award he was still at it, writing an essay originally meant to accompany the Guthrie Theater's production of "The House of Atreus," now making a link between Aeschylus' ancient dramas of the Trojan War and contemporary America: "We can see how our rape of the land in the Nineteenth Century has distorted the American psyche permanently; the contemptuous murders of the Indians, which a hundred years ago seemed such a carefree thing, now permanently sadden us. Our Nineteenth Century murders have started us on a path of contempt toward all savage [*sic*] peoples, and it is difficult for us to leave that path."[15]

Bly continued his poetic attention to that contempt in his third big book, *Sleepers Joining Hands* (1973), including in the poems "Pilgrim Fish Heads" and "Calling to the Badger." In that unusual book's central essay, "I Came out of the Mother Naked," he cites an example of "crude" father consciousness "written by two white men in 1864":

> In the case before us, the Indian races were in the wrongful possession of a continent required by the superior right of the white man. This right, founded in the wisdom of God, eliminated by the ever-operative

---

14 Lewis Hyde, *A Primer for Forgetting: Getting Past the Past* (Farrar, Straus and Giroux, 2019), 233.

15 "The Purple Carpet and Contemporary Life," in *The House of Atreus* by John Lewin (Bantam Books, 1969), 120. Bly uses "carefree" and the word "savage" to represent the negative, pejorative view of the colonizers.

law of progress, will continue to assert its dominion, with varying success, contingent on the use of means employed, until all opposition is hushed in the perfect reign of the superior aggressive principle.[16]

This appalling, repulsive statement, expressing the racist, misanthropic doctrine of Manifest Destiny, explained much of current and subsequent American policy. Bly was intent on revealing this connection.[17]

* * *

Back to this Chapter's chronology. The Civil Rights Movement of the 1950s and '60s across the country drew attention to injustice and discrimination primarily, but not only, against African Americans. At the University of Minnesota in Minneapolis, a committee's report "stressed the need to establish links between the University and Minnesota's eleven federally-recognized tribes to develop recruitment and retention efforts for American Indian students, and to create courses on issues of importance to American Indian communities." Finally, a few years later, in 1969, after "political pressures forced [administrators] to respond to the demands of a growing American Indian student population and the radical activism of the Twin Cities' American Indian community," the Board of Regents approved the

---

16   Charles S. Bryant and Abel Much, A History of the Great Massacre by the Sioux Indians in Minnesota (Rickey and Carroll, 1864). In *Sleepers*, 34.

17   With this and the poems cited above in mind, it's easy at first to suppose that Bly was merely getting on board at the last minute with a trend, the rise in attention to Native American culture. (Much as John Milton seemed to be doing, below.) Not that it would be terribly shameful—better late than never—but was he just recently enlightened? No. He was no latecomer (relatively speaking); this was the manifestation of a process long underway in his consciousness. I trace this process in my forthcoming essay, cited above. There I focus on Bly's own exceptional involvement and interest in Native American history, especially of the Dakota people, as manifested in his first poetry, dating to 1950. This is illuminating information about uncharted territory in Bly's life and career.

formation of the Department of American Indian Studies (the first such autonomous program anywhere). Instruction in Dakota and Ojibwe languages was a key component, as well as the need for general education on "the complexities of historical and contemporary American Indian issues."[18]

Painter and sculptor George Morrison, from the Grand Portage Band of Ojibwe, began teaching in the department in 1970, which was, as he says: "just the right time. Indians were coming up in education. ... It was the result of the Civil Rights movement of the '60s." He also began to give slide lectures at "other institutions in Minnesota, including colleges like St. Olaf; and some colleges in Wisconsin.... I think introducing Indian art in a broad sense into the curriculum was a good idea."[19]

Morrison says, "Though I didn't consider myself an activist...I became a member of AIM, and...did my bit by helping to raise money." He taught a course called "The Arts of the American Indian." There were not many Indian students. "I think it was a valuable course for non-Indian as well as Indian students, introducing them to what was going on in American Indian art from pre-Columbian to the present."[20] After a year at the U of M, he formally joined its Studio Arts Department, teaching painting and drawing.

By 1969, editor John R. Milton had caught on, somewhat. His *South Dakota Review* had a special issue titled, "The American Indian Speaks in Poetry, Fiction, Art, Music, Commentary," which was quickly reissued as a book, *The American Indian Speaks*. Among the many contributors were Simon Ortiz, James Welch, Frank Waters, Patty Harjo, and R.C. Gorman. In a positive development, his magazine's focus on the American West no longer consisted mostly of cowboys and their mythology.

---

18   https://cla.umn.edu/ais/about/history
19   George Morrison (as told to Margot Fortunato Galt), *Turning the Feather Around: My Life in Art* (Minnesota Historical Society Press, 1998), 137.
20   Ibid., 140.

Milton writes in the introduction: "After a century or more of shameful neglect, the Indian is suddenly becoming a popular subject for anthropologists, linguists, editors, writers, do-gooders, hippies and educators—almost all of them Caucasians. There is a danger of exploitation, of wrong motives, of mistaken attitudes, of superiority feelings, and of simple misinterpretation when one race sets out to examine and 'promote' another race." Tell us about it. He continues: "As a close friend of Indians of several tribal groups... I too am tempted to write a long essay which will 'tell the truth' about the American Indian. However, in the communication between the two cultural groups, whether it be Caucasian and Negro or Caucasian and Indian, it seems only fair (and even intelligent) to let the minority groups speak for themselves once in a while."[21] Milton, in a condescending mode, walks a tightrope, comes close to losing his balance, and almost takes a nosedive into what he professes to be avoiding. But it seems that he was trying to do the right thing.

That very summer of 1969, Bly was a teacher at the first Upper Midwest Writers Conference, organized by William Elliott at Bemidji State College in northern Minnesota.[22] Ray Young Bear,

---

21 *South Dakota Review* 7.2 (Summer 1969), 3.
22 Still going, now renamed the Minnesota Northwoods Writers Conference.

an eighteen-year-old poet and recent high school graduate from the Meskwaki Settlement near Tama, Iowa, was a participant through Indian Upward Bound. He records:

> At some point, I was asked by Bly to meet him and David Ray to discuss my work. Hearing my lines being read aloud and critiqued was astounding. Occasionally, Bly would hover moth-like over my Haiku-type poems. … "Now, Young Bear," he asked, "do you see what we're doing here? We like 'Hail of Ice,' but some words aren't needed. Because what you've said, in this part, is adequate, if we make a few changes, like this."
>
> Bly made strikethroughs, something I had never seen. After some lines were deleted or merged with others, in dark green ink, the poem looked and sounded better.[23]

This was akin to weeding, clearing away the obstructions, strengthening the growth of the germ, the real poem. It was a process that any poet showing a poem to Bly would experience (including James Wright at the beginning of their collaboration), if he had deemed it salvageable.

But, initially, the very act of revision clashed with Young Bear's own understanding of poetry: "it took a while to stop believing [that] the English words that flowed from mind to pen and paper, as gifts, were untouchable." On another day, Bly stopped him, as Young Bear continues:

> "Young Bear, I've got some poems you should read."
> He handed over a paperback called the *New American Review*.
>
> "You can have it while you're here."

---

[23] This, and following quotations from: Ray Young Bear, "The Summer of 1969: Children of Speakthunder," in *Native Voices: Indigenous American Poetry, Craft and Conversations,* eds. CMarie Fuhrman and Dean Rader (Tupelo Press, 2019), no page numbers (as they are from the author's own typescript, sent to me).

> He then asked if I had ever heard of James Welch. When I said no, I learned Welch was a Blackfeet from Montana, with several poems in the paperback. As Bly spoke in glowing terms, gesturing as if his hands could read, I scanned "In My Lifetime." Smitten by its structure and clarity, I became an instant fan. It was short of a divination.

Young Bear says that Bly's sharing of Welch's poems "changed my life forever."[24] Maybe Bly's moving hands appeared to be reading, but they were definitely scattering seeds. "Moreover," Young Bear adds, "Bly kickstarted the publishing process by recommending my work to editors. There are no words, at seventy-one winters, that express my appreciation for his literary kindness, no words for having walked a non-ordinary life of poetry writing." It was another fateful, life-changing encounter with gift-giving Bly. The next spring, Young Bear was invited back to Bemidji to do his first-ever poetry reading.

One of those editors to whom Bly recommended him was present at the conference—John Milton.[25] Subsequently, Milton invited Young Bear to contribute to a special 1971 issue of his magazine, to be called "American Indian II." Young Bear's collection of fourteen poems appears there, gaining him due recognition. This time, however, Milton's introduction, instead of showing further improvement, is manifestly patronizing, with his jarring and heedless complaints of having to deal with "Indian time" (i.e., dilatoriness), of Indian writers exploiting their new popularity, of their supposedly characteristic "nomadism," and of their perceived indolence.[26]

---

24 RYB email to MG, 3 January 2022. The first appearance of those poems in book form: James Welch, *Riding the Earthboy 40* (World Publishing Company, 1971).

25 Another may have been Richard Damsten in Minneapolis, in whose subsequent *Black Flag* (see Chapter 9) Young Bear had six poems. Alternatively, it could be that, responding to Damsten's preliminary call for submissions, Bly gave him Young Bear's name and contact information.

26 *South Dakota Review* 9.2 (Summer 1971), vi.

Milton was not done. In 1974, he edited the anthology *Four Indian Poets*, including John Barsness, Paula Gunn Allen, Todd Haycock, and Jeff Saunders. His introduction still fails to avoid condescension. But he recognizes that "even in contemporary times there is a tendency on the part of Indian writers to emphasize traditions, the grandfathers, the longhouses, the continuity of the relationship between Indian and the land, a relationship much closer within the life of the Indian than in any of the other cultures on this continent...."[27] The colonizers' culture had much to learn.

---

27   John R. Milton, ed., *Four Indian Poets* (Dakota Press, 1974), 10.

As laid out in detail elsewhere in this book (see Chs. Nine and Twelve), 1971 was a banner year for new literary magazines in the Upper Midwest. One of those was *Dacotah Territory*, edited by poet and professor Mark Vinz in Moorhead. The name, "not to be confused with the Dakotas, or the U.S. Government's territorial boundaries of 1861. . . is what we now call the Great Plains—the lands originally inhabited by the Dacotah or Sioux nation of tribes, stretching from the Great Lakes and the Mississippi to the Rockies, and from Canada southward to the Oklahoma Territories and beyond. The word Dacotah means 'allies.' To unfriendly tribes it means 'enemies.'"[28] That first issue was dedicated to McGrath, "poet, teacher, friend," who was clearly the primary inspirer, influencer, and encourager, and around whom a literary community was flourishing.

The magazine was founded on "an idea of a healthy and diversified regionalism." Vinz clearly aims to avoid the main hazard of many regional efforts—an insular, narrow-minded, boosterish character. A year later, the magazine's vision was coming more into focus: "The editors are now interested in seeing poetry from 'the territory' (but not 'regionalist poetry'), poetry with some of the elements of surrealism (the image, et al.), a poetry generally open to

---

28   *Dacotah Territory* 1.1 (January 1971), i. The cover illustration was a woodcut, "Sioux Brave," by Bernel Bayliss.

understanding, poetry with social and political commitments [so far, in line with Bly's emphases], poetry of ethnic minorities, particularly the American Indian."[29]

In late 1973, #6, a special Native American issue, was guest-edited by James L. White, whom Vinz had met on a visit to Minneapolis, and included poets from around the country, including Joy Harjo, Roberta Hill, Simon Ortiz, Duane Niatum, Vizenor, Ramona Wilson, and William Witherup. (Ray Young Bear also appeared in a later issue.) Leonard Randolph, director of the NEA literature program, bought 2000 copies of that issue and distributed it to all the state arts agencies in the U.S.[30]

Time of the Indian was a literary magazine begun in 1972, entirely devoted to the writings of Indian youth in Minnesota. Its editor was the same James L. White, who had spent several years working for the Navajo in New Mexico, after which he moved to Minnesota to work in the Poets in the Schools program overseen by Molly LaBerge (see Chapter 15), doing special creative writing work with tribal children. "As a poet I ask only questions and the children answer freely from their spirit world."

The culmination of that, some years later, was the anthology, *Angwamas Minosewag Anishinabeg: Time of the Indian*, which reprinted work from the past six issues of the magazine. Thomas Peacock, a school principal from the Fond du Lac band of Lake Superior Ojibwe, wrote to White: "To Indian children who are grasping for a spiritual and cultural rebirth, your efforts have provided an outlet to air their innermost feelings on being Indian."[31]

---

29   *Dacotah Territory: A 10 Year Anthology*, eds. Mark Vinz and Grayce Ray (North Dakota Institute for Regional Studies, 1982), 4. "

30   Thanks to Mark Vinz for sharing with me a draft of his forthcoming essay, "Labors of Love: Memories of Small Press Publishing in the 1970s and 80s," which alerted me to this last fact.

31   *Angwamas Minosewag Anishinabeg: Time of the Indian,* ed. James L. White (COMPAS 1976), iii. For a later edition of this magazine, edited by David Martinson, see Chapter 15.

Sowing Seeds 165

AIM, as mentioned above, had been founded in large part to focus on urban discrimination, poverty, and abuse at the hands of police, and especially their pernicious effects on Native youth in Minnesota. Two years later, in response to the high dropout rate among Native students at public and Bureau of Indian Affairs-run schools, it announced its aspiration to open "survival schools" that would put Indigenous culture—including traditional practices, and Dakota and Ojibwe language—at the center of its curriculum. Both Heart of the Earth School in Minneapolis and Red School House in St. Paul opened in 1972. Most of the writings in *The Time of the Indian* and the related book came from students at each of these schools, and also from Nett Lake School on the Bois Forte Reservation, Pine Point School in Ponsford on White Earth, and Bizindun Indian School in Duluth. The Walker Art Center held a Heart of the Earth Survival School poetry reading in March 1974.

Also notable is the exhibition, "American Indian Art: Form and Tradition," October 22-December 31, 1972, co-sponsored by the Walker Art Center and the Minneapolis Institute of Art.[32] Most

---

32 A third sponsor was the newly-formed Indian Art Association (which included AIM, the Department of Indian Studies at the University of Minnesota, and other organizations). Later, in 1974, the Walker put on "George Morrison: Drawings," a show of 45 of his pen and ink drawings.

of the 900 objects were functional or spiritual in origin. George Morrison said at the time: "An Indian doesn't have to paint tipis to be an artist." And: "I have never tried to prove that I was Indian through my art ... Yet, there may remain deeply hidden some remote suggestion of the rock whence I was hewn, the preoccupation of the textural surface, the mystery of the structural and organic element, the enigma of the horizon, or the color of the wind."[33] He felt himself caught in the middle, between Indian artists who wanted nothing to do with such an exhibition and those who, "on their own terms, drew their imagery or inspiration directly from Indian life."

Concurrent with this exhibition, Suzanne Weil organized some related programming, with performances of music, dance, theater, and poetry (see Chapter 10). Poets Todd Haycock and Jeff Saunders (whose poems were in the anthology *Four Indian Poets,* above) read at the Walker then.

Vizenor's essay in the exhibition catalog begins: "The poetic images of tribal family people are song pictures and thought rhythms of visions and dreams—timeless patterns of sacred forms of seeing and knowing the energy of life."[34] Songs from oral tradi-

---

33 Morrison, 141.
34 Gerald Vizenor, "Tribal People and the Poetic Image: Visions of

tion were a form of prayer, their words were ritual language. Another description of his quite coincidentally fits even more closely with Bly's penchant for poetry laden with Minnesota images (not to mention his emphasis on inner, spiritual life): "The poetic images of the woodland are the rhythms of life: the drone of mosquitoes and thump of partridge, sprigs of white pine in the nests of eagles, ice cracks running the frozen lakes, the voices of bears, avian dreams of cranes and loons, eagles and crows, visions of hands and eyes."[35]

Wider developments rolled on. At roughly the same time, AIM's leadership—both in the Trail of Broken Treaties caravan to Washington, D.C., in 1972, leading to the occupation of the Department of the Interior building, and in the Wounded Knee Occupation from February 27 to May 8, 1973, on the Pine Ridge Reservation in South Dakota—raised both the organization's visibility in wider American awareness and the pride of Native Americans everywhere as their demands to be granted their long-overlooked rights grew.

In 1975, the Minneapolis American Indian Center opened on Franklin Avenue, its façade being a massive wooden collage designed by Morrison. "Guided by strong Native values," in providing educational and social services the center was planned to "preserve and support American Indian cultural traditions through art, youth and inter-generational programs." There had been a rebirth, its significance much more than literary and artistic. 1975 also saw the Indian Self-Determination and Education Assistance Act signed into law. It was a culmination, for the time being, of the Civil Rights Movement and the Red Power Movement. And another indication of the broad-based renaissance as outlined above.

Nationwide, the first wave of the literary aspect of the renaissance persisted. Abenaki poet Joseph Bruchac started publishing in

---

Eyes and Hands," in *American Indian Art: Form and Tradition* (Walker Art Center and the Minneapolis Institute of Art, 1972), 15.

35   Ibid., 17.

the early 1970s. Blackfeet poet James Welch published his important first novel, *Winter in the Blood,* in 1974. In it, the narrator calls himself "a servant to the memory of death." In 1976, James White's anthology, *The First Skin Around Me: Contemporary American Tribal Poetry,* included poems by Joy Harjo, Leslie Silko, Vizenor, Roberta Hill, Eddie Benton Banai, Duane Niatum, Thomas Peacock, Simon Ortiz, and many others. As the editor writes: "The reason for this book...is to provide a camp ground where Indian artists can share their poem. I think this is how modern presses can be of value to tribal communities. ... I believe it is time (past time, perhaps) for poets who are Indian to enter the mainstream of American poetry."[36]

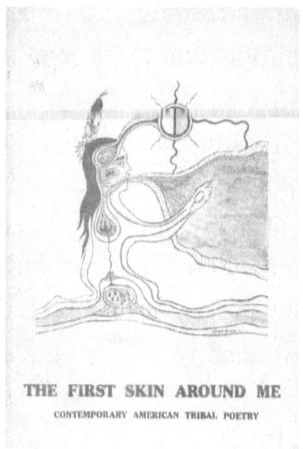

And in 1977, Laguna Pueblo poet and short story writer Leslie Marmon Silko's first novel, *Ceremony,* was published to great acclaim. She had participated in the National Poetry Festival at Grand Valley State College in Allendale, Michigan, in 1975, along with James Welch, Simon Ortiz, Howard Norman, Etheridge Knight,

---

36 James L. White, *The First Skin Around Me: Contemporary American Tribal Poetry* (The Territorial Press, 1976), 7. One of the most prominent and prolific literary figures in the next phase of the Native American Renaissance, with strong ties to Minnesota, is, of course, Louise Erdrich, whose first books came later; *Jacklight* (poetry) and *Love Medicine* (novel) were published in 1984.

Nikki Giovanni, Robert Creeley, Charles Simic, Mei-Mei Berssenbrugge, Robert Bly, and James Wright, among others. Wright was moved to write to Silko after her reading and after he had read her book. They began a correspondence, which resulted in a beautiful book years later.[37]

---

37 *The Delicacy and Strength of Lace: Letters Between Leslie Marmon Silko and James Wright*, edited by Anne Wright (Graywolf Press, 1986).

Chapter 9
A New Crop of Lit Mags: Twin Cities

> In those days, having a literary magazine was a way to build, almost instantly, a kind of community.
> –Jim Moore

In 1958, Bly started sowing seeds with his little magazine *The Fifties* and *The Sixties*, proclaiming the need for a new poetry with a new imagination. It was part of a great wave of little magazines that swept nationwide (esp. east and west coasts), evidence of a revolutionary impulse and an emerging avant-garde in poetry.[1] His second step of sowing, starting with his first book of poems in 1962, which embodied Bly's poetics and, at least to young poets from the North Country, specified a physical, bounded geographical (if also spiritual) place (see Chapter 4), brought a new force to be joined. Soon, within a couple of years, the traces of the sprouting of a new Minnesota poetic community became detectable, even as did Bly's effect on poets all across the country. Then, in 1966, came the important third step of Bly's now trilateral efforts—politics & poetry, specifically in the context of active opposition to the war in Vietnam (see Chapter 6).

---

1 See, especially, *A Secret Location on the Lower East Side: Adventures in Writing*, 1960-1980, edited by Steven Clay and Rodney Phillips (New York Public Library and Granary Books, 1998). Also, in part, *The Little Magazine in America: A Modern Documentary History*, edited by Elliott Anderson and Mary Kinzie (The Pushcart Press, 1978).

Examining the great surge of new literary magazines in the Upper Midwest that began in the 1960s is one way to trace the growing strength and amazing vitality of its literary community. Most of them owed much, at least indirectly, to the example of Bly's surprisingly successful and important magazine. But few of them even approached its "idiosyncratic editing and highly personal critical commentary."[2] Bly the magazine editor was beating a drum, waging a battle, breaking things open, making space for a new kind of poetry. When *The Fifties* was starting out, he and others were reacting against the status quo, and staking a position in a larger conflict. He was certainly in tune with the ethos of the time, attacking his elders, the older generation. And the magazine, aimed at and named for a time, a decade, a generation, and not a region, was nationally distributed from the outset.

But the new wave of local magazines owed even more to the second step and the way that *Silence in the Snowy Fields* had drawn attention to the dignity, the vitality, and the magic of life in this particular place, in the North Country, in Minnesota. In the wake of Bly's magazine, with its ground-breaking done, local magazines meant instead to continue to sow and to reap, to draw together groups of writers, new or little-known writers who were producing

---

2   Michael Anania, "Of Living Belfry and Rampart: On American Literary Magazines Since 1950," in *The Little Magazine in America*, 13.

that new kind of poetry, and to help them flourish and to find an audience. Most of the magazines discussed here were consciously regional, meaning and excited to represent the new status quo that Bly (and others) had helped create. That is to say, their editors were not dissatisfied; rather, they communicated contentment.

Wojahn generalizes:

> The poetics of the Deep Image was the prevailing mode in that era, probably because of Bly, and probably because it was relatively easy to write a mildly surrealist poem about an epiphany in a cornfield in the mode of *Silence in the Snowy Fields*. That's the fare that all the little magazines of the Midwest published. The poetic vocabulary employed was deliberately limited—the work was analogous to what the Georgian Poets were doing in England right before WWI, small in scale, wistfully pastoral. None of us had the ferocity and hurt self-disclosure that made James Wright so great, or the inventiveness of Bly at his best. But they gave us a template.[3]

While each of these magazines below has its own identifiable character, none of them existed in a vacuum. So begins part one (the urban part) of what amounts to a catalog. While it may seem an impediment to forward movement in the overall narrative, I think it the most effective way to convey the reality of their number, their character, their impact, and the corralling of the many poets who were part of the burgeoning scene.[4] As will soon become clear, most little magazines were ephemeral, almost by definition, fizzling out very soon.[5]

---

    3   DW email to MG, 19 July 2020.

    4   I take comfort in knowing that even many-minded Homer relied on catalogues (of ships, women, suitors, warriors slain in battle) for perspective.

    5   My focus is split between "city" and "outstate" magazines in two chapters. The list is not complete, and a few other important local magazines (*Region, Minnesota Review, Carleton Miscellany, South Dakota Review, Sez*) are

Plainsong

Plainsong began publication in early 1967. Edited by Franklin Brainard, an English teacher at Mounds View High School (which I attended) in suburban St. Paul, with help from Ray Smith (another poet), and published by James D. Thueson (a local librarian/publisher), its regional focus is obvious, but there is no statement of purpose or other editorial comment.[6] It is hard to know exactly what to read into its name, "plainsong" being the word for the monophonic, unison singing of Gregorian Chant, but also—in a play on words—possible reference to the poetry of the Great Plains, and/or the plain-spoken free verse poetry that Bly's poems typified. The first issue has mostly poetry, from Brainard himself, Smith, Richard Lyons (at North Dakota State University), Roland Flint (at the U of M, and then poetry editor of *The Minnesota Review*, see Chapter 3), John R. Milton (editor of *South Dakota Review*, see Chapter 8), and novelist Frederick Manfred, who also supplies short fiction. Advertisements are for McCosh's bookstore

---

discussed in other chapters.

6 This little magazine is distinct from another, later *Plainsong*, edited by Frank Steele out of Bowling Green, Kentucky, beginning in 1979, and with which Bly was also associated.

in Dinkytown, and other James Thueson publications (including books by Manfred, Smith, and Milton).

The second issue pulled in Bly, already virtually unignorable, to whom was given the first couple of pages. More poems from Brainard, Smith, and Milton, and first appearances from Manfred's daughter Freya (recent graduate of Macalester College in St. Paul, where she had been a student of Wright's) and John Caddy. August Derleth, well-known Wisconsinite, has both poetry and prose. And there is fiction from another local heavyweight, Le Sueur. More ads, for The Sixties Press and the *South Dakota Review,* show an interest in solidarity and coexistence.

The third and final issue again included Brainard, Lyons, Smith, and Fred Manfred, with the notable additions of Tom Hennen and Michael Kincaid, both of whom will be fixtures on the local scene. The reasons for *Plainsong*'s demise are unclear. Was it lack of a clear vision or position, or money, or Brainard's declining health? The most we can say for certain is that it was a regional magazine with a small core group, and some visual art work of uneven quality. In any case, it was a valiant effort, and the three issues give a glimpse of literary life in Minnesota coming alive under the overarching shadow of Bly's accomplishments. The template that Wojahn identifies above is surely in evidence here.

Nickel & Dime Quarterly

The first of the University's *Ivory Tower* crew (see Chapter 3) to start a magazine was Lewis Hyde, with no little assistance from some of his *Ivory Tower* comrades. But first, his poem, "When We Are in Love," was published in two places in 1968: the Free University magazine *The Minnesota Mama*; and the undergraduate magazine *Academy: A Journal of the Liberal Arts.* Its title, and last line, as many probably noticed, was lifted from Bly's short "Love Poem" in *Silence in the Snowy Fields.* ("When we are in love, we love the grass, / And the barns, and the lightpoles, / And the small main-streets abandoned all night.") Thus it was an early homage and a sign of Bly's influence. Meanwhile, a poetic coterie was forming.

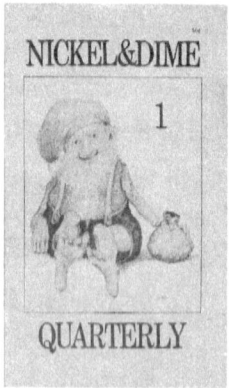 

Hyde's *Nickel & Dime Quarterly* was published in Minneapolis in the late spring of that year. Its apparently self-deprecating name suggests modest aspirations. Although uncredited, Marly Rusoff helped with the physical production (see Chapter 7). Franz Richter, art editor (as also with *Ivory Tower*), supplied the distinctive drawing on the cover and mimicked *kayak* magazine's inclusion of old found engravings and its use of different-colored papers.[7] Poems were from Moore, Hampl, Jonathan Sisson again (also under two pseudonyms: M. Bolus and Jeats Cohen), Michael Tjepkes (another student) and Keith Gunderson (a philosophy professor).

There were translations—by Hyde from the Spanish of Villaurutia, Pablo Neruda, and Vicente Aleixandre, and by Moore from the French of Leconte de Lisle. The always eccentric Gregory Bitz (another local mainstay), under the name "Voltaire Christmas," writes out and draws "The Story of Wee Morris." Hyde has remarked on the excitement of that time among these young poets, the incessant talk and sharing of ideas, all the more lively because

---

7   In national terms, *kayak,* edited by George Hitchcock out on the West Coast, was an early (1964) important offspring of Bly's *The Fifties/Sixties*.

they were *not* all English majors, they were not all studying creative writing, so they were reading in and sharing ideas and outlooks from different fields.

The magazine's second issue, longer and more elaborate than the first (another beautiful job and cover from Richter), came out a year later. It has several new contributors including Chet Corey and some shepherded by Moore, then at the Writer's Workshop in Iowa City. And some repeat contributors: Bitz was there again, in facsimile handwriting with drawings, as was Sisson, with a concrete poem.

Going beyond poetry, Moore writes a substantial essay, "The Journey of Malcolm X," in which he considers the spiritual life revealed in *The Autobiography of Malcolm X* (very much au courant), placing that book in the same league as Augustine's *Confessions* and *The Diary of Anne Frank*. Hampl's help with this issue is acknowledged.

Plans were announced for the next number, including a long interview with Bly. There is also this note: "Though this issue contains no translations, we will carry them in the future. We would like to hear from people who would enjoy making it their job to be familiar with modern poetry in a specific foreign language, to give us translations regularly, and to write short essays on foreign poetry." Sounds very much like continuing a primary mission of Bly's *The Sixties*.

More than just poetry, there was visual artistry, and a move toward critical thinking, and a vision for what lay ahead. Although there had been some advertisements—for Savran's Paperback Shop on the West Bank and Perine's Bookstore and The Podium (Music and Tobacco Shop) in Dinkytown—not enough money was available to continue. So the magazine was discontinued. But these people would all be heard from again.

Black Flag

Also printed on the West Bank (by the Mad Bomber Press), a year later, was *Black Flag: Poems for the Resistance,* edited by Richard Damsten.[8] The black flag had long symbolized anarchism—its anger, outrage, and resolve and strength in opposition to every form of hierarchy and inequality. In physical format, this is by all appearances a literary magazine. Yet it is further subtitled "A One-Shot Poetry Bomb" (in apparent reference to the Black Flag brand of insecticide, and maybe also to the notorious "mad bomber" himself, George Metesky). It commemorated Flag Day, June 14th, 1970 (the black flag being the negation of all flags), and was sub-subtitled "Poets from Minnesota & Other Stations in the Cosmos." Apparently, no additional issues were planned.[9] Illustrated and with some old found engravings, it leaned in a surrealist direction, was predominantly regional, and plainly antiwar, as the initial statement suggests:

> Welcome to the Resistant Troubadour-Machine.

---

8   Damsten was from Duluth, and later changed his name to Waara, discarding his step-father's name.

9   An anomaly and one-off, it may not strictly belong in this chapter, though it does have advertisements: for United Farm Workers; and for *Beaver* 55 (a literary magazine).

The full moon is in its eclipse.
Grab your straight-razor and come with me:
The time has come to dissect the Eye of USA.[10]

The list of Minnesota contributors overlaps with those in *Plainsong* and *Nickel & Dime Quarterly,* evidence of growing community cooperation once again: John Caddy, Gunderson, Richard Shaw, Sarah Shaw, Michael Kincaid, Brainard, Tjepkes, Corey, Tom Hennen; and it also includes newcomers Dale Jacobson (a student of McGrath's), Michael Berryhill, Roy McBride, and Timothy Baland (who had been working with Bly). Two were from neighboring states: Doug Flaherty, editor of *The Road Apple Review*, had just moved to Oshkosh, Wisconsin; and Ray Young Bear (a Bly protégé, see Chapter 8) was in Iowa. From further afield, Gary Snyder's "Smokey the Bear Sutra" was at the top, courtesy of the fact that the poem comes with the customary directive of the gift economy, "may be reproduced free forever." David Ray was Bly's friend and co-founder of Poets and Writers Against the Vietnam War.

The Lamp in the Spine

1971 was an *annus mirabilis* for new literary magazines (four of

---

10   Note the apparent reference to a gruesome scene in the 1929 surrealist film "Un Chien Andalou," by Luis Buñuel and Salvador Dalí, which was once again in vogue. (I saw it around the same time.)

them) in the Upper Midwest. First was *The Lamp in the Spine,* edited by Hampl and Moore, though still in Iowa City. Former undergraduate staffers of *Ivory Tower*, they both had received MFA degrees from the Iowa Writers' Workshop in poetry at the University of Iowa. Moore had recently been released early from federal prison in Springfield, Missouri, having served ten months for draft resistance.[11]

The magazine's unusual name comes from Virginia Woolf's extended essay, "A Room of One's Own," in which she contrasts the fine meals furnished at men's colleges in Oxford and Cambridge with those at women's colleges. She writes:"a good dinner is of great importance to good talk. One cannot think well, love well, sleep well if one has not dined well. The lamp in the spine does not light on beef and prunes." Thus, the magazine's feminist slant is at least implicit in the title.

Hampl adds: "she writes about not being interested in the hard little electric light of the intellect, but in the lamp in the spine—meaning the imagination." Of course, Bly's often underscored distinction between the imagination and the intellect was fundamental to his view of the new poetry.[12] Hyde first offered his friends the chance to take over his defunct magazine, *Nickel & Dime Quarterly*. But they were intent on launching with a new name.[13] Another *Ivory Tower* associate, Gregory Bitz, did the first front cover.

It was an ambitious undertaking and, seen whole, it seems

---

11   This was at the Federal Medical Center, as Moore says, "commonly known as the asshole of the system." It was a friend from the *Ivory Tower,* Sam Heins, now a law student, who realized that Moore's sentence should be shortened because of the Supreme Court's recent Gutknecht Decision—based on the case of a Minneapolis draft resister and activist, David Gutknecht. As Moore says re Heins: "I owe him an eternal debt." MG interview with JM, 7 January 2020.

12   He rejected most submitted poems on the grounds that they were "written with the intellect, not the feeling." For more, see *Born Under*, 115-131.

13   Hampl rues in retrospect: "Garrison Keillor…was (rightly) repelled by the title, and tried to get us to change it. Why didn't we listen? Well, you tend not to listen to good sense when you're that young and passionate about something." PH email to MG, 19 March 2020.

closer to *The Sixties* (although with many important differences) than any of the other magazines under consideration. In the "similar" column, content included poetry, translation, essays, criticism, politics, even some parody. Also a powerful editorial outlook. In the "dissimilar" column (beyond the obvious as discussed at the top of this Chapter), *The Lamp* had a much broader aesthetic range and a greater quantity and variety of content and contributors. It also held feminism as an explicit and basic value, and it evinced a growing and related interest in journal writing. In this way, it was also about the task of sowing seeds. Hampl says:

> Jim and I wanted our magazine to "connect poetry and politics." I think we used those words or ones very like. We felt that literary magazines were still mostly just "literary," collecting dumps of poems without any reason to be together except they were considered "good." Such little magazines were, to us, not enough content-driven…. We had the double impulse of the war (still raging for another four years) and the rise of feminism as the engines of our ideas about "poetry and politics." … We had a simple editorial plan—we would publish poetry, never our own, and we would publish essays, often or usually our own. The essays would give the magazine editorial drive and distinction.

The bit about essays is similar to *The Sixties*, though most of Bly's were focused narrowly on poetics in support of the revolution he was leading. Still, Moore says that he himself "probably wouldn't have written [the essays] if it wasn't for Robert." Bly, of course, published his own poetry and translations—not out of vanity but because examples of his idea of the "new poetry" were hard to come by in those early days. Also, Hampl and Moore followed his example by not sending printed rejection slips, but personal responses—a labor intensive, time-consuming, and, generous practice.

Moore says: "We were engaged in the cultural and political happenings of the time, and it seemed that starting a literary magazine—a lot of people were doing it—was a way to participate in what was happening.... In those days having a literary magazine was a way to build, almost instantly, a kind of community. Also, we were looking at what Robert had done with *The Sixties*, wanting to do our own version with a more feminist slant—still the antiwar slant, but more feminist, more in tune with the cultural changes that were happening."[14] He continues: "We tried to do a range of stuff the way Robert did, but looser. His magazine looked so elegant.... We were doing ours on a shoestring and typing up the proofs—if you made a mistake, you had to start all over again. We ran the earlier issues off and stapled them ourselves. It was cheap to do."

For the abundance of varied and far-flung contributors to *The Lamp*, the editors drew from their poet friends and acquaintances in Iowa City and in the Twin Cities—by 1973 they had returned to St. Paul—and further spun off from connections made with writers in both places. While they attracted well-known (and soon to be well-known) writers like Wendell Berry, Greg Kuzma (editor of *Pebble*), William Matthews (a Bly friend, and co-editor of *Lillabulero*), Gail Godwin, David Ray, Albert Goldbarth, Denise Levertov, Marge Piercy, Naomi Replansky, Hayden Carruth, Ted Kooser (editor of the *New Salt Creek Reader*), Philip Lamantia (whom Bly had recently published in *The Seventies*), and Gregory Orr (ditto), they also used many who would be recognized as regulars in the Minnesota posse.[15] Michael Moos, for one, says that publication in *The*

---

14   MG interview with JM, 7 January 2020.

15   Veterans of *The Ivory Tower* and *The Nickel & Dime Quarterly*—Keillor, Hyde (who helped much behind the scenes), Galt, Richter, Bitz, and Sisson—as well as Mike Finley, Kirkpatrick, Wendy Salinger, Mark Vinz (*Dacotah Territory*), Michael Moos, Thomas Dillon Redshaw, David Martinson, John Engman, Phil Dentinger (*Steelhead*), Louis Jenkins (*Steelhead*), Jenné Andrews,

Lamp "made me feel as though I was part of a larger family of poets, and inspired in me a greater courage to send my poems out to more magazines."[16] These contributors were, it might go without saying, on top of the well-represented "big three," Bly, McGrath, and Le Sueur, on whose shoulders they quite consciously rode.

In addition were occasional translations—of Attila József, Neruda, Björn Håkansson, Ivan Goll, Miroslav Holub, and a few others—fewer parodies (i.e., Salinger's "W.S. Merwin Rewrites Shakespeare's Sonnet 146," McGrath's "Driving Toward Boston I Run Across One of Robert Bly's Old Poems," and an anonymous rejection slip from *The New Yorker*), some fiction, various quotations and excerpts, including antiwar pieces, reviews, other intermittent oddities (poems from children, concrete poems, drawings, even Vachel Lindsay), and increasing attention to journal writing by women, Le Sueur being the exemplar. There also was the interview with Bly, promised originally for the third issue of *Nickel & Dime Quarterly*, conducted by Hyde and Richter.

The essays by Hampl include "What Shall Zelda Do?", "Writing from Desire," (in which she mentions Bly, Ginsberg, and Snyder as male poets "worried about the traditional male trait of domination—of nature, of women, of other men"), "The Love of Comrades," and "A Book with a Lock and Key." Moore writes a three-parter, "American Poetry in and out of the Cave," a very critical, Bly-like take, first on Kinnell, Merwin, and Wright (including the statement, "Ten years ago there was a revolution in poetry," that points directly to Bly's work), a second essay on Levertov, and a third on Ignatow and Rainer Maria Rilke. Hyde's are more broadly-based, more deeply philosophical: "Come, Let Us Reason Together or What Occurred to Me While Reading Ludwig Wittgenstein" and "The Tuber Mind."[17]

John Rezmerski, Browne, Joe Paddock, and Wendy Knox.
    16   MM email to MG, 29 May 2024.
    17   Remaining essays are by Keith Hjortshoj, "Poetry and Myth," W.G. Roll, "Psychical Research in the Seventies," and Jack Litewka, "The Socialized Penis."

In the last issue, number nine, Moore wrote, "Why I'm Quitting *The Lamp in the Spine* and Why Poetry is Essential to the Revolution," followed by Hampl's much shorter "A Letter to Our Readers." That was the fall of 1974. Moore had written to Hyde: "As you can see, we're giving up *The Lamp*—we both feel that the next few years will be crucial to our own work as poets and lives as people...."[18] In fact, both Hampl and Moore subsequently saw publication of their first books.[19]

The North Stone Review

A second locally important literary magazine to start up in 1971, *The North Stone Review* from Minneapolis, is an outlier, in a sense, mainly because of the obdurate nature of its editor, James Naiden, who was kind of a lone ranger, but also because he kept it going, very irregularly, until 2002.[20] While a few editors—at least of those considered

---

18 JM to LH, 15 July 1974.
19 James Moore, *The New Body* (University of Pittsburgh Press, 1975); Patricia Hampl, *Woman Before an Aquarium* (University of Pittsburgh Press, 1978).
20 There were fourteen issues in all. It might have gone longer, except that in 2003 he went to prison for "attempting to entice a child through the internet and mails to engage in unlawful sexual activity and attempting to induce a child to travel for unlawful sexual activity." https://case-law.vlex.com/vid/u-s-v-naiden-891385825 In any case, it might already have gone too long, as it seemed

here—might be absolved for dealing in a noticeably kind or favorable fashion with their friends, Naiden flipped that practice. He was an astute, fierce, and uncompromising critic, *à la* Bly, but also a vindictive one, by reputation. If he felt slighted by a fellow poet, crossed by a publisher, even jilted by a lover, he could lash out in print.

Naiden had recently, in 1970, settled in Dinkytown after some incomplete study in creative writing at the University of Iowa. The first issue, in the spring, was all poetry with the exception of Naiden's book review. Several of the contributors shared that Iowa connection, as did the two poets under review (Anselm Hollo and his student Ray DiPalma). Other names we have already seen: Brainard (editor of *Plainsong*), Tjepkes, Kincaid, and Warren Woessner. It is noteworthy, surely, that one of Brainard's short poems here is entitled "Robert Bly":

> His silent snows shimmer
> like affection around the cells
> that hold the lonely man
> upright under the sea
> walking as if on water.

This is as strong an indication of Bly's predominant position in Minnesota at the time as we might find.

In Naiden and Kincaid's subsequent interview, Brainard acknowledges Bly's generosity and generativity: their readings together; Bly's suggestions, both about his poems and where to submit them, often with resultant acceptance; the importance of Bly's emphasis on the surreal image; and the translations of earthy Spanish and South American poems. "None of us in our group, I think, would follow him, like we were following a guru—but we listen very carefully to what he's got to say."[21]

---

to start imitating itself.

21 "A Discusssion with Franklin Brainard," *The North Stone Review* 3 (Summer-Fall 1972), 23.

The few issues following in the 1970s indicate Naiden's increasing reliance on Minnesota poets—both for poems and for reviews—as well as the expansion of content to include some translations and a variety of prose, with special emphasis on poetry reviews. He certainly was in line with Bly's conviction, first articulated in *The Fifties*, that poetry needs criticism for its health, that young poets need criticism from other young poets, that there is too much praise, that harsh criticism has its place. Political matters appear to have no place in Naiden's magazine, however.

The growing list of contributors includes Rakosi, Paddock, Caddy, Vinz, Jenkins, Dentinger, Allan Kornblum, Greenberg, Sisson, and many others.[22] Of course, Bly is represented (also some of his translations), as are his friends like Ignatow and Stafford. At least a couple of issues include advertisements, again for Dinkytown and West Bank businesses.[23]

Given these signs of extraordinary growth and verdancy in the literary life of Minnesota, this might be the right place for a brief aside, to consider a plan Bly had for the next issue of his own magazine. *The Seventies 2* was long slated to be a "Young Poets Issue," pointedly meant to publish good poets—in Bly's estimation—who had been left out of Paul Carroll's 1969 anthology, *The Young American Poets*. Along with many other nationally known poets (a varied list), Bly was including locals Hennen, Kincaid, Don Olsen, Woessner, Holm, Moore, and Hyde.[24] It would have been nice exposure for them beyond Minnesota's borders. But, alas, the issue never appeared, as *The Seventies* 1 (Spring 1972) proved to be the final one.

---

22   In addition to the core group from the first issue were John Daniel, Redshaw, Corey, Engman, Philip Gallo, Doug Blazek, Robert Damsten, Martinson, Richard Shaw, Sarah Shaw, Caroline (Vogel) Marshall, and Peter Mladinic.

23   Perine's Campus Book Center, Savran's Paperback Shop, Savran & Rusoff Bookdealers, The Podium, and others.

24   Cited in *Born Under*, 295. It may be of interest to note that, among the thirty-seven poets on the list were also Audre Lorde, Sonia Sanchez, Rosellen Brown, Kathleen Marshall, Jeanne Hill, Carol Morris, Jane Kenyon, and Duane Niatum.

Moons and Lion Tailes

After graduating from Minneapolis Southwest High School, as a U of M undergraduate Jim Perlman studied mostly in the English Department. He lived on the West Bank near Wilson Library, and was poetry editor of the short-lived *The American Flyer and Other Suspensions,* which, after one issue, became *ONE,* distributed free in the *Minnesota Daily* (though there were only two issues).[25] Contributors included Browne, Minczeski, Hennen, Dochniak, and three poems by Helge Schjotz-Christensen, a Dane.

Schjotz-Christensen soon suggested to Perlman—who knew a little bit about printing (both as co-editor of his high school literary magazine, and having worked a short while operating an AB Dick offset printing machine, not to mention a stint in the warehouse of The Bookmen, Inc., the wholesale book distributor run by his cousin, Norton Stillman)—that they start a new literary magazine together. They had attended the launch reading for the Minnesota Writers' Publishing House (MWPH) in Morris, which made an impression (see Chapter 13). Perlman says that, at that time, his "triune poetry gods" were Le Sueur, McGrath, and Bly. And Helge, he says, "was keen on soliciting work from Bly." He adds: "Helge and I viewed

---

25 Will Weaver was the fiction editor of *American Flyer.* Michael Bliss edited *One.* The *Ivory Tower* was by then defunct.

Bly as a primary force of that era—we pursued his cooperation and wanted his respect and support for our magazine."[26]

They set about assembling poems, translations, essays, and book reviews. The name, *Moons and Lion Tailes,* was drawn from the early Sixties Press book, *The Lion's Tail and Eyes* (see Chapter 4). Richter, veteran illustrator for *The Ivory Tower, Nickel & Dime Quarterly,* and *The Lamp in the Spine* (as well as Bly's Seventies Press book, *Twenty Poems of Tomas Tranströmer* and the first two titles for MWPH), drew the "Man in the Moon" image for the front cover, which became the magazine's enduring logo (a trait it shared with Bly's magazine). The first issue in Spring 1973 was done on a typewriter, and it and the second issue were assembled, folded, and staple-bound by hand. The publisher of the magazine was the Permanent Press, which, Perlman says, was "just me trying to be clever." Beyond clever—prescient, it turns out, given his presence on the scene a half century later.

This, on the face of it, may seem the most Bly-influenced of all these mags. The poems are largely from the Bly template. Contributors at the outset included: Marisha Chamberlain, Hennen, McGrath, Mike Finley, Caroline Vogel, Brainard, Hyde (his translations of Vicente Aleixandre, later published by Bly's Seventies Press), and the editors. There is one book review, of Brainard's book, *Raingatherer,* from the Minnesota Writer's Publishing House (see Chapter 14). (The magazine carefully reviewed each MWPH book as it appeared, showing great care for nurturing the young poets on the local scene.) The first issue's back cover features a four-line poem by Bly. "A Doing Nothing Poem":

> There is a bird that flies through the water
> It is like a whale ten miles high!
> Before it went into the ocean,
> It was just a bit of dust from under my bed!

---

26 JP email to MG, 12 December 2020.

Issue two included Minczeski's poem, "Variations on a Line by Robert Bly," beginning:

> Driving a car through Minnesota
> you see things you have never seen before
> blue turtles, blue monkeys,
> everything's blue in Minnesota
> guitars are blue and people.[27]

Also, Wendy Knox's poem "Realization," maybe in response to Bly's poem above, begins: "I read Robert Bly, his / whales flashing."

Subsequent issues expand the number of reviews and that list of contributors who are, of course, mostly locals.[28] There were also Bly's far-flung friends and contemporaries (most of whom he had published and critiqued), Wright, Ignatow, Levertov, Louis Simpson, George Hitchcock, Russell Edson, and Philip Levine. Surely, Bly urged these and other friends to submit, vouching for this magazine. Again, while attempting to encompass the whole country, the primary and honorable purpose seemed to provide an outlet for local poets and to give them opportunities to criticize and be criticized.

In 1976, Knox was added to the masthead; in 1977, Perlman's name fell off as he and Helge parted ways; in 1978, the magazine folded after eight issues. Perlman's summation of Bly's influence was that they had seen him "as a means to help our magazine gain regional and national fame, which it did." Schjotz-Christensen then disappears from the record, but Perlman's Holy Cow! Press, as we shall see (Chapter 14), has been an everlasting part of the landscape.

---

27 There are several "driving" poems in *Silence in the Snowy Fields*.
28 Including Jenkins, Gunderson, Freya Manfred, Roberts, Tjepkes, Mary Logue, William Meissner, Dochniak, Wojahn, Machado (tr. Bly), Rezmerski, Candyce Clayton, Moore, Vinz, Doug Blazek, Hampl, Jill Breckenridge-Haldeman, Hanson, Hasse, Stephen Dunn, Andrews, Dentinger, Sutter, Mary Karr, Greenberg, Charles Waterman, Jeanette Ferrary, Robert Hedin, Jonis Agee, Rakosi, Cardona-Hine, Jacobson, and Nancy Paddock. But also Marge Piercy, Carolyn Forché, and Franz Wright.

Magazines, as the epigraph to this Chapter proclaims, were a means of building a community, as one thing led to another. Jenné Andrews writes: "A journal in Minneapolis published me, and its editor invited me to my first all night literary party, in the topmost story of a warehouse in some run-down inner city neighborhood. The place was filled with marijuana smoke, the wine was flowing, and everyone talked books, writing, art."[29] As she continues, soon after, "with new women friends who wrote," she helped to found Women Poets of the Twin Cities, and after that, with one of those friends, Caroline Marshall, she founded the Smith Park Poetry Series (see Chapters 10 and 11). "What golden hours and golden days."

The Medicine Man

The first and only issue of this was published in early 1973 by a collective, Poets Probably, a group of women that included Betty Schutte, Diana Wolfe, Roth Roston, Polly Sander, and Barbara Meyer Lipp. Everything that I have been able to learn about this group, whose name does not exactly exude confidence, comes from this

---

29 Jenné Andrews, "Loquaciously Yours, Memoir and Ruminations: Time and the Poet," https://loquaciouslyyours.com/2010/03/22/time-and-the-poet/

one-off magazine in which they all have a role.[30] Diana Wolfe does the illustrations, and her opening poem gives the mag its title, and maybe also its character:

> There is only one MEDICINE MAN
>
> She has big blue eyes
> and smokes a cigar.
>
> She will tell you anything
> And you'll never be sorry.
>
> I saw her yesterday with her cinched waist
> smoke rolling from her body:
>
> She looked happy.

The Lake Street Review

In south Minneapolis, the Lake Street Writers group was a loose collective, about whom Margot Fortunato Galt says: "We…were undoubtedly influenced by feminism, though we contained as many men as women."[31] Soon they decided to put a more formal stamp on the group by starting a magazine named after the locally famous (or infamous, as often somewhat intimidating to anyone visiting from rural Minnesota) major east-west thoroughfare. The first mimeographed issue, in 1976, was edited by Lar Burke, and included a poem by Sisson, "To St. Paul," about Lake St. and the Lake St. Bridge. Succeeding issues were edited by poet Kevin Fitz-Patrick and included more regulars on the scene.[32] At one point, the "grounds for selection" were said, waggishly, to "include proximity

---

30   To be clear, I was unable to find any more information beyond that on Ruth Roston, the only member of the group whose name is found later on the record. Her book of poems, *I Live in the Watchmakers' Town* was published by New Rivers Press (Minnesota Voices Project #5) in 1981. And she co-edited books with Emilie Buchwald for Milkweed Editions in the 1980s.
31   "Note on the Laurel Poetry Collective," a flyer.
32   Like Bitz, Naiden, Finley, Minczeski, Hasse, Kincaid, Sue Ann Martinson, plus Mary Kay Rummel, Sigrid Bergie, and Ethna McKiernan.

of writer's residence to Lake Street (in St. Paul—Marshall Ave.), artistic excellence or promise, the quality of other submissions, and the critical mood of the editors." That sounds about right.

Sing, Heavenly Muse

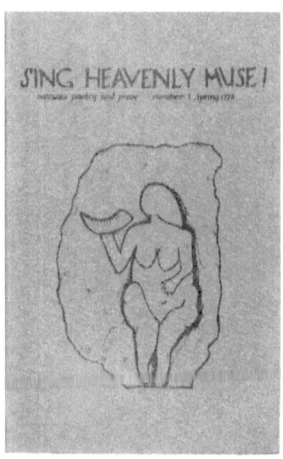

In spring 1978, Sue Ann Martinson, who had been coordinator of the Loft a couple of years earlier, and editor of the Loft Newsletter, put together the first issue of *Sing, Heavenly Muse! Women's Poetry and Prose* in Minneapolis. (Its name is from line 6 of Milton's *Paradise Lost,* as he follows the epic convention of invoking his source of poetic inspiration.) Contributors included many of the local stalwarts, all women.[33] A subsequent announcement for the magazine may seem surprisingly tepid: "The magazine is women-centered, but not intended to be a strong feminist magazine in any sense. The requirement for submission is simply that a piece be by a woman, and/or about women's concerns. We recognize that poems written by men may be appropriate for our magazine."[34] It lasted until 1997, with twenty-three issues.

---

    33   Kate Green, Florence Dacey, Roston, Nancy Paddock, Martinson, Le Sueur, Caroline Marshall, Ellen Kennedy, Knox, Carol Connolly, Bea Williams, Hasse, Marilyn Nelson, and others.

    34   *The Loft Newsletter,* April 1979.

Preview

At first, this was the monthly program guide, in pamphlet form, for the fledgling Minnesota Educational Radio—the vision of Father Colman Barry at St. John's University in Collegeville, implemented by Bill Kling—which went on the air in 1967. Hardly a literary magazine, and thus its inclusion here may at first be questionable. But after six years, in February 1973, Hampl (*Ivory Tower* veteran and then current co-editor of *Lamp in the Spine*) took over as editor—an idea she had pitched to Kling at Keillor's suggestion—with a new glossy format and expanded content. In the initial issue she wrote: "we do plan to give a look at various poets, writers, artists and craftspeople in the area." This was an understatement, as uninterrupted attention would now be paid to the poetry scene in Minnesota. Surely she was given free rein by Kling. He also wanted more from outstate, so Hampl enlisted Carol Bly to provide a regular "Letter from the Country," written from her home in rural Madison, another bridge between urban and rural Minnesota (see Chapter 13).[35]

In the April issue, Hampl wrote a long piece on the West Bank's Snoose Boulevard Festival. And the May cover featured a drawing by Franz Richter and a few lines from a Brainard poem. Moore has a long article, "Keeping the Poets down on the Farm: The Minnesota Writers' Publishing House." He writes: "Cooperatively run publishing ventures like this are beginning to appear elsewhere in this country and in Canada... These publishing cooperatives are started for many of the same reasons food co-ops keep springing up: to provide a human alternative to the huge institutions which have such a stranglehold on important human needs. ...such counter-institutions want to meet them more effectively and more cheaply...."[36] And

---

35   These were later collected in book form, *Letters from the Country* (Harper & Row, 1981).

36   *Preview* 7.5 (May 1973), 5-6.

his focus turns to Minnesota in particular: "At the heart of all kinds of regionalism is the belief that an individual needs to be in direct contact with his or her own roots to survive psychically and sometimes economically. … But there is more to regionalism than this. Each region is unique and will give its own particular form to what may well be universal needs. In fact, it *must* be allowed to do this if it is to survive as a living area and not become a kind of historical curiosity."

A "one page anthology by a few Minnesota poets" includes Andrews, Jenkins, Hennen, Brainard, and—no surprise—Robert Bly. Future issues printed more poems,[37] book reviews, articles on the local (both urban and rural) scene (by Kirkpatrick, Gruchow, Hampl, Patricia Monaghan, Chamberlain, and Moore), interviews (with McGrath, by Moore, with Rakosi, by Mary Ellen Shaw), even poet and videographer/filmmaker Mike Hazard's pareidolic photographs (which have proved to be a life-long pursuit).

Milkweed

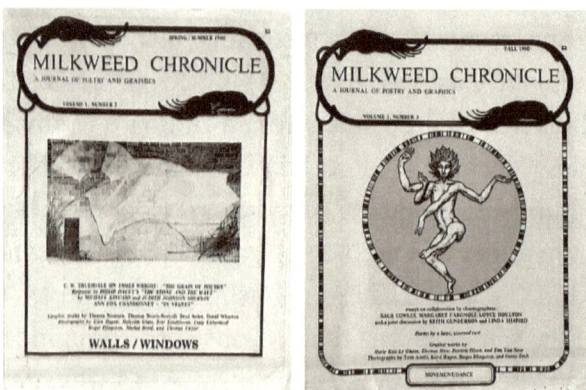

This book's account ends in 1980, a year that saw the initial issues of this important, large (almost folio size) magazine, which eventually gave rise to the key independent publishing house, Milk-

---

37   By Kirkpatrick, Le Sueur, Andrews, Neruda (tr. Hyde), McGrath, Logue, Sisson, Brainard, Cary Waterman, and Joe Paddock.

weed Editions. It happened as a direct result of a process long underway, and the story of its founding involves the original sower himself, Bly. Emilie Buchwald writes how, in 1978, she and artist Randy Scholes were now on the Loft's board. She describes: "It was early one afternoon before a Loft reading by poets Etheridge Knight and Robert Bly [see Chapter 7]…that Randy and I first considered the ideas behind what would become *Milkweed Chronicle*….we…began a conversation about the work of the poets we were about to hear…."[38]

So ends this catalog of Twin Cities literary magazines and periodical publications.[39] But now we turn to the related and overlapping in-person activity that was an even more effective means of building a sense of community among young poets in the Twin Cities—the essential and foundational phenomenon of the public poetry reading. This is, of course, how poetry had begun in ancient times, long before the invention of alphabets or books and before widespread literacy. Rebirth was in order.

---

38 Emilie Buchwald, *A Milkweed Chronicle: The Formative Years of a Literary Nonprofit Press* (Milkweed Editions, 2021), 4. Senator Eugene McCarthy had been scheduled to read with Bly on May 20, but an airline strike forced him to cancel. Knight took his place, likely at Bly's suggestion.

39 Here are a few contemporary kin publications:

Kedemi Mike Finley became the editor of *Academy*, the University's literary magazine. He says: "Like Caesar crossing the Rubicon, I took this tired student rag and reshaped it into a 70s lit mag, renaming it *Kedemi* (the first e is actually a schwa, an upside-down a), an idea I got from Marcel Duchamp. First rule—student work was strongly discouraged!"

Machete This was a tabloid publication with which Jonathan Sisson was at least intermittently involved.

Many Corners 1973-74 (or 85?), a monthly newspaper for Cedar-Riverside and surrounding communities, fairly mainstream, with contributing editors including Finley, Al Milgrom, Mary Ellen Shaw. It was focused on the Seven Corners area of the West Bank, and included an occasional poem.

Chapter 10
Poetryapolis: Twin Cities Poetry Readings

...that old bastion of tweedy stodginess.[1]
–Patricia Hampl

Though poetry is written alone, not for yourself, but written in solitude, a poetry reading makes clear that the poem only lives in a community.[2]
–Robert Bly

Roy C. McBride writes of his introduction to the local poetry scene in a brief essay felicitously titled "Poetryapolis":

> Remember the first poetry reading I ever attended. At the Unitarian Society on Mt. Curve. Open reading. In the basement. Organized by Michael Kincaid. Robert Bly was there. He had just won the National Book Award. I had never heard of Robert Bly. I had never heard of the National Book Award! He read a wonderful poem about three presidents. He cracked the binding on his newly arrived soft-covered edition.

---

1   Hampl, "The Poet as Troubadour," *Preview* 8.6 (June 1974), 4.
2   In Mike Hazard and Greg Pratt's film, "A Man Writes to a Part of Himself: The Poetry of Robert Bly" (The CIE, 1978). https://www.youtube.com/watch?v=MVGvTgyEbOM&t=99s

> Franklin Brainard read poems about his parents. He published a magazine called *Plainsong*. He was from New Brighton. I thought New Brighton was in the Boundary Waters. Poetry coming together in Minneapolis in 1968. I wanted to come along. That night I wrote a poem about a duck in Loring Park.[3]

McBride—newly arrived in Minnesota from Arkansas via Michigan, one of the few Black students at Macalester College in St. Paul—signs his name to this as "Roy C. McApolis," and come along he did, as poetry came together.

From his comment, one might guess that, more than "Three Presidents" and other antiwar poems, Bly also read his two-line poem "Ducks."[4] He was showing the possibilities of the new poetry. Here is another sign of a poetic community in the process of awakening and becoming, and its salutary impact on young poets. McBride was a large, beloved, bountiful presence and a driving force in Twin Cities spoken word poetry (as we shall see) for decades afterward.[5]

The now-popular phenomenon of a public poetry reading—in which a poet mainly reads their own work—was in those days still quite recent. Readings had first taken hold in academic settings, on college and university campuses, usually sponsored by the English Department. No surprise there. They were to be studied and judged as literature, and were "always culturally reverent, stuffy events."[6]

---

3   "Poetryapolis," in *Blues Visions: African American Writing from Minnesota*, ed. Alexs Pate (Minnesota Historical Society Press, 2015), 9. I have corrected the text's date of 1967, as it was definitely 1968 when Bly won the NBA for his 1967 book, *The Light Around the Body*.

4   This comprised the entire contents of a recent booklet from Ox Head Press (see Chapter 13).

5   See Roy McBride, *Secret Traffic: Selected Poems* (Nodin Press, 2013). Also see Mike Hazard's film, "A Poet Poets: Roy McBride," (The CIE, 2011): https://www.youtube.com/watch?v=3udIV_4peb4

6   Hampl, "Midwestern Sublime," 8.

Their increase came about, in part, as creative writing programs started to get a foothold in academia in the 1960s and 70s.

Albert Camus said: "One of the temptations of the artist is to believe himself solitary, and in truth he hears this shouted at him with a certain base delight. But this is not true. He stands in the midst of all, in the same rank, neither higher nor lower, with all those who are working and struggling."[7] Poetry is written in solitude, but fledgling poets need to find friends with whom to share their poetic lives. This can happen by accident or, better, by design. As Diane Seuss put it recently: "We're all in this together. We're writing. What ludicrous and difficult work it is. Let me offer you my hand."[8]

So, poets congregated. The outlines of community start to come clear by various means. One, as we have seen and shall see (Chapters 9 and 12), is through the literary magazines that draw poets together. Another is through chapbooks and other publications of small local presses (Chapter 14). But best is through public readings when poets gather, bodily, to hear other poets (and they celebrate with one another afterwards). And through the organizations or structures that gave rise to readings (see Chapter 11). The richness of this new scene is evident in all these modes.

This was when the art of poetry was reasserting itself, breaking away from its stodgy and elitist reputation, reverting to its origins as song, a part of oral tradition, and a celebratory communal event. Again, Bly's example is central, especially for the Upper Midwest. Soon, even young poets without publications were giving readings, to be experienced and enjoyed by an audience, if also emulated and learned from. Long before the "poetry slam" was a thing, there were open-mic readings, lottery readings at the Loft, and free-for-alls at the Walker Art Center, where any amateur brave enough could get

---

    7   Camus, "The Artist and His Time," in *The Myth of Sisyphus*, tr. Justin O'Brien (Penguin Books, 1955).

    8   https://www.nybooks.com/daily/2022/06/18/the-oversoul-speaking-to-the-undercarriage/

up and read their poems to the assembled listeners.

The reading thus became a social phenomenon, a fun opportunity for give and take, and a foremost means of building camaraderie. Attending a reading could also be another life-changing experience. Wojahn remembers: "I was a sophomore at the University of Minnesota when I heard Bly and Tranströmer read together in the fall of '72. I came away from that reading with the feeling that from that point on my sole ambition was to be a poet."[9]

Although the start of Bly's own career in oral poetry reading might be dated to his Harvard commencement in 1950, when he delivered the "class poem," it was many years before he did another public reading. In April 1958, his poem "On the Sioux Trial" was read aloud at Macalester College in St. Paul—not by him but by the Drama Choros, Macalester's verse-speaking choir of thirty-two voices, whose longtime director, Mary Gwen Owen, did much to elevate choral reading as an interpretive art form.[10] Typical programs included poetry by Vachel Lindsay, Carl Sandburg, Edgar Lee Masters, or Ogden Nash, passages from the Bible, Euripides, or Dr. Seuss, occasionally with some contemporary work added. Of course, it worked best with formally metrical poetry (as Bly's was, at the time) and poems with end rhymes. We might say, given this awareness, that in 1958 a young poet from Minnesota started sowing seeds in another way—this time by proxy.

Soon, after the birth of *The Fifties*, and after the 1959 appearance of his "Poems for the Ascension of J.P. Morgan," Bly, now broken free of formalism, stepped out on his own. In the ensuing years, he read his poems or translations at Harvard, at New York's 92nd St. Y, and at New York University, where he also was briefly

---

9   DW email to MG, 19 July 2020.

10   This and three other winning poems (just announced) from the Minnesota Centennial poetry contest were on the program, as mentioned in the *Minneapolis Tribune*, April 16, 1958. For more on this, see my forthcoming essay, cited above in Chapter 8.

in charge of the reading program.[11] But his situation changed significantly after the publication of *Silence in the Snowy Fields* in late 1962 (see Chapter 4).

Don Olsen, then a graduate student at the University of Minnesota, was present at Bly's first poetry reading after that book came out, in the basement of the University's Newman Center. He describes the scene:

> There were 25 or 30 people at the reading, sitting here and there on metal folding chairs. There were enough chairs set up for 100 or so people, so it felt a little empty.
>
> Bly was wearing a striped, off-white seersucker suit, white shirt and tie. The suit was a little small for him, but he looked every part the gentleman poet. And he was nervous as he read…
>
> He gave very little introduction, if any, to his poems, and he read with a dull kind of monotone style of delivery, his eyes looking downward most of the time and not at the audience…he would read the poem rapidly and move on to another poem. There were occasional comments that drew laughter from the small audience.[12]

Around the same time, Bill Holm, an undergraduate at Gustavus Adolphus College, in St. Peter, attended Bly's reading on that campus. As Holm describes it, Bly arrived, having driven from Madison, in his "rusty old Buick… He read from *Silence in the Snowy Fields*, and from his translations of Neruda and some Scandinavians. His reading was quiet and diffident—almost shy—as if

---

11   See *Born Under,* 57-8. In those days, Bly typically spent half of the year in New York.

12   Don Olsen, "Notes on Robert Bly," his typescript made in 2002 (and given to me), from his much earlier handwritten notes.

he wondered how he could fill up an hour with such small poems."[13] These two recollections are remarkable for the way they contrast with what later came to be Bly's signature style as an exceptionally charismatic reader and performer with a commanding stage presence. "Nervous," "quiet," "monotone," "diffident," "shy"—really?

A few months later, however, at Carleton College in Northfield, Olsen noted a transformation, which was also manifesting itself physically, as though Bly were slowly emerging from a cocoon, getting ready to fly:

> He was wearing the same seersucker suit, which was now getting a bit threadbare and appeared to have shrunk a little. There were tears on the edges of the pockets. The suit fit him too tightly. He seemed about to burst out of it.
>
> ... Bly's stage presence had progressed considerably. He read beautifully from his early J.P. Morgan poems. One line, "Roosters leap up and fall dead in the snow," elicited laughter from the audience.
>
> Bly had the academic audience in his hands with sharp, sarcastic comments about Alexander Pope, T.S. Eliot, Robert Penn Warren, and others.

As Bly's influence continued to spread in ensuing years—via his magazine, his translations in the Sixties Press books, his own book, and his readings in support of them—the number of reading opportunities increased around the region and the country. Both locally and elsewhere, Bly began to share the stage with other young and younger poets. This activity in fact now became, and would long remain, his primary source of income.

But what caused Bly's skill and visibility as a reader to surge most rapidly was the growth of the antiwar movement (see Chapter 6). As he says, "Reciting political poems at Vietnam gatherings, I

---

13   BH to MG, 20 August 2000.

experienced for the first time in my life the power of spoken or oral poetry."[14] Even then, as Bly was "sounding the dark truths," poet William Heyen said, "of all the poets I've ever heard, you establish the sense of community and love during your readings."[15] His readings became much more than the word "reading" connotes; they were exuberant performances, happenings, mind-altering experiences for the audience. To Wojahn they were "the poetic equivalent of a [Grateful] Dead concert—on and on but always *very* on."[16]

The rest of this Chapter will list and describe some (not all) of the various reading series/venues around the Twin Cities as they emerged—an astonishing profusion, really—most of which Bly had a part in. Throughout this period Bly was bringing other poets to Minnesota, like Tomas Tranströmer and Rolf Jacobsen, whom he had translated. He also helped to attract his friends from elsewhere, including Creeley, Ignatow, Levertov, Hall, Simpson, Ginsberg, Stafford, Kinnell, and many others.

The First Unitarian Society

At 900 Mt. Curve Ave. in Minneapolis (just up Lowry Hill from the Walker Art Center and the Guthrie Theatre in its original location), this was the site of a series beginning in September 1967, overseen and organized by poet Michael Kincaid (as described by McBride at the top of this Chapter). Readings were scheduled for the second Tuesday of each month. Early readers included Bly, Olsen, Hennen, Tjepkes, Richard Shaw, and Brainard. Later came Gunderson, Vizenor, Caddy, and two Macalester College students, Charles Baxter and McBride. This series continued for at least the next few years.

The Walker Art Center

---

14 Selected Poems, 62.
15 "An Argument about 'Universal' Versus 'Political' Art," an Interview with Gregory FitzGerald and William Heyen, in Robert Bly, *Talking All Morning* (The University of Michigan Press, 1980 [orig. interview 1970]), 82.
16 DW email to MG, 19 July 2020.

It was also the late 1960s when the Walker Art Center, the fine contemporary art museum in Minneapolis, began to become truly multidisciplinary. Suzanne Weil, the Walker's Performing Arts Coordinator from 1969 to 1976, put together a staggering array of musical performances, also establishing residencies for composers, choreographers, and dance and theater companies.[17] (Most of these

---

    17   The following is <u>only a partial</u> list of performers on the stage of the adjacent Guthrie Theater, 1969-1976, by genre (loosely!):

- **Rock:** the Who, Led Zeppelin, the Grateful Dead, the Mothers of Invention, Alice Cooper, Neil Young, Jethro Tull, Joe Cocker, Mott the Hoople, Emerson Lake & Palmer, Todd Rundgren, Elton John, Steely Dan, Bruce Springsteen, Roxy Music, the Mahavishnu Orchestra
- **Jazz:** Weather Report, Miles Davis, Elvin Jones, Charles Mingus, Herbie Hancock, Keith Jarrett.
  Folk/Country: Tom Waits, Randy Newman, Cat Stevens, Randy Newman, Ry Cooder, Janis Ian, John Prine, Arlo Guthrie, Gordon Lightfoot, Emmylou Harris, Laura Nyro, Kris Kristofferson, Leonard Cohen, Wendy Waldman, Waylon Jennings, Tammy Wynette, Bill Monroe, Roger McGuinn, Jerry Jeff Walker, Taj Mahal, (plus locals) Leo Kottke, John Koerner, Dave Ray, Tony Glover, Willie Murphy.
- **Blues:** B.B. King, Howlin' Wolf, Sonny Terry and Brownie McGhee, John Mayall, Bonnie Raitt,
- **R&B/Soul:** Curtis Mayfield, Bobby Blue Bland
- **World Music:** Scandinavisk Musik, Aliza Ngono
- **Classical and sacred**: Aaron Copland, William Bolcom, (and locals) the St. Paul Chamber Orchestra, Philip Brunelle, the Bach Society, the Minnesota Chorale, the Dale Warland Singers
- **Avant-garde:** Steve Reich, John Cage, Philip Glass, Meredith Monk, Electric Stereopticon
- **Choreographers and dance companies:** Merce Cunningham, Twyla Tharp, Dance Theatre of Harlem, Pilobolus Dance Company, (local) Nancy Hauser Dance Company
- **Theater companies:** Mabou Mines, El Teatro Nuevo, (local) Illusion Theater
- **Other:** (local) Dudley Riggs' Brave New Workshop, Rick Shope Mime Troupe

    This material is from the Walker Art Center's institutional records. The finding aid for Performing Arts Records, Coordinator, Suzanne Weil, 1969-1976

performances were on the thrust stage of the adjoining Guthrie Theatre.) She brought poetry readings as well, not only by well-known poets from elsewhere, like Ginsberg, Diane Wakoski, Patti Smith, and Ignatow, but also by many young poets from Minnesota. She even sponsored "free-for-alls," at which anyone could read. Again, the attention to and encouragement of local talent is laudable, and had a beneficial effect on the local scene.

In February 1970, the Walker Art Center and the West Bank Arts Festival collaborated and presented "Poetry on the West Bank" during four consecutive weeks. Readers included Bly, Gunderson, Kincaid, McBride, Robin Raygor, Bitz, Keillor, Caddy, and Tjepkes at the Guild of Performing Arts, a music and dance school at 504 Cedar Ave. (wedged between Palmer's Bar and the Electric Fetus Record & Head Shop).[18]

A "Poetry Show" at the Walker Art Center in November 1971 featured poet/artist Bitz, Raygor, photographer Tom Arndt, and Keillor, who says that Bitz and Arndt were the first to lure him to perform. "They were the impetus, the tempters, the compadres."[19] He has also more recently thanked Weil for being "the first person to ever put me on stage."[20] In his memoir, he calls the Walker Art Center "the HQ of cool," says that Weil "liked what she liked," and that, with a friend like her "I was a made man."[21]

Later came "Prairie Home Entertainment" in September 1972, Keillor alone in 1974, and the full-blown "Prairie Home Companion" show in August-October 1975. The program of Walker Art

---

is at https://s3.amazonaws.com/wac-imgix/cms/PA_Weil_FA.pdf.

18   Presented in conjunction with this was an innovation: "Dial-A-Poem." One could call 339-3001 on weekday evenings and on Saturday and Sunday to hear readings by each of the poets in the series.

19   Mary Abbe, "Old Friends, New Combinations," *Minneapolis Star-Tribune* (December 9, 2010).

20   This was at the last performance of "A Prairie Home Companion" in 2016.

21   Garrison Keillor, *That Time of Year: A Minnesota Life* (Arcade Publishing, 2020), 142.

Center readings began to accelerate in early 1972, as Weil fully embraced the local poetry contingent, including Browne and Keith Harrison, Alvin Greenberg and Carl Rakosi, Gunderson and Stanley Kiesel, McGrath and Stephen Dunn (then at Southwest Minnesota State College in Marshall).

To accompany the 1972 exhibition, "American Indian Art: Form and Tradition," Weil added much related programming—dance, music, theater, and poetry performances (by Navajo poets Jeff Saunders and Todd Haycock) (see Chapter 8). Vizenor read in 1973. April 1973 saw no less than four readings by a group of the Women Poets of the Twin Cities (see Chapter 11), and again in 1974. Freya Manfred and Vizenor in 1974. The year ended with a flurry of readings in December, including Martha Roth and Femi Fatoba, Madelon Sprengnether Gohlke and McBride, Browne and Gunderson. And 1975 began with Keillor and Ditz again, followed by monthly readings, including the usual local crowd, the Fort Mango trio (Bitz, Sisson, and Hushcha, see Chapter 11), and James Lenfestey, Hasse, and Andrews.

Weil's successor, Nigel Redden (1976-1982), did well with the pattern she had set, although the poetry readings, while including many local poets to begin with (Minczeski, Moore, Hampl, and others), gradually moved to more nationally known poets. Thus, her departure ended an era for the Walker and Minnesota poetry.[22]

North Stone Reading Series

Poet James Naiden moved to Minneapolis in 1970, and bumped into Tjepkes in a Mexican restaurant in Dinkytown. Naiden says, "Bly was one of the few poets Tjepkes respected enough to say so." Through him, Naiden met Kincaid, Caddy, and Brainard, "then desperately ill with leukemia but still able to write fine poems with

---

22   The finding aid for Redden's tenure is at https://s3.amazonaws.com/wac-imgix/cms/PA_Redden_FA.pdf.

Bly's encouragement."[23] Soon after his new magazine, the *North Stone Review* (see Chapter 9), was underway, "somehow the idea of a poetry reading on the West Bank at the Guild of Performing Arts to feature poets in the magazine materialized. The first reading was held in July 1971."[24] It became a series, and a powerhouse.

Photo courtesy of Hennepin County Library

While Naiden was putting up posters at the nearby Coffeehouse Extemporé, its manager, Ron Sjoberg, convinced him to hold readings there, too. Though both sites were regularly used, the Extemp (then at 325 Cedar Ave.) became its more regular location This was an important new opportunity for local poets. April 18, 1972, the readers were Brainard, Tjepkes, Mary Pat Flandrick, and Lyn Lifshin. On 3 June 1972, as Naiden says, Bly "generously agreed to do a benefit reading to raise money for a third issue," along with

---

23 James Naiden, "Early Stages of a Literary Culture in Minneapolis," the *North Stone Review* 14 (2002), 213.

24 Ibid., 214.

Brainard.[25] (Naiden was charging $1.00 for admission at first.) Many others already named, such as Le Sueur, Mike Finley, and McBride, participated early on, and many poets were, of course, in the audience.

Knox, then a student at Macalester, describes her introduction to the reading scene: "Roy [McBride] and Muggsy [Margaret Falk] and their whole household was a bunch of weirdoes and very smart, creative people, he was an excellent poet and storyteller, and she a wonderful artist and writer. They got me involved in the poetry readings at the Café Extemporé, and I was hooked."[26] At the same time, she says Naiden was "a real 'my way or the highway' sort of guy. Very contentious."[27] She adds that it seemed like he "always had four men and one woman reader at every reading…." (Stay tuned.)

There were usually parties following the readings, cementing connections with heady schmoozing, networking, and the various inevitable hookups (as in sexual encounters). Lyle Daggett, still in or just out of high school, and awestruck, remembers being "wary of the backstage infighting and maneuvering that invariably goes on at such events and in such scenes." Nevertheless, these gatherings were one more cardinal piece of the community building process.

Further insight into some inevitable tensions of the growing poetry community comes from Mike Finley, who called Naiden "a big, boorish man…sort of the poetry czar of the Twin Cities for a few years—no one saw print or found an audience except through him. He was exceptionally easy to dislike…." Then writing for the *Minnesota Daily,* Finley took, as he says, a "cheap shot." "I wrote a 'review' of the local poetry scene in which I characterized him as having 'the personality of an axe murderer'… In my mind, he was so transparent—so mean-spirited, so full of himself, and so unlik-

---

25   Ibid. This is especially notable—Bly did not carry a grudge—given that Naiden had recently trashed Bly in a review in the *Minneapolis Tribune.*
26   WKC email to MG, 16 November 2021.
27   WKC email to MG, 18 September 2021.

able…"²⁸ Still, "people put up with him, because at least he did the scutwork of holding the readings, and they did not want to jeopardize the bennies he distributed." Naiden retaliated in various publications, calling Finley an anti-poet, a bad poet, a poetaster, a poetizer, and his poems "pseudo-poetry" and "excremental offerings." It is no secret that Naiden, despite his very important role, was not widely liked. As Wojahn says: "He made a point of alienating just about every person in the community."

With two readings a month, Naiden also decided to type up a short monthly newsletter, *Caesura,* to publicize the coming readings. This became a great, invaluable asset. In 1973-74 its purpose broadened, and it gained support from the Minnesota State Arts Board. Then, without Naiden, it morphed into *Minnesota Literature Newsletter* (which continued publication until 2008), serving as the essential clearinghouse for all local literary events and information.²⁹

Churches

Churches were pressed into action, too. Beginning in the late 1960s, Walker Methodist Community Church, in the Powderhorn Park neighborhood in South Minneapolis, became a hub for grassroots political and social activism and for the arts (dance, music, and theater—most notably the Powderhorn Puppet Theatre and At the Foot of the Mountain).³⁰ And it was the site of many poetry readings. One such event with Keillor and Bitz combined activism, poetry and music (and tomfoolery!).³¹ Walker Church was also where the enduring

---

28   Mike Finley, *The Offset Revolution: A Writer's Memoir* (Kraken Press, 2001), 56.

29   This is a slot now filled by Rain Taxi's online Twin Cities Literary Calendar.

30   Named after the same lumber baron, Thomas Barlow Walker, as were the Walker Art Center and the northern Minnesota town of Walker, on Leech Lake. (He also founded the Minneapolis Public Library.)

31   From 1974; the Cedar Riverside Environmental Defense Fund had arisen in late 1973, in opposition to the massive planned expansion of Cedar

KFAI Community Radio station began in 1978, its studio in the bell tower (then moving to the West Bank in 1986).

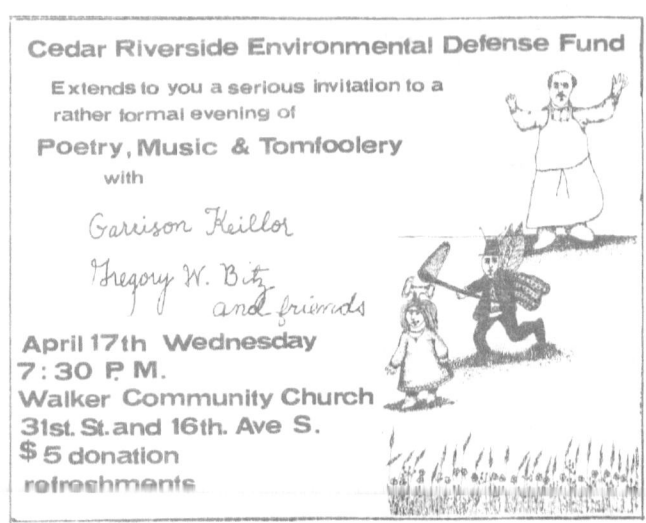

In 1972 a monthly series of "Open Poetry Readings" was initiated at One Groveland, the name for a basement space of Plymouth Congregational Church at the corner of Groveland Ave. (19th St.) and Nicollet Ave. on the edge of downtown. Jim Perlman, a poet, future editor and publisher (see Chapters 9 and 14), helped to organize these for a while. One never knew in advance who would show up, but they were invariably local poets.[32]

World Famous Poets

Mary Logue, who wrote for the *Minnesota Daily* as a University student, met Wojahn, Michel Krug, and Coco Weber in Moore's first class at the book loft in Dinkytown (see Chapter 7). The four of

---

Square West, making "city within a city" and completely altering the neighborhood. The construction did not go ahead. This pairing of Keillor, Bitz, et al., was also seen at the inaugural sign-up dinner for the Loft. See Chapter 7.

    32   Much to my surprise and delight, my research revealed that my poetry-loving father, Henry Gustafson, was then on the One Groveland subcommittee (with Pam Hanold) of the Plymouth Neighborhood Board.

Sowing Seeds

them kept getting together after the sessions had ended, and soon she and Wojahn (both of whom also had been in Browne's U of M class together) decided to initiate their own reading series with this tongue-in-cheek name.[33]

They secured the initial funding and soon got more help from the State Arts Board and the NEA. Unlike many of the other reading series, which typically charged $1.00, their readings were free. The regular venue was in the basement of the Newman Center on campus (where Bly had given his early reading, as described above, more than a decade earlier). These city readings welcomed poets from around the state, from Moorhead, Marshall, Duluth, and Northfield, as well as from the Twin Cities. In 1976 and '77, readers—always two per reading—included Hasse and Stanley Kiesel, Alvaro Cardona-Hine and Grayce Ray, Mary Karr and Marilyn Nelson, James L. White and Thomas Peacock, Barbara Hughes and John Engman, and Philip Dacey and Craig Volk. The better balance, gender-wise, is obvious.

The Loft

Once the Loft got rolling in the mid-70s, (see Chapter 7) its forward movement was unstoppable. And it seemed to involve almost everyone. Soon the schedule in the Loft newsletter showed a reading almost weekly: lottery readings, publication readings, benefit readings, themed readings, workshop readings, anniversary readings (marking Halloween, Christmas, Emily Dickinson's birthday). Also, lunar events: in 1977, Full Moon Poetry Workshop with Dochniak,[34] and in 1978, Knox and McBride's read-

---

33 ML email to MG, 10 November 2020. Logue herself soon taught Baudelaire and Rimbaud at the Loft, was involved with WPTC, and worked for PITS and COMPAS and the like (see Chapter 15).

34 "Let's Go Down by the River, Drink My Daddy's Wine," on the three full moons of the summer at Father Hennepin Park, across from Pracna on Main, "will gather poets, writers, funkists, and dedicated listening 'to read and celebrate the tidal energy of the Big Swiss Cheese in the Sky.'" Cost: "food and

ing "A Celebration in Poetry: Lunar Eclipse/Good Friday/1st Full Moon in Libra/Vernal Equinox/Unconscious to Conscious." These included poets from all over the state and from bordering states, sometimes accompanied by music or dance. Also, occasionally Loft readings were co-sponsored with another reading series, Third Century Poetry and Prose of the West Bank Union (University of Minnesota). Not just poetry, then, but non-fiction, drama, traditional tales, and children's stories, too. Plainly, the Loft readings were many and various, as befits the all-embracing literary organization it was quickly becoming.

Smith Park Poetry Series

A principal poetic enterprise was the Smith Park Poetry Series (also called Minnesota Poetry Outloud, though later the two became distinct—see Chapter 13), across the river in St. Paul. It was perched on the cusp of or overlapped with several important developments. The location for the readings was the Variety Hall Theatre (soon to be the Park Square Theatre) opposite Smith Park (soon renamed Mears Park) in Lowertown. The series started as an extension of the Smith Park Gallery, located on the second floor of what was then the headquarters of the upstart Minnesota Educational Radio (soon to be renamed Minnesota Public Radio).[35] Change was in the air!

The ambitious venture was started by Jenné Andrews and Caroline Vogel,[36] with initial help from the Minnesota State Arts Coun-

---

drink, new poetry, and a little blood for the mosquitoes. 'In case of rain, we can smoke cigarettes under the bridge (or move to The Loft).'"

35 We might note that poet and *Ivory Tower*'s former editor Garrison Keillor's *A Prairie Home Companion* began its regular broadcasts in 1974 at the Park Square Theatre (after the initial July 6 broadcast from Macalester College). (He had been doing a morning radio show with KSJR, subsequently KSJN, since 1969.) Also, that Patricia Hampl served as the editor of *Preview*, the station's monthly magazine (which became *Minnesota Monthly* in 1976), and Patricia Kirkpatrick and Carol Bly wrote for that magazine, too (see Chapter 9).

36 AKA Caroline Rasmussen or Marshall, elsewhere in this book.

cil. They were well aware that the writing community had been growing, and that "the women's movement, which is keen on poetry, has created a new audience."[37] Their opening statement in the booklet created for the 1973-74 season is a summation of what was going on in the state:

> More "voices" are to be heard in Minnesota poetry than ever before, and they constitute a diverse and fascinating chorus. Some are well-known—like those of Meridel Le Sueur, Tom McGrath, and Robert Bly. Others—dozens from the North Woods and the plains, from deceptively quiet small towns and the Twin Cities, from universities and colleges and school language arts departments around the state—are becoming increasingly familiar. Equally interesting are those of previously silent Minnesota writers, many of them women, who are producing fine poems and reading them aloud whenever they can.
>
> Thanks to "little" magazines and small press series of chapbooks, to an increasing number of readings, and to an ever-greater use of live, local poets in state classrooms, poetry is being woven into the fabric of Minnesota life more every day. As a result, more and more poems—most of them reflecting the rich psychic energy and spiritual heritage of this region—are being stimulated. The Smith Park Poetry Series was begun to provide a hearing for them.[38]

---

37 Hampl, "The Poet as Troubadour," *Preview* 8.6 (June 1974), 4.
38 *Smith Park Poetry Series: Minnesota Poetry Outloud: The First Season*, (n.p.,1973).

Andrews' own introduction is entitled "Creating Community." "We've begun to think of poetry outloud as community-coming-alive in the way, perhaps, as Tom McGrath has written in his book, *Letter to an Imaginary Friend,* of the *communitas* born of chopping wood in winter," a solidarity beyond "fraternity or camaraderie." She continues:

> Poetry outloud makes instantaneous testimonial to poet and listener's experience, together. As such, it is a way of bonding. A young poet has effusively written that listening to Robert Bly read is like sitting before a crackling, generous fire. It may be said that to listen to Meridel Le Sueur read is to hear, to use her phrase, the woman-river. It is the commitment made by the poet to touch our personhood, what we are, were, and will become.

That is, a commitment to being on the side of the future.

All of this is congruent with Bly's repeated emphasis on poetry as performance—that poetry is meant primarily to be read or recited aloud and heard; it is a living thing, not a "well-wrought urn," an artifact for the page, to read in silence.[39] (While this may sound obvious to some of us—given poetry's pre-literate, communal origins—it was not so obvious when poetry readings were still a newish phenomenon in the midcentury United States, and when most young people first encountered poetry in the tattered pages of their high school textbooks.) This is an emphasis that Etheridge Knight powerfully resonated with (see Chapter 11). Surely one reason for McBride's attraction to Bly, too. And for many others.

Here we are a far cry from "that old bastion of tweedy stodginess" of a decade earlier. Andrews and Vogel shared "a conviction that the Minnesota poetry scene is fat with anarchy and genius."[40] They intended a "relatively unstructured organization," or "organized anarchy." The plan was that they would encourage a collective of readers, "once they are chosen, to participate in the planning of their programs, choosing special staging or musical accompaniment, for example." That first season ran from November 1973 to June 1974, and most of the participating poets have been noted previously in this book—mostly from the Twin Cities, and others from more distant communities closely associated with certain magazines.[41] The first reading included Andrews, Phebe Hanson, and Michael Moos, who drove down from Moorhead. He says it was "my first experience of taking my poetry on the road. It was very exciting, and I felt there was a magic in the air that night!"[42]

---

39   The title of a 1947 book by Cleanth Brooks, a prominent New Critic (see Chapter 3).

40   From a flyer for the first scheduled reading on November 29, in the Caroline Marshall papers, MNHS.

41   Andrews, Hanson, Moos, Rezmerski, Vogel, Greenberg, Caddy, Martinson, Finley, Mary Ellen Shaw, Hampl, Kirkpatrick, Moore, Brainard, Madelon Gohlke, Knox, Browne, White, both Blys, Jenkins, and Freya Manfred.

42   MM email to MG, 29 May 2024. His first chapbook, *Hawk Hover*, had just been published (see Chapter 14).

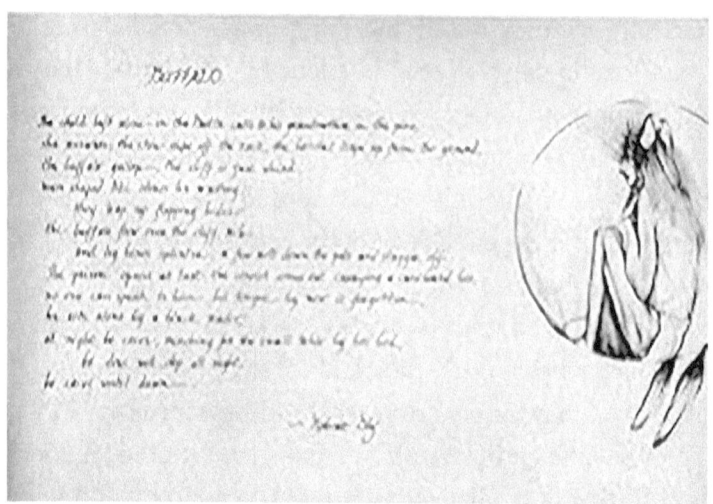

All the poets were also represented by a broadside of one of their poems, available for the price of admission ($1.00). Most of them were illustrated either by Annie Hayes or Ellen Kennedy. This combination of words and visual images is a notable step.[43] The series was wildly successful and very well attended—the broadsides were also part of the attraction, as was the free "lively" (i.e., spiked) cider. Minczeski says: "the Smith Park series was the most important for me, and the one that helped the poetry community gel."[44] It also helped it to grow.

* * *

This look back at a remarkably lively scene may give it the sheen of a golden age. Better is to see it—somewhat fancifully, given the short time frame—in larger historical perspective as the period of what we may call the "early" renaissance, in advance of the "high" renaissance of the years 1980-2000, and beyond. One of the youngest of the poets

---

43   Later in 1976-77, Vanilla Press did something similar with *A Coloring Books of Poetry for Adults*, and eventually, at the end of the decade, Emilie Buchwald and artist Randall Scholes conceived the *Milkweed Chronicle* with a comparable and fully-developed vision.

44   MG interview with JM, 25 June 2020.

in that arena, Mike Finley, has a wistful poem on those days in the Twin Cities, a candid and broad view that may stand as fitting conclusion to and a sort of summation of this Chapter:

"All the Young Poets" (for Phebe Hanson)

> I remember readings at the Unitarian Society, Marly Rusoff's, and the Extemporé
> and how we vied with the others for reading time.
> I always sat with the surrealists like Richard Waara and Jeff Beddowe,
> There was always the danger of a recalcitrant ice tray,
> always a poet from one of the colleges talking about the Lakota
> and the lonely strand of barbed wire
> looping across the prairie.
> Women poets wept and pounded their fists about their betrayals and rejections.
> University professors looked long in the tooth in their denim sportcoats
> and gleaming goatees, the guy who had a chapbook out and read the whole thing
> until even people without watches were glancing at their wrists.
> The nervous boy who rattled his papers, as if these people in folding chairs
> Were even listening.
> How surprised he was after a week of planning and dreaming to open his mouth

and sound strangled and the boy couldn't believe how bad he was
until he opened his mouth and hated how young he was.
Penelope Suess disgusted with the men,
Mary Ellen Shaw peering over her spectacles,
Jonathan Sisson, intelligent and hostile,
Englishman John Daniel's classy roundelays,
Crazy Robin Raygor's blunt impossibilities,
John Rezmerski, the funniest and humblest of them all
Speaking truths against the evening's pomposities.
Gregory Bitz with his mad persona and shrapnel-riddled
hole going right through his upper arm
and grinning Michael Tjepkes, rocking Byronic on his cane,
Jim Naiden pulling his pants up by the belt,
and Michael Kincaid as grave as the grave as the grave,
Caroline Marshall chaste as a feather,
Keith Gunderson spouting passages from the thesaurus,
Mary Pat Flandrick with her Kenneth Patchen letters,
Wendy Knox antsy for something good to happen
and Garrison Keillor's tales from the pea patch
and Phebe Hanson's tales of the town of Sacred Heart,
Margaret Hasse sharing her delicate songs
and Jenné Andrews, who'd seen too many troubles to recount
and Tom McGrath, kinder than he needed to be,
Robert Bly presiding like a piecemeal prince,
Frank Brainard lifting his Styrofoam cup,

and afterwards the bars and the cold cars,
everyone clutching the coats against the Minneapolis wind,
an image, a hiccup, a gesture, a disease
these were the years of clapping on one another's armor
and galloping off to the action,
it seemed at the time we could do it forever
and a few of us did, but where did the rest go?[45]

---

[45] *The Rapture* (Kraken Press, 2011), 55.

Chapter 11
Poetryapolis: Other Gatherings

Diversity makes the prairie resilient.[1]
   –Paul Gruchow

The Minnesota scene is fat with anarchy and genius.
   –Jenné Andrews & Caroline Vogel

Often, as was common in those counterculture days of the 1960s and 70s, after meeting and finding common ground, writers and other artists naturally grouped themselves in non-hierarchical (even anarchic) cooperatives, or collectives. This might be in support of shared interest in writing/poetics and in art-making but also in the interest of eventual public readings, and/or eventual publication, as we shall see. Women poets and artists did so along gender lines, too, for good reason. So, we might think of these gatherings in part as first steps that inevitably led to more poetry readings in an urban setting. A hodgepodge follows.

Women Poets of the Twin Cities (WPTC)

The feminist movement (in its second wave in the U.S.) was manifest locally in this dynamic and prominent collective that formed in later 1971. A handful of women, including Penelope Suess and

---

[1] *Grass Roots*, 77.

Beryle (Bea) Williams, conceived and organized a first joint reading at the Guild of Performing Arts on the West Bank. This was their formal start, a breakthrough. Williams says:

> We organized because we weren't hearing women's poetry and weren't getting acquainted in private ways. It grew out of our need. We needed to write and share and have it heard.[2]

As seen in Chapter 10, the poets selected to read in local reading series and the ones doing the selecting were, with rare exceptions, men—misogyny in action.

At least as important as the readings may have been their regular meetings, as Williams indicates. Membership in WPTC was open to any woman who wrote poems. It was, as Caroline Marshall described it, an "energetic and elastic sisterhood."[3] When they congregated, they read their poems and offered one another criticism, advice, and support. Regional subject matter continued to be foregrounded but was also purposefully expressed through their roles as women—as daughters, sisters, mothers, and lovers. They wanted to build a community, which soon became a larger network affording collaborations and close friendships alike.

Two examples convey a sense of how good and enriching this sisterhood was. Hampl recalls her "instant friendship" with Phebe Hanson, whom she met "in January 1972—in Jenné Andrews's Summit Ave. apartment in fact, at a Women Poets meeting—the first I had gone to. I'd just come back to St. Paul. I don't know who invited me. I showed up with Patricia Kirkpatrick, and we were warmly welcomed."[4]

And Wendy Knox conveys a sense of how it felt, just after she had graduated from Macalester:

---

2 As quoted in Pat Monaghan, "WPTC: Imaginative Transportation," *Minnesota Daily* (November 12, 1973), 11-13.

3 So she wrote on a WPTC folder found in the Caroline Marshall Papers, P2754 Box 1, MNHS.

4 PH to MG, 19 February 2020.

> WPTC was my first "women's consciousness raising group," though those hadn't been invented yet… I had absolutely no concept in my mind that I was a writer until I walked into Phebe Hanson's living room and saw about twenty people there, all of whom were women and called themselves poets. Wow!… Walking into that room gave me twenty completely different role models…and I could go back to them and learn more from them every month. We brought our own poems, read poems by other women writers we'd discovered, and tinkered with poems we'd read before and brought them back to see if they "worked better" next time and get some advice. We may have begun meeting in response to Jim Naiden's "one (quiet) token woman" readings, the "fight for the mic" at the Extemporé…but we met and met and kept on meeting, mostly at Phebe Hanson's Minneapolis and Bea Williams' St. Paul homes.[5]

More public readings followed. What came to be known as the "rape reading" was held at the Theater in the Round on Seven Corners in November 1972, co-sponsored by the Rape Crisis Center. There were twelve readers plus musicians Judy Larson (of the Sorry Muthas) and bluegrass singer Jan Johnson. Also, later that month, WPTC poets read accompanied by Coexistence, a jazz band, to benefit victims of assault and attempted rape. The reading was referred to as "an amalgam of art and politics."

As Pat Monaghan wrote:

> The Women Poets themselves are perhaps best described by the continuums upon which they fall: from teen-aged to middle-aged, from counterculture to middle-class, from gay to straight, from politically radical to moderate, from just embarking on a literary career to semi-established. Their rather anarchic

---

5   WKC email to MG, 16 November 2021.

organization slides across other continuums, from private to public, from personal to political, from poetic to polemical.[6]

Bea Williams acknowledged their limitations, however, in her introduction to the anthology *Women Poets in the Twin Cities,* published by Vanilla Press in 1975 (see Chapter 14). "One variety we lack, not by design, is that of race. Where are the women writers of this area who happen to be black, Indian, non-white?... this anthology suffers in failing to include the ubiquitous experience of women."[7]

Many readings followed at various venues, including college campuses. A few stand out. In 1975, a Candlemas Reading was held on February 1, which was the Feast of Brighid, a Celtic goddess. Forty to fifty poets, the bulk of WPTC's membership, read at the Burbank-Livingston-Griggs house on Summit Avenue in St. Paul, with the closing ceremony at midnight. They had a Valentine's Day reading at the Walker Art Center, soon after. The permanent record of this was a book, *Love from Women Poets,* published by Smith Park Press (a spin-off from that poetry series and its broadsides).[8] Another reading on December 16, 1976 was held at the WARM (Women's Art Registry of Minnesota) Gallery (see below). WPTC also started a Poetry in Public Places project, putting poem posters on city (MTC) buses.

---

6 Pat Monaghan. "WPTC: Imaginative Transportation," *Minnesota Daily* (November 12, 1973), 11-13.

7 Bea Williams, "Introduction," *Women Poets of the Twin Cities* (Vanilla Press, 1975 [2nd ed. 1977]), v-vii. The editorial committee was Andrews, Marisha Chamberlain, Jan Drantell, Mary Ellen Shaw, and Williams. Poets included are the editors plus Nancy Beckwith, Breckenridge-Haldeman, Margaret Falk, Jeanette Ferrary, Mary Pat Flandrick, Hampl, Dale Handeen, Hanson, Kirkpatrick, Knox, Elizabeth Lowell, Natasha (Katy Sheehy), Marge Sucoff, Penelope Suess, and Vogel.

8 This was edited by Caroline Vogel, all in her calligraphy. Poets include most of those in the note above, plus Ellen Kennedy, Candy Clayton, Jean-Marie Fisher, Pat Monaghan, Susan Zeni, Ethna McKiernan, and Margaret Hasse.

Love from Women Poets (1975)

When Knox later enrolled in the writing program at the University of Massachusetts, Amherst, she realized the great value of what she had experienced here. "The WPTC, weak on the technical side, but strong on support and empathetic understanding, were a lifeline to sanity, and I think we provided much-needed balancing in the Minnesota community, too. We showed not only that it could be done, but done well, with new and exciting ways of writing and seeing the world."[9] This was a key to a healthy ecosystem.

Le Sueur referred to the women as "forgotten, beaten down, dispersed, alienated, scattered and silenced… The male experience makes a one-sided, patriarchal neurosis without the corresponding female experience. It makes a cultural monstrosity, a retarded, mutilated social image… As much as the Black or Indian experience, the images of women have been distorted." And, also put characteristically: "To hive together, to be published together, is necessary," thereby creating a "womanscape."[10]

---

9   WKC email to MG, 16 November 2021.
10   *Women Poets of the Twin Cities*, ix-xi.

Gold Flower

Another outlet for this community, before the formation of WPTC, was this collective enterprise, a tabloid publication, a "feminist monthly" edited by Shirley Heyer, which first appeared in 1971 and ran for several years. Contents included news stories, reviews, personal and political commentaries, art, photography, and poetry by and for women. It came to have a regular poetry page, with poems from Vogel, Andrews, Hampl, Shaw, and others. On July 21, 1974, at the Pillsbury-Waite Cultural Arts Center, a benefit poetry reading for *Gold Flower* was put on, where readers included Knox, Coco Weber, Mary Logue, and Astrid Bergie.

The Ithunn Apple Occasional Poets Collective

This group, in Minneapolis, reportedly, was conceived by Justin Thyme (a.k.a. Jonathan Sisson, a man of several pseudonyms) in the fall of 1970. Coordinated by Sisson, it was "dedicated to getting poets out of old patterns and poetic egos."[11] (Thus, a perennially necessary mission.) It soon consisted of thirty-five or so poets who put on occasional readings. Bitz was one; another participant was Bea Williams, also a founding member of WPTC. Ithunn (or Idunn/Idun/Iduna) in Norse mythology was the keeper of the magical apples by means of which the gods were able to maintain their eternal youth. She also happened to be the wife of Bragi, god of poetry.[12]

Fort Mango

Visual artists were also banding together in place. In 1975, Scott Seekins, Dick Brewer, Leon Hushcha, Herb Grika, and others, including poets Greg Bitz, Jonathan Sisson, and photographer Tom Arndt, formed this cooperative, which changed its location a cou-

---

11   *The North Stone Review 3* (1972).
12   Likely it's just a Minnesota coincidence that the Norse god Odin and his horse Sleipnir, plus the two ravens, Huginn and Muginn, were the logo for Bly's magazine and press.

ple of times during its eight-year run, eventually ending up above the Loon Bar in downtown Minneapolis. About two dozen patrons supported them, paying studio rent and expenses in exchange for selecting art pieces once a year. Journalist Mary Abbe wrote:

> Artists were reclaiming empty warehouses in downtown Minneapolis during the 1970s and launching cooperatives with fanciful names like Fort Mango, which Hushcha co-founded on 1st Avenue N. as a combination studio, showroom and print shop. He met Keillor at Fort Mango when the wannabe writer from Anoka dropped in with their mutual friend [photographer Tom] Arndt. Keillor credits Arndt and another show participant, poet/artist/songwriter Gregory Bitz, with first luring him onto the stage.[13]

So there was some literary overlap.[14] But the fact that those artists were all male, especially given the times, was a glaring fault to be remedied.

Women's Art Registry of Minnesota (WARM)

Poet Margo Fortunato Galt writes: "WARM emerged early from the tide of feminist protest and discovery that, in the early 1970s, flooded American culture. WARM threatened the local art establishment that was almost completely male... But it soon succeeded in becoming one of the best shows in town."[15] A collective of women meeting first in homes and studios, it unofficially began in the Art Department at the College of St. Catherine in St. Paul. The gallery finally and officially opened in April 1976, in the Wyman Building on 1st Avenue North, downtown Minneapolis (not far from the Loon Bar). Among the thirty-seven co-founders was Hazel Belvo. It went on to great success and national recognition. There was intermittent over-

---

13   *Minneapolis StarTribune*, December 9, 2010.
14   As evidenced by a few small press books in Chapter 14.
15   "The History of WARM," https://thewarm.org/History.htm.

lap with poetry readings, including by WPTC, as events there made their way into the schedule in the *Minnesota Literature Newsletter*.[16] We have seen and will see more evidence of how literary enterprises like the Smith Park Poetry Series, Vanilla Press (see Chapter 14), and the *Milkweed Chronicle* were using visual art to complement literary art.

Roy C. McBride & the Church of Saint Vincent Van Gogh

1973 Macalester College Directory

McBride's early enthusiasm for and commitment to the Minneapolis poetry scene (see Chapter 10) grew. He began to sponsor his own programs at his home at 120 Groveland Ave. *Minnesota Literature* advertised in December 1974: "EXORCISMS / Poetry Readings / Floor Shows / Prices on Request." And two months later: "CONJURE COMPANY performs poetry, music, dance, and song" After two more months: "Open Reading / Boogie / Benefit." But there

---

16 A WPTC reading (see above), and, as seen in *MLN* (February 1977), a gallery exhibition of work by Phyllis Meloff and Wanda Brown.

was plenty more to come from him, ever resourceful, as he strove to bring people together.

By mid-1975, the Pillsbury-Waite Cultural Arts Center in South Minneapolis was sponsoring jazz and poetry events. The next year it was announced that McBride had been appointed their writer in residence. "Among his many schemes are: a readers' workshop, the upcoming Mayday Festival and Twin Cities Writers' Conference, and other madnesses." Lyle Daggett remembers his own experience in McBride's workshop, the "Church of Saint Vincent Van Gogh" as McBride called it:[17]

> We met Wednesday evenings, more or less weekly, around eight or ten of us initially, and gradually a few more people began showing up sometimes. We would write and read our poems together, and from time to time we did group readings at various places around the community and the city at large.
>
> Besides Roy, other participants I remember from that time are Jim Dochniak, Linda Bryant, Kevin O'Rourke, Ivory Giles, Ruth Magler, Dale Handeen, Steve Linsner...and myself; around the time I began showing up, poets Etheridge Knight and Mary McAnally began participating. Sometime after that poet Mike Finley started coming, and poet Mary Karr...

Then he tells of one apparent "madness":

> One sweltering hot Wednesday evening, sometime in July 1976, five of us (Roy, Kevin, Mary, Steve and I) got on a bus in south Minneapolis headed toward downtown at evening rush hour, and began reading poems to the bus riders. (Roy had talked to the driver about it ahead of time, so he wouldn't think a bunch of people were going crazy on his

---

17 See McBride, *Secret Traffic*, 132.

bus.)… People on the bus were agape and thrilled and spellbound. People's jaws dropped and their eyes widened like the moon. We took turns reading, whoever had a poem ready. People clapped, offered comments, a few people stayed on the bus two and three blocks past their regular stops to finish listening to our poems. It was joyful and giddy…[18]

This embodies the already quoted remark: "Things were like that—casual improvisational, free-spirited and ripe with possibilities."[19] Those were the days of unpredictability, as the seeds of poetry were being scattered freely and widely.

One part of the (second annual) Mayday Festival at Powderhorn Park in Minneapolis, on May 1, 1976, was billed as a McBride-run Twin Cities Poets Workshop involving more than twenty-five poets, plus music and mime. Later that month the Twin Cities Writers' Conference was held at the Arts Center. On the schedule was a workshop held with local editors, publishers, and an attorney specializing in laws affecting writers, plus a workshop with members of the Arts Board Literature Panel, COMPAS, PITS (see Chapter 15), and others. Last was a tentative discussion of a Midwest book fair or writers' conference, an apparent preliminary to the First Annual Midwestern Writers' Festival & Book Fair held that October (see below). This was a distance from that first reading the newcomer McBride had attended eight years earlier. And there was still much more to come.[20]

---

18 Lyle Daggett, http://aburningpatience.blogspot.com/2011/08/poet-roy-mcbride.html

19 Mary Abbe, "Old Friends, New Combinations," *Minneapolis Star-Tribune* (December 9, 2010).

20 In the 1980s and 90s, including: Poetry for the People, the Powderhorn Writers Festival, the Continental Historical Reclamation Project, and Dream Band.

Etheridge Knight & The Free People's Poetry Workshop

Other opportunities also brought poets together to discuss their work, to learn from one another, and to do an occasional public reading. This famed workshop was the undertaking of Etheridge Knight, a compelling Black poet who lived in Minneapolis from 1972 to 1977. His book, *Poems from Prison*, had brought him fairly widespread attention in the poetry world.[21] Donald Hall first invited Knight to read at the University of Michigan in 1969, and began to tell him more and more about his friend Bly. Eventually, in early 1972, when the final issue of Bly's magazine—the "Leaping Poetry" issue—appeared, Knight wrote to him. "I've known you for a long time, through Donald Hall… The paper you did about 'The Leap' in the latest issue of *The Seventies* is outta sight."[22] Bly, who by then had heard plenty about Knight, undoubtedly wrote back. Shortly after that, Knight and his new wife Mary McAnally moved to Minneapolis.[23] As Minczeski remembers, when he asked Knight why he had come there, of all places, he replied that it was largely because of Bly. Rusoff agrees that Bly was the main attraction for Knight.

---

    21   (Broadside Press, 1968).
    22   EK to RB, n.d.
    23   Interesting that in 1974, Bly did a recording, "Black Box Three," with Sonia Sanchez, who had married Knight in 1968, and who was also a key member of the Black Arts Movement.

Knight was part of the Black Arts Movement, and for him—as for Bly, coming out of a very different heritage—poetry was an oral art with a long oral tradition, written to perform; a sound to be heard, not an artifact for the page and the mind alone, not to be read in silence.[24] "Poets are sayers, singers, and chanters," he liked to say. By this time, Bly had long been an overt performer at his readings, not merely a reader, which was part of his potency. He demonstrated the power of poetry to move, to agitate, to mesmerize, and, of course, to plant a seed. Thus the mutual appeal these two enjoyed.

Bly also introduced Knight to the work of Jung. Knight participated in the second Great Mother Conference in 1976, up on Burntside Lake near Ely, along with other locals, Bill Holm, Rusoff, and Nor Hall (as well as Coleman Barks, Rita Shumaker, Ann Igoe, and others). John Rosenwald recalls:

> Knight's impact was huge. I recall no persons of color at the first conference. Knight changed that. His booming voice as he read "Ilu, the Talking Drum"; his streetsmarts as he did the dozens on "I Sing the Shine"; his life as a Korean War vet, junkie, ex-con; his physicality, his presence as a street singer, his commitment to the oral tradition, all made his weight felt. Even in comical ways.[25]

---

24   The Black Arts Movement was a counterpart of the Black Power Movement, and had been started by Amiri Baraka (aka LeRoi Jones), the poet, playwright, and editor with whom Bly had had some contact early on. The hub for Black Arts (esp. art, music, and dance) in Minneapolis was the African American Cultural Center. Two young visual artists, Seitu Jones and Ta-coumba T. Aiken, were active at the "Afro Center" in those early days.

25   John Rosenwald, "Small Engine Repair: Thirty-Five Years of the Annual Conference on the Great Mother and the New Father, Organized by Robert Bly," in *Robert Bly in This World: Proceedings of a Conference held at Elmer L. Andersen Library, University of Minnesota, April 16-19, 2009* (University of Minnesota Press, 2011), 124.

Bly was bringing people together everywhere he went, leaping over what might be obstacles for others.

Mary Karr, then a young poet who had attended Macalester College for a couple of years, went to the 1975 National Poetry Festival at Grand Valley State College in Michigan, where she encountered Knight for the first time (the same Festival where Wright encountered Silko; see Chapter 8). She recollects the workshop this way: "Two nights a week, Etheridge held a private poetry workshop in his house, charging young writers like me a pitiful hundred bucks to sit for four months in his living room while he conducted our discussions from the sagging trough of a chenille armchair."[26] She describes his house as "green and imploding," and adds, "Everything about Etheridge's place was off-kilter."

Not only that, "he was an addict of the first caliber. Allegedly sober, Etheridge ran his own beer- and marijuana-maintenance program. While he spouted lines from Dickinson, he kept a forty-ounce of Colt 45 malt liquor between his knobby knees." He was on a Methadone program, but was also known to be shooting up heroin. As Terrance Hayes says, "During the course of one weekend in Minneapolis, Mr. K borrowed money from three poets, one poet's girlfriend, one poet's wife, another poet's ex-wife, and a former poetry student."[27] He was trouble, a storyteller, a crafty liar, a bullshitter extraordinaire, "often blowing smoke, as they say."[28]

He nevertheless was in state of grace of sorts, and endeared himself to the poets who attended his workshops. They included Karr, Andrews, McBride, Kate Green, Minczeski, Logue, Wojahn, Marilyn Nelson, and, as Karr recalls, Bly, "maybe a quarter of the time." And there were occasional visitors, including Kinnell, Quincy Troupe, Levertov, and Audre Lorde. Karr paints a picture: "You

---

26 Mary Karr, *Lit: A Memoir* (HarperCollins, 2009), 52.
27 Terrance Hayes, *To Float in the Space Between,* (Wave Books, 2018), 91-2.
28 Ibid., 13.

gotta imagine twelve or fifteen people in this house in Minneapolis and it's 30 below outside and you're slow dancing with Audre Lorde."[29] Again, a far cry from where we began (although it's still as cold as Tyrone Guthrie found—see Chapter 2).

Marilyn Nelson recollects it this way: "It started with a limited time span, but continued for months. I think I was involved for a year or more." More than that, "it started as a 'normal' workshop, discussing and critiquing our poems. Then Etheridge started taking us out into the community to present unannounced public readings. They were wonderful. You really learn something about writing when you stand up and read poems before a group of strangers who didn't expect to be listening to 'poetry,' and you capture their attention so they don't get up and leave."[30] This, reminiscent of McBride's workshop's bus ride (above), fits, if somewhat crookedly, with Bly's distinction between a true "community" and a network (see Chapter 13).

Wojahn remembers: "Etheridge had his demons but he was charismatic and encouraging to us all. When Bly came, his comments were a little more harsh and acerbic, though never unfair."[31] Although Nelson remembers Bly at Knight's workshop, she says, "better than that was his coming to our readings. He seldom spoke to us, but if he liked a poem, he grunted loudly. Getting a grunt from Bly became the goal of the reading."[32] This was another gift from Bly—his full attention. Bly's presence and his pre-eminence was

---

29 As quoted in Ibid., 131.
30 MN email to MG, 23 October 2020.
31 DW email to MG, 19 July 2020.
32 This conforms with Galway Kinnell's poem for Bly, "The Groans," which begins: "When Poet X comes out with a startling / metaphor a melody of appreciative groans / ripples up from somewhere in the front; / and I know Robert Bly is in the audience." And at the end: "these groans…/ …must be the glow / …from the pleasure / of paying full attention to another, made audible." In *Walking Swiftly: Writings in Honor of Robert Bly*, ed. Thomas R. Smith (Ally Press, 1992), 80-82.

also confirmed by Karr's humorous poem "about all of the Minnesota poets mushing in dogsleds to Bly's house, and upon arriving, falling on their knees in the snow and genuflecting."[33]

A kind of culmination of Knight's workshop was the first (and last) annual Free People's Poetry Festival held at the Cedar-Riverside People's Center, which included readings by Kinnell, Bly, Jessica Hagedorn, and Knight himself. (Jim Sitter attended this with Karr, and remembers that Knight had been hanging around the Hungry Mind.) The workshop gained a new formality with a public announcement that it "will be continuing through September and October. Each Thursday night there is an open reading to the public at the Seward Café on Franklin Ave. in Minneapolis (at 22nd), and the following Friday evening a critique session at Knight's house."[34]

These workshops represent an important opening for a small number of poets of color, an opening that Dochniak and other poets would attempt to widen in the near future (see Chapter 6). In this regard—and others, including gender—the current literary scene in Minnesota has evolved far beyond the limitations of its past. Always in flux, continually renewing itself as the gifts keep moving.

McBride's poem in "Poetryapolis" seems an astute augury of our present. His antennae had been working:

> black poet. white poet. red poet. yellow poet. brown poet. woman poet.
>
> black. white. red. yellow. brown. woman. poet.
>
> black. black. black. black. black. black. black.
>
> poet. poet. poet.
>
> white. white. white.

---

33   So recalled by Marilyn Nelson. MN email to MG, 23 October 2020. Repeated pleas to Karr have elicited nothing further.

34   From *Minnesota Literature Newsletter* (September 1976).

poet. poet. poet.

within the circles of Poetryapolis. root fruit. history. herstory. ourstories.[35]

Hungry Mind Bookstore & Reading Series

Minneapolis' twin city, St. Paul, had more than the Smith Park Poetry Series to offer. The Hungry Mind Bookstore was founded by David Unowsky on Grand Ave. in 1970. He says: "Bill Savran and Savran's Books was my model when I started. I wanted to be the St. Paul equivalent of Savran's."[36] He more than succeeded. The founding of the Hungry Mind—as of other contemporary literary institutions— happened wholly in the spirit of the social and political outlooks and activities of the American countercultural movement. In 1970, protestors were in the streets, were even getting killed there (i.e., Kent State), the Civil Rights Movement was continuing, the Women's Liberation Movement was gaining momentum, and the Gay Rights Movement had started publicly.

Macalester College was then the center of antiwar and leftist political activity in St. Paul.[37] Unowsky says: "I wanted to be part of it. I also believed that books can change the world and books can

---

35 *Blues Vision,* 10. Not everyone was in tune. For example, the *Minnesota Poets Anthology* 2.1 (St. Cloud State College, 1973), edited by Stephanie Borden, included fifteen poets, all of them men, and all white (with the exception of Michael S. Harper who had visited the state, briefly). Armand E. Falk states, somewhat obtusely: "The poets you will be reading are men who share in some ways the experience of living in Minnesota. They have poetry as a common vehicle and the results are as diverse as could be expected from any group of humans."

36 DU email to MG, 18 December 2020.

37 I remember being in an antiwar march to protest the invasion of Cambodia in the spring of 1970, from the University of Minnesota in Minneapolis to the State Capitol in St. Paul. Organizers warned us, as we neared the crowds from Macalester on Summit Avenue, to be wary of the radical students there, as though they had a greater potential to incite violence.

change a person's life, and so I wanted to be in the book business."[38] The store opened in October. "I knew nothing about the book business.... I learned by the skin of my teeth, I learned the hard way. ... I was mostly motivated by political stuff."[39]

Above, we have seen the important roles played by McCosh's Books, by Savran's Paperback Shop (for both, see Chapter 5), and by Rusoff & Co. (Chapter 7), all in Minneapolis. They were nodes, useful and essential gathering places where not only could one stay on top of and purchase what was being published, but one could run into other poets and meet new ones. Places where seeds were flying about, via conversation and books changing hands. Places of all-important connection for these solitaries.

The Hungry Mind also became Macalester's official bookstore, so at first the customers were mostly students. "In those days, students actually read books and were very politically active." The first in-store poetry reading in the fall of 1971, was Macalester English professor Alvin Greenberg. Intermittent readings followed. Eventually, Jim Sitter, a Mac grad from Fargo, started working at the Hungry Mind in July 1975. "Stunned" by the lack of a reading series at Macalester (he was accustomed to the one run by Mark Vinz at Moorhead State College), he soon organized one at the Hungry Mind. Minnesota poets were highlighted at the beginning.[40]

As Sitter says: "Once it started it couldn't seem to stop."[41] During

---

38 From David Wilk interview with David Unowsky on "Writers Cast: The Voice of Writing," May 31, 2017, https://www.writerscast.com/david-wilk-interviews-hungry-minds-bookstore-founder-david-unowsky/

39 His experience was in the family liquor business. Unowsky interview, May 2, 2017 https://anchor.fm/jewbalations/episodes/79-David-Unowsky-ekcfbc

40 Including Greenberg, Vinz, Roberts, Clayton, Chamberlain, Moore, Hampl, McBride, Keenan, Hazard, Karr, Knox, Mary Ellen Shaw, Cardona-Hine, McGrath, Stanley Kiesel, Dale Handeen, Ellen Kennedy, and many others.

41 JS email to MG, 9 May 2022.

the first season, readings were mostly held in the basement of the college's Weyerhauser Chapel, until they moved upstairs. "The first season concluded in May 1976, with Moore & Hampl and a party. The series helped the store establish itself as THE literary bookstore destination (when most people wouldn't cross the river for books)."

Sitter estimates that he put together sixty or seventy-two readings until he took on the role of managing Bookslinger, another book distribution outfit. Unowsky says: "It took a couple of years to get a vision of what a bookstore really could be, and to recognize that there were people like me doing this all over the country." So this was another Minnesota version of a national trend. And one thing led to another. "I think the sense that this was a place of community gathering grew sort of organically."[42]

Wojahn says: "The Hungry Mind had a wall of poetry as big as the one at Grolier's [in Cambridge, Mass.]. Lots of small press stuff...." Sitter acknowledges: "David Unowsky allowed me to lose his money building the poetry section at the store. About two and a half years in, he finally said, 'well, you are actually turning that inventory.' The reading series was done basically on my time in the evening...so the real financial loss in the early days for David on the literary side was the poetry section. ... David once called me 'The Big Wind from North Dakota.'"[43]

Starting out, the main book supplier was The Bookmen, Inc. (run by Norton Stillman and Ned Waldman), and magazines came from Gopher News.[44] Unowsky again: "The poetry section really

---

    42   DU email to MG, 21 December 2020.
    43   JS, op. cit.
    44   In 1972, Norton Stillman, also publisher of Nodin Press, opened Micawber's Books on Carter Ave. in the St. Anthony Park neighborhood of St. Paul. The cozy, quaint space lived up to the always hopeful expectation of the clerk, Mr. Micawber, in Dickens' *David Copperfield,* that "something will turn up." It proved to be a good fit for that "small town within a city," with its both well-educated (with many University of Minnesota faculty) and relatively staid (not counterculture) populace.

grew in the mid-70s, influenced by Truck Distribution (David Wilk) and then by Jim Sitter. ... In my mind, the combination of Savran's, the Loft, the Hungry Mind, and MPR were major factors in making this great literary community. The small press show at St. Kate's was also important. ... It worked both ways: got small presses interested in us, and got us more interested in small presses."

Midwestern Writers' Festival & Book Fair

The first of these bookfairs in the Twin Cities, sponsored by the then recently incorporated Associated Colleges of the Twin Cities, was held at the College of St. Catherine in St. Paul in October 1976. Readings were spread out across the five member colleges, but the exhibitors were there at St. Kate's, "alternative press publishers from across the country, but...especially the wealth of presses in the Midwest. In addition to the...displays, there will be workshops on starting and running a small press, publishing in little magazines, small press distribution, etc."[45]

For the first two years, writer Jonis Agee (then married to David Wilk), teaching at St. Kate's, was the coordinator. In 1978 it moved to nearby Macalester (where it was managed by Jim Sitter—as he says, "actually the colleges 'hired' me through the Unowsky/Wilk/Hungry Mind/Truck Distribution Service partnership that controlled my life for a couple of years"), and then the fourth Great Midwestern Bookfair (as it had come to be called) was at Augsburg College on the West Bank in March 1979. Readers at that time were Stanley Elkin, Audre Lorde, Lisel Mueller, Edward Dorn, and Kelly Cherry, with 200 small presses represented. Later venues included Butler Square on 1st Ave. N. in downtown Minneapolis, and then Willey Hall on the U of M's West Bank. Dochniak was the coordinator for that one on April 24, 1981.

---

45 From *Minnesota Literature Newsletter* (September 1976).

This was a pivot point, as Sitter says: "The gatherings resulted in various people and presses moving to the metropolitan area. Michael Tarachow and Pentagram Press from Milwaukee, Gerald Lange and Bieler Press from Madison, Wisconsin, and the most important, the Kornblums."[46] Allan and Cinda Kornblum, of Toothpaste Press in West Branch, Iowa, came up to exhibit at the fairs and witnessed the vibrant literary scene and community in Minneapolis, so they decided to move here eventually (establishing Coffee House Press). Of course, the gatherings also stimulated writers and readers, and bookpersons of various types, in ways impossible to account for.

So also did bookstores. At least now, with the Smith Park Poetry Series and the Hungry Mind's, there were two good literary reasons to go to St. Paul. More than two, actually, with readings at Hamline College, the College of St. Catherine, and the suburban (White Bear Lake) Lakewood Community College. The poetry readings' center of gravity—in Minneapolis—had shifted somewhat as the imbalance between the two Twin Cities was lessened to an extent. The state capital and eastern twin had merged with its larger neighbor to become fully part of "Poetryapolis."

Amazon Bookstore

But the scene west of the Mississippi also continued to grow. Concurrent with the Hungry Mind's early life was the start of the Amazon (no, not *that* one) Bookstore. In June 1970, Rosina Richter and Julie Morse (who had started the *Female Liberation Newsletter* in 1969) carted some boxes of books on women's liberation and feminism (bought with $400 left after the death of a father) to a house in the Seward neighborhood (adjacent to Cedar-Riverside). It was the Brown House commune at 2418 26th Ave S., dedicated to draft resistance and other political activism (including the expanding food co-op movement). Don Olson, soon to be more widely known as one of the Minnesota Eight (who in July were arrested while attempting

---

46 JS email to MG, 9 May 2022.

to destroy draft files in Selective Service offices, and sentenced to five years in federal prison), had lived there. (Eventually he, too, became a key member of the literary community as longtime distributor of magazines to the Hungry Mind and other independent bookstores in the Twin Cities.)

Richter and Morse started selling books (and soon, journals and newspapers) about, by, and for women. It was a scrappy operation at the start, done by appointment only, with very limited hours, from the porch. But they were trying to change the world. In this revolutionary spirit they envisioned and soon founded what was the first feminist/lesbian bookstore in the United States, independent and collective, choosing the name of a tribe of women warriors from Greek mythology.

Their venture was a model in the forefront of a national movement, the proliferation of women's bookstores, another important aspect of second wave feminism. Over several years in the early 1970s, as the collective grew, its location shifted around south Minneapolis until settling at 2607 Hennepin Ave. S. The store quickly became a central meeting point for and a fixture in the bookish feminist/lesbian community in the Twin Cities—a safe space, a site for readings, a hub for grassroots organizing, and a clearing house of information. It thus was an essential component of the larger community, the literary ecosystem in Minnesota.

Chapter 12
The Crop of Lit Mags: Greater Minnesota

> A nation's body of literature does not depend wholly on the great, and since the magazines have served as a seedbed for each generation of creative writers they have also helped to preserve the very impulse to literary creation.[1]

Literary communities around the state kept themselves inspired and writing in good part by creating, supporting, reading and contributing to regional little magazines. Some of these defied the normal life span and hung on for a long time, and they also helped to forge a link with other communities in Minnesota and neighboring states. The variegated catalog of the veritable cornucopia begun in Chapter 9 continues.

---

1   "Statement of the Association of Literary Magazines of America," a flyer for an organization spearheaded by Reed Whittemore and formed in St. Paul on November 11, 1961. Bly was on the executive committee (with Whittemore, Tate, and Henry Rago). See above, Chapter 3.

Crazy Horse

Thomas McGrath and his wife Eugenia launched the irregular *Crazy Horse* in 1962 (see Chapter 8). It was initially published in New York, but McGrath soon moved homeward to start teaching at North Dakota State University in Fargo and then, just across the Red River, at Moorhead State College in Minnesota. This was an idiosyncratic and rebellious little magazine that had some of the freshness and verve that made Bly's magazine stand out. At the start, many of the contributors were McGrath's friends from his years in Los Angeles, known as the Marsh Street Irregulars and "Incognoscenti."

The masthead reads: "*Crazy Horse* is an irregular publication edited by a dead Sioux chief who is presently reincarnated in a group of Western Poets." McGrath declared: "*NO MORE CATTLEMEN OR SHEEPMEN—WE WANT OUTLAWS!!*" His focuses on the West, on Native American lore, and on the language of revolution, of class struggle and communism, attacking American capitalism and imperialism from the vantage point of, as he put it, the "unaffiliated far left," was unmistakable. And his poetic horizons were broad, plainly excluding the academic establishment. As stated eloquently in the manifesto, he was after:

> a poetry where the surrealist lions of Lorca and the classically magnetic lambs of Marvell and Crane fly up together: as a great beast of affirmation: absolute light. A poetry grand, armored, bawdy, seditious of death; of a violent elegance; as of clouds full of diamonds and lightning; of suicidal assaults on new states of being; of ultimate daring; of love, rage, generosity, failure, truth.
>
> And, at the other pole, the lone crow and darkness: Bashō, Issa, the poetry of the moon.
>
> In between, the destructive element of a practical poesy—everything to help blow up the system: satire, japery, extravagance, humor, Brecht, case histories, parody, practical jokes, criticism.

Bly's declaration of independence, voiced in the first few issues of *The Fifties* and *The Sixties*, had had an effect on what McGrath, in his singularity, saw as possible.

However, under McGrath's editorship *Crazy Horse* consisted of poetry above all. Consider this exception (in #3, 1967), under the rubric "Notes Toward a Newer Criticism":

> 1. To _____ as the poet with the most inflated reputation. (Fill in the blank and send him a copy. You may vote any number of times.)
> 2. To Marianne Moore for the worst book of a promising year.
> 3. To Allen Ginsberg for the worst poem—"Washita Cortex Syndrome.".
> 4. To *Time-Life* for continuing disservice to the Old Girl and to poetry generally.

These comical jabs were almost straight out of Bly's and *The Sixties*' satiric/critical playbook.

As he became more re-settled in his home region, McGrath mustered his own band of local poets ("outlaws")—a satellite community, as it were, of the Twin Cities—whose poems began to appear in the magazine: Vinz, Richard Lyons, and students from McGrath's poetry workshop including Dale Jacobson, Michael Moos, James Fawbush, Tom Poindexter, and others. Moos speaks of their gatherings at McGrath's house and elsewhere: "he was a strong, welcoming, guiding force in the lives of young poets trying to find their way."[2] Indeed, the fifth issue of *Crazy Horse* included first publications for seven of his students, next to poems by Bly (one dedicated to McGrath) and a Vallejo translation by Bly and Wright, an experience that Moos calls "extraordinarily encouraging for me."[3] This is a fitting snapshot of poetry in Minnesota coming alive.

Alvaro Cardona-Hine, another California friend, came to Fargo to be NDSU poet-in-residence, and then settled in Minnesota for a decade or so. For a while, the magazine was put out under the auspices of the Institute for Regional Studies at NDSU. Then, after issue #5, the demands of full-time teaching were such that McGrath decided to transfer responsibility for the magazine to Southwest Minnesota State College in Marshall. Thus, his powerful editorship came to an end. Philip Dacey took over in 1970, with help from Bart Sutter, Larry Levis, and others.

There it continued, if much more tamely (minus the political edge, among other things), and under Dacey's direction seemed to take its cues even more from the pattern established by Bly's magazine. Each issue had poems, reviews, an interview and a parody.[4] The poems were by a mix of nationally known (mostly) and locally

---

2   MM email to MG, 29 May 2024.
3   Ibid.
4   E.g., interviews of Donald Justice, David Ignatow, Charles Simic, and Theodore Weiss; and parodies of John Ashbery, James Dickey, Allen Ginsberg, Mark Strand, and Bly.

prominent poets. In 1977, Howard Mohr took the helm, again giving it a more decidedly local emphasis.[5]

That issue included Olsen's "The Cowshit Poem," a parody of Bly that—as parodies should do—speaks the truth, in this case of Bly's connection to the fertile (fertilized) land and his diffuse influence as a successful sower of seeds (and of a first generation of poets):

> Friends, I've gone back to the land!
> I can open the kitchen window and smell cowshit for breakfast!
> I travel only the dirt roads. And I love it. I love the land!
> I love the dust that sticks to my body.
> The good musty breath of the earth covers my skin.
> I walk the bean fields, I walk the potato fields, I walk all kinds of fields.
> Yesterday, I walked five miles of abandoned railroad tracks.
> I saw abandoned barns, I saw abandoned farms,
> I saw abandoned cars, I saw abandoned people.
> I felt abandoned.
> And it was good. It was night. I feel abandoned best at night.
> So I stood in a cornfield,
> my arms raised to the sky. I was like a tall plant,
> and the green darkness a blanket over my body.
> I was alone among the stalks of corn!

---

5   #17 (Summer 1977). Those local poets included: Olsen, Chamberlain, Rezmerski, Joe Paddock, Charles Waterman, Nancy Paddock, Vinz, and Holm.

> And the sun rose, and I looked around, and I was not alone!
>
> This was not a field of corn
>
> but only long, long rows and rows of poets,
>
> hundreds and thousands of poets
>
> standing in even, cultivated lines,
>
> their arms raised to the sky—an aging, dried out crop
>
> left over from last year's harvest.[6]

Then the magazine left Minnesota for Kentucky and forever.[7]

Dacotah Territory

DACOTAH TERRITORY 5

As indicated above (in Chapter 9), 1971 was an especially fruitful year for little magazines with a strong Minnesota connection, all four of them with patent connections to Bly. Two in the Twin Cities, and two sprouted up in northern Minnesota. They were also proof of the literary proliferation happening in the region, a bumper crop of poets (as Olsen's poem points to, exaggeratedly).

---

6   *Crazy Horse* 17 (1977). Many references here to Bly's work, of course, including his translation with Christina Paulston of the poems of Gunnar Ekelöf, *I Do Best Alone at Night* (Charioteer Press, 1968).

7   *Crazy Horse* did not meet its demise until 2022.

One was *Dacotah Territory*, edited by poet and professor Mark Vinz in Moorhead (see Chapter 8). "The name refers to 'the Great Plains'—the lands originally inhabited by the Dacotah or Sioux nation of tribes.... The word Dacotah means 'allies.' To unfriendly tribes it means 'enemies.'"[8] That first issue was dedicated to McGrath, "poet, teacher, friend," the primary inspiration, influencer, and encourager.[9] By this time, due to McGrath's influence and charisma (and the ground broken by *Crazy Horse*), there was a solid community of writers thriving in the Fargo-Moorhead area. Vinz was surely carrying the baton, utilizing the McGrath posse with students Dale Jacobson, Michael Moos, and Tom Hagen as associate editors.

However, Vinz readily acknowledges that Bly's "inspiration and encouragement" was also central from the outset, with him contributing and encouraging submissions. His home of Madison was "only 130 miles away, he was a frequent visitor, and, needless to say, his zeal had an effect on us all."[10] In fact, the first issue includes Bly's poem, "Driving Toward Dacotah Territory," dedicated to McGrath, and a Rilke translation.

Dacotah Territory, says Vinz in retrospect, began as "a small and simple and mostly regional publication," and grew "to a much larger and nationally distributed one." It was both beautiful and highly intelligent. Its modest aspirations, founded on "an idea of a healthy and diversified regionalism," stood in contrast to Bly's magazine's original aspirations that were—for reasons discussed earlier—more wide-ranging and non-territorial from the beginning.

---

8   *Dacotah Territory* 1.1 (January 1971).

9   Note that one of the associate editors, Dale Jacobson, another student of McGrath's, had contributed to *Black Flag*. Also, the first issue incorporates some content of what David Martinson, yet another student of McGrath's, had gathered a year earlier for his little magazine, *North Forty*, conceived but then aborted.

10   *Dacotah Territory: A 10 Year Anthology*, edited by Mark Vinz and Grayce Ray (North Dakota Institute for Regional Studies, 1982), 4.

Vinz is eloquent on the need to avoid the main hazard of many regional efforts—an insular, narrow-minded, boosterish character. He says: "what we always sought was twofold: to tap into the poetry of place flourishing around us, but never to be simply limited by it; to take a stand against the placelessness of American society, but not with 'down-homeism'…" Of course, Bly had effectively enabled this, as his efforts, outlined in this book, had made crystal clear that poets and readers did not have "to take their cues from far away and thus overlook much of what was in their midst."[11]

Starting with the third issue, in 1972, the magazine's vision came into sharper focus: "The editors are now interested in seeing poetry from 'the territory' (but not 'regionalist poetry'), poetry with some of the elements of surrealism (the image et al.), a poetry generally open to understanding, poetry with social and political commitments, poetry of ethnic minorities, particularly the American Indian." The template of Bly's image-centered poetry is plain, not to mention his political poetry. Although attention to Native Americans was, as I have shown (in a forthcoming essay, cited in Chapter 8), explicit from the beginning of Bly's own poetry and on into the 1970s, it was hardly a concern for his magazine or press. *Dacotah Territory* made noble and notable headway by giving attention to the poetic work of the original inhabitants of the region and North America. (Also see Chapter 8 for details of the special Native American issue.)

McGrath guest edited two issues, too. In fact, issue #3 was made up primarily of material McGrath had gathered for *Crazy Horse,* just when he lost control of it. Issue #11 was a "Minnesota Poets in the Schools Anthology" (see Chapter 15). The final issue, #17 (1980), was another anthology, all poems about fathers. The latter may be due to Bly's influence, as his attention had begun turning to men and the particular issues they face. Also, Holy Cow! Press had just published *Brother Songs: A Male Anthology of Poetry* (see Chapter 14). The

---

11   All quotations in this paragraph, Ibid., 1-3.

magazine's poetry-heavy issues included reviews, too, notes from the editor, and, less often, translations, interviews, and essays.

The list of contributors over the decade is long, and includes virtually all of those mentioned in this book as important members of the Minnesota poetry community. Many of these poets had been or were or would be editors of their own little magazines, evidence of the mutual support system and interrelatedness that seemed to arise spontaneously.[12] Moos adds: "Being part of *Dacotah Territory* put me out into a larger orbit of other poets and editors."[13]

Vinz also mentions how a meeting organized by small press advocate (and psychiatrist) Marvin Sukov in Minneapolis in 1972 led to his own growing involvement with the larger community. "Something exciting was definitely happening within the region, and centered in the Minneapolis-St. Paul area." He met dozens of poets in succeeding years, and notes the importance of bookstores in the Twin Cities and other literary organizations (e.g., Poets in the Schools). "Even though I always fancied myself an emissary from the Far Edge, both I and *DT* were accepted into the center of activity in the Twin Cities."[14] Vinz did not feel that there was an unbridgeable chasm between urban and rural on the poetry map.

He also brought several nationally known poets to do readings at Moorhead State, including Robert Creeley, Galway Kinnell, John Berryman, and William Stafford. The amount of inspiration they offered to young poets in the area should not be underestimated. Because of the vibrancy of the local *Dacotah Territory* scene and the

---

12 The poet-editors include Bly, McGrath, Brainard, Milton, Moore & Hampl, Vinz, Naiden, Jenkins & Dentinger, Philip Dacey, Howard Mohr, Robert Schuler, and John Judson. Notable outsiders (i.e., based elsewhere but widely or fairly widely known) include Ignatow, Stafford, Merwin, Snyder, Richard Hugo, Kooser, Carolyn Forché, Sharon Olds, Louis Simpson, David Ray, Frank Stanford, Gene Frumkin, Doug Blazek, Joseph Bruchac, most of whom have a demonstrable link with Bly.

13 MM email to MG, 29 May 2024.

14 Vinz, *Dacotah Territory*, 5.

stellar presence of McGrath, in 1974, North Dakota State University held "City Lights in North Dakota," a week-long conference of Beat poets, including Allen Ginsberg, Gary Snyder, Kenneth Rexroth, Gregory Corso, Michael McClure, Lawrence Ferlinghetti, and others. Surely, this too made the local poets feel importantly placed.

He sums up, beautifully: "In the most important sense, a magazine is not a *thing*, impersonal and intangible. No, it's a spirit, a particular sense of taste and judgment, and maybe even a vision—something that's ultimately non-transferable."[15] And so it ended after nearly ten years.[16]

Steelhead

The fourth important debut in 1971, *Steelhead*, was edited by poets Louis Jenkins and Philip Dentinger in Duluth, on the other side of the state from Moorhead, also a good distance from Minnesota's metropolitan center. The steelhead is a type of rainbow trout that lives in Lake Superior and spawns in some of the larger rivers on the North Shore, especially the Knife River (a translation of the Ojibwe *mokomani zibi*).

---

15   Ibid., 12. This is obviously apropos of what happened with *Crazy Horse* when McGrath was no longer involved.

16   It should be noted that in 1977, Vinz briefly became editor of *Dakota Arts Quarterly,* a literary magazine from Fargo. That fact shows in part how the scene was flourishing in the region.

Thus, again, the magazine's title was a testament to a particular locale. Jenkins had come to Minnesota via Oklahoma, Kansas, and Colorado, finally transplanting himself in his wife's home town.

After encountering *Silence in the Snowy Fields,* and then poring over issues of *The Sixties,* he had begun a correspondence with Bly several years earlier, sending poems and receiving Bly's generous and encouraging critiques. Once in Duluth, he met Dentinger, another aspiring poet and a friend of his wife's family, and they decided to start a magazine, inspired by Bly's example. Jenkins had taken a printing course in high school. They began with a letterpress and some worn-out type, first putting out two little collections entitled *Salted in the Shell.*

Steelhead: A Magazine of Poetry first appeared in December. Its stated aspirations were relatively broad, seeking "all types of quality contemporary poetry and translations," though surely that meant poetry in line with the template Bly had supplied. Later issues, however, included some prose, reviews, more illustrations, even a cartoon. Editorial voice and position were only detectable, if at all, in the choice of the submissions they printed, most of which were from the region. Contributors to the first issue included Bly with a translation of Tranströmer, and Bly's friends Ignatow and John Haines, whom he surely steered *Steelhead's* way. Most of the others were local—from Duluth and environs, from further out in Minnesota, and from Wisconsin. They include Dacey (new editor of *Crazy Horse*), Woessner (co-editor of *Abraxas*, in Madison, Wisconsin), Olsen (editor-printer-publisher of Ox Head Press), Waara (formerly Damsten, editor of *Black Flag*), and Sisson (who seems ubiquitous). The mutual support system that Vinz noted above is again in evidence.

The next issue was only short poems (*à la* the Sixties Press book, *The Sea and the Honeycomb*), which Bly not surprisingly told Jenkins he liked a lot. It included Bly's translation of Jan Erik Vold and Harry Martinson, Olsen's of Machado and Gerardo Diego, plus a poem from William Stafford. Another issue was an anthology of sixteen Minnesota poets.[17] The editors themselves rounded out other issues. By #5, Dentinger was no longer co-editor (in his stead were Katherine Basham, Robert Hart, and Timothy Kachinske; plus a note that *Steelhead* was published by the English Department at the University of Minnesota, Duluth), as he had departed for New Mexico.[18] The seventh and last issue was in 1979.

Dentinger reminisces: "Looking at these old publications, I am struck by what a diverse, lively, ad hoc poetry scene we had in Duluth in those early years, with lots of open readings at various venues attended primarily by the poets themselves—some serious, some not—and their current or soon-to-be significant others. Party to follow."[19] Readings and the magazine were the glue that bonded them. But there were two more magazines in the region's lively poetry scene that overlapped with *Steelhead*.

A Lake Superior Journal

---

17   #4 (1974). Including Bly, McGrath, Moore, Freya Manfred, Rezmerski, Olsen, Browne, Robert Damsten, Andrews, David Martinson, Kincaid, Vogel, Chamberlain, Hennen, Wojahn, and Breckenridge-Haldeman.

18   One of the new later contributors was Connie Wanek, with whom Dentinger had connected in Las Cruces, New Mexico. And the rest, as they say, is history....

19   PD email to MG, 8 May 2023.

First put out in 1975 by the Lake Superior Association of Colleges and Universities in Duluth, this magazine, edited by Linda Hastings, was aiming high. The cover listed contents: Poetry / Art / Photography / Prose. Although welcoming work "with a regional theme, our basic goal is quality work from any quarter." Contributors are mostly local, and mostly associated with local academia. But the first poem—of course, once again lending legitimacy to a new magazine—is by Bly (who also contributes his translation of *Han Ola og Han Per*, a Norwegian American comic strip), and other contributors include Browne, Jenkins, Dentinger, Rob Damsten, Basham, and Rezmerski. The second and final issue included Cary and Charles Waterman, Al Zolynas, Siv Cedering Fox, David Kubach, and gave even more attention to translation.

The Great Circumpolar Bear Cult

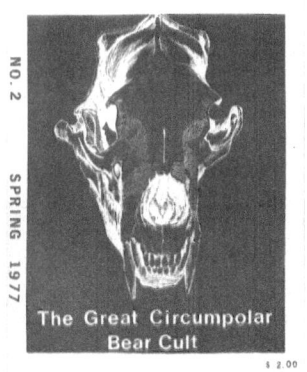
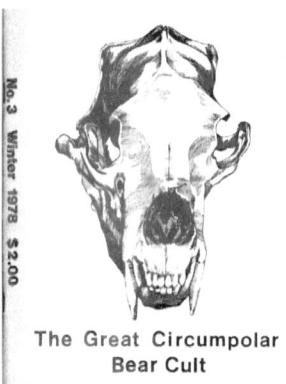

Edited by David Kubach and Rick Penn, this came out of Ashland, Wisconsin (home of Northland College), on the south shore of Lake Superior, in 1976. They stated in the first issue: "We have...a shared interest in the north, living here by choice not far from where the descendants of the kalevala milk their cows and bands of Anishinabe still preserve some of the traditional ways of woodland life... So it's natural that we should be particularly hospitable to writing from and about the north." They were staking out a region, including the original Indigenous inhabitants and the more recent Finnish immigrants, while also acknowledging literary indebtedness to Bly and Snyder. Of course, Dentinger and Jenkins from Duluth had poems there.

Quickly the magazine attracted more poets primarily from Minnesota and Wisconsin, including Finley, Vinz, Young Bear, Wojahn, Logue, Hasse, Peter Mladinic, Dacey, Robert Hedin, Woessner, George Roberts, and many others. There were translations of Rilke by John Michel. And outsiders, Connie Wanek (via Dentinger), Joseph Bruchac and even Kenneth Rexroth. The magazine had three issues in three years.

Loonfeather

Elsewhere in the Northland, literary activity continued with the publication of *Loonfeather: Minnesota North Country Art* in Bemidji in 1979. William Elliott, poet/professor who had founded the Upper Midwest Writers Conference at Bemidji State College in 1969 (see Chapter 8), was the editor to start. He writes: "North central Minnesota has always enjoyed a talented group of writers and artists, but their work has never had a steady regional outlet." The plan was modest, to keep expenses low and help assure longevity. His model was the success and survival of *North Country Anvil* (see below).

Still room for fancy, however: "No other bird, with its unique but lonely call, could better illustrate the artistic voice of the writer. And no other bird represents the artist's invisible yet dramatic influence as it flies over the woods and lakes of our region than the loon." This was to be a "small, uncomplicated regional magazine."

The first issue was dedicated to "our state bird (our mentor)" and to "Bob Dylan." And, once again, this new magazine's first poem was by Bly, "Late Morning." Other contributors include Susan Hauser, Dacey, Vinz, fiction by Jon Hassler, and an interview with Browne. He explains his long ago and successful transplantation (to Minneapolis, and up to a cabin near Benedict): "I don't think I'm a midwestern poet. ... I was living in Finland and read these poems of Bly's and Wright's about lakes and silences and forests, and by accident came to stay very close to the place where the poems had been written—near here. And now I have a house here...I was drawn by the energy of the poetry."

The North Country Anvil

Back to southern Minnesota and a giant on the magazine landscape. Beginning in 1972, *The North Country Anvil* was a regional publication, deeply rooted in agrarian life in Minnesota, and plainly founded in and reflective of the countercultural movement and antiwar sensibilities of the period. Here was an example of an alternative community that was synthesizing politics, social theory, and the arts into a lifestyle. It "expected its readers to think and react. ... the magazine demands serious readers willing to take a long hard look at their society and the way their lives function—or don't function—within it."[20] Much more than a literary journal, although it had a strong literary component, it was, one might say, more in step with the times than any we have considered. It also aligns most closely with our overriding ecosystem metaphor.

Gruchow writes regarding this magazine: "The countercultural movement of the late 1960s and 1970s was actually based on stoutly old-fashioned ideas: the democratization of labor, self-reliance, social equality, anti-materialism, and the power of nature to inform culture." He continues, "The counterculturalists were the proponents of what, in American society, really are the traditional values."[21] This sounds much like what the poets in Minnesota were about.

It was about the (so-called) return to the land, moving back to nature, with an idealistic vision of the way things once were—or were imagined to have been. Reflecting the disillusionment of the younger generation, the magazine was anti-industrialism, anti-materialism, anti-consumerism, and anti-technopoly, decrying the accompanying dehumanization and environmental destruction. The adjectives leftist, libertarian, progressive, radical, communitarian, feminist, are all well-applied. Perhaps Le Sueur was the figure whose sensibility and stances most closely aligned with the *Anvil*'s. (Indeed, she had been a contributor, along with Richard Wright, Nelson Algren, and Langston Hughes, to the original *Anvil* [1933], a magazine devoted to proletarian themes.) Or perhaps not.

---

20 James Moore, "A New *Anvil* Hammers it out in the North Country," *Preview* 7.10 (October 1973), 12.

21 Gruchow, "Introduction," in Rhonda R. Gilman, ed., *Ringing in the Wilderness* (Holy Cow! Press, 1996), xv. Of course, as he importantly notes, the countercultural movement in rural Minnesota was essentially white and middle-class.

Although turned out by an informal collective, the magazine was very much the vision of its editor, Jack Miller. The fact that he insisted that the drive for social change be spiritually based, that it involve the search for meaning, also shows his alignment with Bly's thought, as does the insistence on being rural and regional—coming out of Millville, Minnesota, a town with approximately 130 residents (Coincidentally about twenty-five miles east of Pine Island, the original business address of *The Fifties*; another coincidence is that Miller had spent his high school years in Montevideo, a town about twenty-five miles east of Madison, Bly's home base.) He wrote in the first issue (June 1972): "We need to start close to home. To be better citizens of the world, we need to understand our families, our communities, our regions, and our various cultural heritages. We need a sense of where we come from to know where we need to go."[22] All well and good.

Miller also wrote in the second issue, showing the artificiality of my division of magazines (and also of poetry readings) into urban and rural:

> The countryside offers sanctuary... In a broader sense, this entire region, cities and all, is countryside: Even the cities take their character from the great farmland, woodland, and lakeland that stretches from Illinois to Canada, from the Dakotas to Lake Michigan. Partly because of this country character, the region is a place specially blessed. It has grown up healthy and strong, with some sense of its locale, with some feelings of community and, most importantly with a closeness to the land and the seasons. If there is a place where new ideas can grow and reach fruition, this North Country is it.[23]

Miller and most of his comrades had moved from the city to rural Millville.

---

22 *NCA* 1 (June 1972).
23 *NCA* 2 (October 1972), 33.

The primary focus of the *Anvil* was always on social and political matters, with much attention paid to AIM (founded in Minneapolis in 1968) and subsequent ongoing struggles at Wounded Knee and Pine Ridge in South Dakota, to local and national politics, and to organic farming, mining, alternative schooling, activism, communes, religion, outdoor life, gardening, homesteading, bicycling, pollution, nuclear power, food cooperatives, strikes, and resistance.

But, in addition, there was ample attention to literature, especially to poetry (with the editorial vision of Ray and Mara Smith) as an important component of an alternative lifestyle. Literary contributors include Le Sueur, Bly (poetry and more), and McGrath, as well as a host of others.[24] The magazine lasted until 1989, and its character changed somewhat over time.

Bly chose the *Anvil* as the most appropriate vehicle to convey his first public announcement of the formation of the literary collective, the Minnesota Writers' Publishing House, in 1972 (see Chapter 14). A few years later, there is a two-part interview with Bly, the first entitled "Politics & the Soul," and the second "Searching for Culture and God in the Midwestern Wasteland."[25] In the latter he bemoans the fact that Norwegian Americans and Swedish Americans have mostly lost touch with the languages, literatures, and cultures from which they came, that they have lost their groundedness, their roots. This despite the fact that decades earlier they had planted the seeds of a political and social radicalism that could still be detected in Minnesota.

There is also significant space given to reviews, from Moore (on McGrath and Adrienne Rich), Jenkins, Finley, Charles Waterman, and Emilio DeGrazia. Naiden has a four-part look at Minneso-

---

24   Including Vizenor, Rakosi, Kincaid, Brainard, Tjepkes, Redshaw, Cary Waterman, Finley, Lyons, Naiden, Vinz, Dentinger, Sutter, Dacey, Paddock, Corey, Hennen, Sisson, Freya Manfred, Caddy, Minczeski, Clayton, Mladinic, and Rezmerski.

25   *NCA* 20 (Dec.-Jan. 1976-77); 21 March-April 1977).

ta poetry, worth treating in some depth. The first part, "Minnesota's Lively Poetry Scene," begins "The territory, suddenly, is full of poets and poetry journals, and some of them are spectacularly good... good enough to get you hooked on poetry even if you've always disliked it."[26] He considers *Black Flag,* his own *The North Stone Review* (shamelessly), *Dacotah Territory, Steelhead* (harshly), *The Minnesota Review, Crazy Horse, The Carleton Miscellany,* and *The Lamp in the Spine* (briefly). He also mentions Bly's *The Seventies* and writes that he is hoping for another issue.

Naiden adds, much in tune with the broader message of this book:

> Bly has been criticized for being "too powerful" and for being many other things in Minnesota "literary circles," and in the poetry scene generally around the country. But no one can question his generosity and kindness toward other deserving writers, especially the younger ones; his energy and willingness to help any sincere writer is probably part of the reason, aside from his winning the National Book Award for poetry in 1968, that his influence is so strong in this state, not to say across the country generally.

In "Minnesota Poetry – II," Naiden moves on to books by Mc-Grath and Bly, and then the first two books from the Minnesota Writers' Publishing House. He likes the newer issues of *Steelhead* and *The Lamp in the Spine,* but is hard on the first issue of *Moons and Lion Tailes.*[27] In part three he is mostly positive, on new issues of *Dacotah Territory, Crazy Horse,* and *The Lamp,* and on new books by Greenberg, Kincaid, James L. White, Bea Williams, Tjepkes, and Ray Smith.[28] Finally, he keeps praising *Dacotah Territory,* and the new, short-lived magazine, *The Beggar's Bowl.* Books by William Lamppa, Marjorie Sucoff, William Elliott, and James Fawbush are treated mostly kindly.

---

26   *NCA* 6 (June-July 1973), 65ff.
27   *NCA* 7 (August-September 1973), 59ff.
28   *NCA* 8 (October-November 1973), 54 ff.

Great River Review

Founded by Emilio DeGrazia in the Mississippi River town of Winona (forty-five miles from Millville), in 1977, this magazine had an initial emphasis on prose. It befitted the developing literary landscape in Minnesota, with the Loft's influence and its growing attention to much more than poetry. DeGrazia's retrospective statement is also in tune with the zeitgeist, with emphasis on the region and political matters. He writes:

> My ambitions for *GRR* developed out of my sense that new writers, especially of fiction, needed a literary journal of some girth and quality to support their efforts. These writers, I hoped, would come mainly from the Minnesota region and would, conspicuously in their work, affirm the value of place. Moreover, I wanted these writers to represent and articulate an aesthetic worthy of the best values of the anti-Vietnam war generation, with its concerns for ecology, social justice and peace. *GRR* would provide new work that was homegrown, well-made, intelligent, and conscience-driven.[29]

---

29 "Introduction," in *Great River Review,* 36 & 37 (*Keys to the Interior: Twenty-Five Years of* Great River Review, eds. Richard Broderick and Robert Hedin). iii.

Remarkably long-lived, *GRR* has changed editors and locales over the decades (most notably Robert Hedin in Red Wing), but still sits on the bank of the mighty Mississippi (in Minneapolis, with Peter Campion).

This catalog is necessarily incomplete, but I have tried to highlight in the text those most significant for the story I mean to tell. There were several other little magazines in the area, as noted in this footnote (and surely more that I've missed).[30]

---

30 They included:

Northeast, Lacrosse, Wisc., 1966, ed. John Judson

Uzzano, Mt Carroll, Ill., 1967, ed. Robert Schuler (Not from a bordering state, but Schuler says *Dacotah Territory* made him want to start his own magazine. In the first issue were McGrath, Gunderson, and Brainard. And it eventually moved to Menomonie, Wisc.)

Road Apple Review, Oshkosh, Wisc. (relocated there from Albuquerque after #1), Winter 1968-1969, eds. Doug Flaherty & James Bradford

Sunday Clothes: A Magazine of the Fine Arts, Hermosa, S. Dak., 1971, ed. Linda Hasselstrom

The Beggar's Bowl, Albert Lea, Minn., 1972, ed. Alan Altany (a Franciscan tertiary). Yet another debut in which Bly had a poem: "Written in a Journal."

Spirit that Moves Us, Iowa City, Iowa, 1975, ed., Morty Sklar

Oakwood, Brookings, S. Dak. (SDSU), 1975, eds. Doug Cockrell & David Allan Evans. Not far from the Minnesota border, the first issue contained poetry by students (mostly, but with a few professors, like Phil Dacey, editor of *Crazy Horse* in Minnesota, and another Minnesotan Freya Manfred). Unapologetically regional, it proves that there was something going around in "Siouxland," and they had caught it. Later contributors included Hasse, Meissner, Dave Etter, Kathleen Norris, Siv Cedering Fox, and Greg Kuzma.

Voices, Marshall, Minn. (from the Southwest Minnesota Arts and Humanities Council), 1976 (This represents an evolution of the SMAHC newsletter, was hardly a literary magazine, though it published an essay by Bill Holm, reprinted a review of books by Bly, etc.)

Chapter 13
Building Bridges Outstate: Poetry Outloud

> Many Midwesterners live in small towns of the kind Sinclair Lewis made synonymous with emptiness, and Babbitry is everywhere encountered, yet [some] poets…find it possible to love what even Sinclair Lewis could not fully hate.[1]
> –Lucien Stryk

My distinction between city poetry readings (above, in Chapters 10 and 11) and those in greater Minnesota (here) will prove to be less than accurate, in line with Jack Miller's comment above: "In a broader sense, this entire region, cities and all, is countryside: Even the cities take their character from the great farmland, woodland, and lakeland that stretches from Illinois to Canada, from the Dakotas to Lake Michigan." While Bly's influence was surely felt more strongly in urban areas, given the higher concentration of poets there, his attention to rural Minnesota—where he was from and had chosen to remain—never flagged. He was interested in building bridges over the urban-rural divide.[2] So he exemplifies the subject matter of this

---

[1] "Introduction," *Heartland: Poets of the Midwest*, vol. 1, ed. Lucien Stryk (Northern Illinois University Press, 1967), xix.

[2] It so happens that the urban-rural divide in Minnesota was also deliberately bridged by the Farmer-Labor Movement decades earlier.

Chapter. And the larger project, with many other poets following his lead, must be counted an impressive success.

Sometimes, even readings on college campuses in small towns seemed to get closer to making that connection (partly because many of the students themselves were from small towns). *Black Flag* (see Chapter 9), sponsored a "Black Flag Poetry Fest" at the University of Minnesota – Morris campus (150 miles WNW of Minneapolis) in December 1970.[3] Twelve poets published in the magazine were there for two days "to meet with classes and individual students, conduct a workshop, and give several readings."[4] In addition, there was "an informal, free-for-all reading," in which "all members of the campus community are urged to read their own works and listen to those of others." The "instant" community of readers and writers created on the page by a magazine was hereby substantiated in person and, importantly, outside of the Twin Cities.

It is no surprise that a deeply felt sense of place became paramount for many or most of the poets involved in the Minnesota Writers' Publishing House (see Chapter 14). After that program got underway, at another poetry festival in Morris (with participants including McGrath, Hennen, Rezmerski, Jenkins, Bitz, Brainard, and Andrews), sponsored by the Minnesota Prairie Poets Association (launched at that event), Bly remarked that, in Minnesota at least, the poets were not confined to the Twin Cities. Rather, there were poets scattered all across the state. He then, keeping at his sowing/wilding, generating ideas and always looking to community building and the entire ecosystem, openly imagined a poetry anthology in which all eighty-seven counties of Minnesota would be represented, either by residents of or visitors to each county. It was an appealing and kooky suggestion, typically Blyish.

---

3   As reported in the student newspaper, *The Vanguard* 11.10 (3 December 1970).

4   They were: Richard and Sarah Shaw, Kincaid, Brainard, Tjepkes, Raygor, Richard Damsten (the editor), McBride, Tim Baland, Hennen, Chet Corey, and Caddy. (Rezmerski joined them, too.)

A couple of years later, he indicated that he had been pursuing the idea, thinking it somehow suitable for the MWPH. "What we'd like is one poem for each of the counties, and a poem that gives some sense of the physical being of that county, its foliage, or the mood of one of its towns." Poets were responding to the call. For a while, Bill Holm was designated co-editor, and they received poems from twenty counties.[5] But there was an unforeseen problem, as Bly had indicated earlier: "most of the poems do not really touch the county."[6] A poem about a lake, for example, seemed like it could be about any Minnesota lake. He wanted poems to be more specific and topographical, so he gave up on the scheme.[7]

* * *

It is notable how some individual poets, who customarily were city residents, sought out rural experiences for themselves, apparently emulating (however briefly) the way Bly managed to live and work. Hyde and Moore visited Bly's farm a few times, and were once put to work digging a new outhouse hole in preparation for the honeymoon of James Wright and his new wife, Annie. Physical labor was not the only thing; in 1971, Hyde spent two weeks on the farm, helping Bly by proofreading the text for two Seventies

---

5   *Minnesota Literature Newsletter* (February 1977). The announcement also said: "There are 65 counties not yet covered, and 20 or 30 more are hoped for before the book goes to press in March or April. Poems should deal with the landscape of, or the life of people in the county."

6   "The Writer's Sense of Place," *South Dakota Review* 13.3 (Autumn, 1975), 74.

7   To commemorate the 150th anniversary of Minnesota's statehood, the League of Minnesota Poets revived the idea. The resultant book was *County Lines: 87 Minnesota Counties, 130 Minnesota Poets*, eds. David Bengston, Charmaine Pappas Donovan, Angela Foster, and John Calvin Rezmerski (Loonfeather Press, 2008). One of the editors, Rezmerski, had been present when Bly made the original suggestion. Granted, Bly's exacting (and impossible?) standard had been relaxed.

Press books of Bly's translations.[8] He made other subsequent visits tending to literary matters.

In the summer of 1972, Hyde and his girlfriend Mary Hilmer, Moore and Hampl, and Wendy Salinger (a poet friend from the Iowa Writers' Workshop) all moved into an abandoned farmhouse near Canby, about twenty miles south of Madison. Carol Bly had alerted them to the house's availability; and it was very cheap, at $10 a month per person. Moore says "we thought of it as a commune, it was intentional, not just like sharing an apartment."[9] The five of them competed to see who could spend the least money when grocery shopping for the household. Hampl, however, remembers it differently: "We strongly rejected the word commune—that suggested a hippie farm life and style we weren't about. And we knew it was just for the summer—the place had no heat. Oh and the mice scurrying around! We all wanted to be writers—and with the exception of Mary...that's what we did."[10]

The point of that venture was to focus on their own work—in some semblance of a rural writer's residency, remote from the city's distractions/demands—and, at least implicitly, to get in touch with the poetic rural life that Bly had brought to the fore in *Silence in the Snowy Fields*. Also to heed his relentlessly repeated emphasis on any poet's need for solitude. It was *not* to make contact with other poets nearby, such as in Marshall. Moore says: "We were pretty high on ourselves." Hyde adds: "We were the center of the universe."

Bly, says Moore, "was very helpful." Hampl remembers: "I can still see a beat-up car bumping over the unpaved road to the farmhouse, Carol, Robert, Tom McGrath, Ruth Ray... They came to visit, brought food, I think. I don't remember the visit itself, but imagine they were amused and curious about us living this romantic

---

8   *Lorca and Jiménez: Selected Poems* (Beacon Press, 1973) and *Friends, You Drank Some Darkness* (Beacon Press, 1975).

9   MG interview with JM, 7 January 2020.

10   PH email to MG, 19 February 2020.

marginal life." Hyde recalls that the young women gave McGrath a hard time that day "because he was so macho."

Hampl also made a subsequent visit to the area, to Bill Holm's house in his hometown, Minneota, with Moore, Hanson (who grew up in nearby Sacred Heart), and Rusoff. In 1973, Hyde actually moved to nearby Clarkfield, thirty-five miles from Madison, where Franz Richter (art editor of *Ivory Tower, Nickel & Dime Quarterly,* and illustrator of various books and magazines) lived. And he had a job for a while as an electrician at the Moduline Mobile Home factory in Montevideo.

Yet others made a similar move, but with a key difference—they got involved with the people who lived there, as poetic emissaries of a sort. Wendy Knox left the Twin Cities for Minneota, at first house-sitting for Holm after his mother died and while he was away as writer in residence at Lakewood Community College (in White Bear Lake). She settled in, doing much more than the solitary labor of writing poetry, working for the Southwest Minnesota Arts and Humanities Council (SMAHC) from 1976 to 1979, first in the Poets in the Schools program (see Chapter 15). And a Macalester College friend, poet Dale Handeen, lived in nearby Montevideo.

Joe Paddock, who grew up in Litchfield but had been living in Minneapolis, was "called back," to the region, to the town of Olivia, in 1975, to be Poet in Residence with an NEA pilot project, "Poets in the Community." He recalls: "I rather quickly discovered that the residency wasn't to be about me so much as the community of people with whom I worked. My poet-pride somewhat dashed, I came to terms with the fact that more than anything I was to become a channel for the poetry of the people of the community, much of it in the form of actual poetry written by individuals of all ages, writing that I facilitated."[11] The resultant book, *The Things We Know Best: An Oral History of Olivia, Minnesota, and Its Surrounding Countryside,* was "an expression of what community is... In the face of the frightening alienation of our time,

---

11   Joe Paddock, *Infinity's Edge,* 214.

there is that heart and soul of community, a sense of closeness, which permeates nearly every page of this book."[12]

The next year, from November 1976 to August 1977, Joe and his wife Nancy held a regional poetry residency, called Poetry Alive!, sponsored by SMAHC and the NEA. In that time and in that twenty-one-county area, as he says, they "traveled these 13,758 square miles and their 163 towns... Like a pair of old-time pack peddlers. A rich experience, during which time we met many, many poets." He adds: "Southwestern Minnesota has been especially fertile ground for poetry. Tough growths of poetry everywhere out here, like the cattails and bastard grass which once claimed the lowlands of these prairies." They then put together an anthology marking this prairie restoration, *Poets of Southwestern Minnesota,* a mix of forty published and unpublished poets (but mostly the latter), nicely putting them side by side.[13] And each Paddock also produced a chapbook of their own, under the same auspices. Incidentally, in the fall following their residency, Southwest Minnesota State University in Marshall held a conference on "Literature of Place," with participation by Bly, Holm, Anselm Hollo, William Kloefkorn, and William Stafford. More encouragement for local poets.

---

12 Ibid., 217.
13 They included Bly, Fred Manfred, Phebe Hanson, Holm, Hennen, and Phil and Florence Dacey. Illustrations by Franz Richter.

Now to move toward the main subject matter of this Chapter: the poetry reading. This turn from urban areas and college campuses across the state to rural Minnesota, to (so to speak) "real" people, that is, people other than poets and assorted eggheads/literati, was a significant and bold move, also in line with the Poets in the Schools and other COMPAS programs (see Chapter 15).

For the summer months of July and August 1974, Caroline Vogel (co-founder of the Smith Park Poetry Series in St. Paul) and John Rezmerski (professor at Gustavus Adolphus College in St. Peter), organized three outstate tours to bring poetry to the people. The first was to western Minnesota: to Olivia, Marshall, Cottonwood, Ghent, Minneota, Taunton, Canby, Dawson, and Madison. This was one journalistic summation:

> The purpose of the Poetry Outloud project—believed to be the first of its kind in the nation—is, in the lofty words of the State Arts Council, to "revive the oral tradition of literature that existed in the Dark and Middle Ages when poets roved the countryside, performing a vital function in stimulating a sense of community through their roles as celebrants and bearers of spiritual news."

However new and innovative Poetry Outloud may have seemed, it was plainly the re-emergence of an age-old practice. More evidence of a renaissance, in fact.

Schedule for the first Poetry Outloud tour, 1974

The cultural scene in small towns in the Upper Midwest had been aptly, if archly, described by Lewis in *Main Street*. The small town leaders, virtually all of them men (including successful and respected farmers like Jacob Bly), saw themselves as the upholders of American "civilization," represented by money, politics, hard work, and religion. Their wives were often the ones who pushed for the less visible cultural infrastructure: public libraries, their children's education, local theaters, and reading groups. Some of them also wrote poetry now and then. Carol Bly, in a "letter from the country," referred to this as "the ladies' friends-of-the-arts syndrome."[14]

* * *

---

14   Carol Bly, "If a Thing Is Worth Doing, It's Worth Doing Badly," *Letters from the Country* (Harper & Row, 1981), 27. We might note that she was behind the community effort that transformed the old First Lutheran Church in Madison into the Prairie Arts center in 1973.

In the early 1970s, Bly was writing a column for *American Poetry Review*. The one titled "The Network and the Community" goes a long way toward explaining how he saw his role in his hometown and in Minnesota.[15] It is also thought-provoking, and provides a useful way to distinguish between Bly's impact and connections nationwide/worldwide, and those on his home turf. And more to the point, it is especially relevant to this Chapter's subject matter. Please bear with me.

The sources for his thoughts were Jung's *Psychological Types* and Philip Slater's *Earthwalk*.[16] In a previous column, "Developing the Underneath," Bly had laid out Jung's idea that inside each of us there are four "intelligences," cognitive functions or ways of dealing with the world—feeling, thinking, intuition, sensing—and that one of the four is dominant. Of the remaining three, one is distinctly inferior.

Bly goes on to define his terms. A network "is often composed of people with the same dominant function developed," people who are therefore significantly in accord, who have the same freedoms. And a network does not have any particular territory. It is comfortable, because it is where people understand us; like a college or university English Department, or, for that matter, a so-called "community" of poets. (It is essential to note that this is how I, and others, use the word "community" just above and throughout this book, *not* in the way particular to Bly's essay, as defined here, and in the rest of this Chapter.)

"A network is lovely if you also have a community." A true community, that is. "A community," Bly says, "has old people in it, and feeble-minded people; there are babies, and people with entirely different ways of grasping the world than yours...." They may live "entirely on a physical plane," and they have duties instead of freedoms, "and what binds them together are similar restraints." A community is experienced "as water in which you swim."

---

15   *APR* 3.1 (Jan/Feb 1974), 19-21. All quotations in the following paragraphs are from this.

16   The latter had just been published (Anchor/Doubleday, 1974).

So, we begin to see where this is going. Bly is, in part, working out an understanding of his own place in Madison and the consequences of his choice to return and remain there, even though he was not farming. A community is "a closed circuitry. Certain ideas and emotions and habits go round and round, generation after generation, with a [centripetal] force."[17] He continues:

> Once in a while…one man in the group would suddenly fly off straight out, instead of obeying the force. He would go out into the desert, or somewhere out into the solitude far inside him, stay there a long time, and discover something amazing… Usually then he returns and announces his discovery…most prophets are thrown away, and the community ignores both the message and the prophet. But once in a while it opens just enough to take in the new idea, all the time attacking the bearer…—then the community closes again, but its internal circuitry is now changed—slightly.

Thus, the community is modified by the "flying fragment" that returns to it.

This starts sounding like an ecosystem. "The important thing is the community itself and its continuity, because it is a living forest of people, ecologically sound; that is important, not the flying fragment." Everybody wants to be a flying fragment, Bly says. "In fact, the flying fragment these days does not actually return to the community at all with his gift… He now…tends to return and offer his gift to a network."

The column becomes more overtly autobiographical, as Bly acknowledges: "I grew up on a farm, near a Norwegian Ameri-

---

17   Bly actually uses, mistakenly (I think), the word "centrifugal—as inside a washing machine, in which the clothes "flee the center"—confusing it with "centripetal" the force that "seeks the center." The flying fragment *is* centrifugal.

can community... I went off east to college, then lived alone for about three years. Alone, I did fly off in a straight line, and I did learn something no one else in my family has known before." But, he admits, when he returned home he did *not* give that gift to the community, instead isolating himself so he could write more poetry. He started a magazine, and he responds to the submissions he receives from all over the country. But this is a perfect example of a network. "When I publish a book...I try to give something to the community, but my day-to-day work seems to be entirely done for the network."[18]

Bly characterizes poetry readings as "mainly network affairs." Which is not to diminish their importance. And although he doesn't make the distinction here, he mainly means the city and campus readings from the last Chapter. Young poets want to join the community of poets, but of course it's another network. "That's all right, as long as everyone is clear. All you can do to a network is give to it; you can't expect it to give much of substance to you..." Still, networks are nourished by ideas from other networks. Communities, unlike networks, "are self-sustaining, like a long standing forest..."

His antiwar leadership (see Chapter 6) was important for fostering the literary network, both nationally and locally. As he writes: "Much of our so-called revolutionary poetry is written not for the community, but for a network of like-minded people. (The antiwar readings of the sixties involved, I think, about half community and half network.)" While he was cultivating the poets in their Minnesota network, he also encouraged them, especially those in smaller towns, to be part of their communities.

Then he draws an interesting contrast. "In South American political poetry—Neruda's is an example—the ground emotion is often love for the community. The ground emotion in North American political poetry is often hatred for the only real community the

---

18 This might be the place to recall that, when young Bly joined 4-H and F.F.A., he pledged himself to his community. See Chapter 1.

male or female poet knows, namely the ordinary people that surround his or her parents." Surely this schism—the divergent points of view on society, politics, and traditional values—had widened (then labeled the "generation gap") during the social and cultural upheaval of the 1960s. Whether or not we accept this understanding of "ground emotion," it speaks volumes when, as we shall see below, Bly himself and many other Minnesota poets began to focus not (only) on their own comfortable network, and the receptive audiences in the cities and in colleges and universities, but on small towns (sometimes their own), old people's homes, libraries, etc. This was gift-giving, sharing the wealth of poetry for the good of all, seeking to ameliorate the pains of division.

Bly next tells of the first time he "ever tried to bring back anything I had learned and offer it to the community." In the winter of 1972-73, he offered a five-lecture course for adults called "The Ideas of Freud and Jung and How They Apply to Life in Madison, Minnesota." Carol Bly writes that the course was "funny, charming, friendly, and very succinct."[19] She continues: "All thirty-five to forty people who came took part—laughing, telling things from their own lives, without frigidity or fear, because they grasped that psychology is simply a body of truth which we all take part in." Bly himself says they "were astonished at how helpful [Freud's] ideas [of the unconscious, the superego, ego, and id] were in understanding such things as rebellions in high school, aloof administrators, and marriages." He says they found Jung's ideas "even more helpful, even luminous."

Thus, "in a community what one species gives off, oxygen for example, another species needs." This again sounds very much like an ecosystem with its many reciprocal operations, essential for the continuance of life. Holm wrote about Bly: "I have heard him read in small Minnesota towns for farmers who thought Longfellow was

---

19 Carol Bly, 77.

a radical and an eastern snob. He read with tenderness and intelligence, giving them ideas, the gift of feeling, a sense of community. He gave them, damn it, love and brains!"[20]

Despite the differences in outlook, despite the vast gulf created by his education at Harvard College, a few years living the garret life in Manhattan, the Iowa Writer's Workshop, and his Fulbright year, Bly didn't feel himself above or better than those in and around Madison, Minnesota. He did not condescend or view them with contempt. He didn't wear a Harvard tie. After all, this was where he had grown up. This was his community. He knew so many of them personally, and many of them remembered him as a boy.

At the same time, neither did he subscribe or submit to the dominant social code, nor allow its insularity to hold him back from exercising his intellect, pursuing his interests, saying what he felt, doing what he intended to do, or being who he wanted to be. He plainly revered the place and its people, no matter the disagreements or the distance between their cares and concerns and his. He remained connected to family and friends. He—despite everything—enjoyed rural life in a place he loved. Regardless of the vast reach of his impact, and his endless comings and goings, Bly always knew that this was his place on this planet. He was grounded/rooted here.

* * *

Enter Poetry Outloud (again). When the caravan got to Madison, something happened that seems readymade for this book. And although Bly had been sowing seeds around the country and around the state for many years, this was new, as a journalist reports:

> Eighteen poets read for three hours; it was *the first time Bly had read his poems in his home town*. "They hadn't had rain for weeks," said Ms. Vogel, "so they

---

20   Holm, "Why I Live in Minneota," *Walking Swiftly*, 71

told us, 'If you bring rain, we'd love poetry forever.' And in the middle of the reading it got black and windy, and started raining, so they loved us."[21]

Bly and others apparently function as more than sowers—as rainmakers, too. It was as if they made the weather, presumably also providing the sunshine (!).

There were five poets on that tour—Vogel, Rezmerski, Jenkins, Cary Waterman, and Al Zolynas. Waterman says: "We were supposed to camp, but, fortunately, we were invited by sympathetic poetry lovers to stay in their homes."[22] Others participated when the troupe came to their hometown, as did Bly in Madison, Howard Mohr in Cottonwood, and Holm in Minneota. But their ranks often swelled further with locals who, with some encouragement, felt emboldened to read their own poems. "Bly introduced some of the townspeople who read, though it took considerable coaxing to get them to pull the poetry out of their back pockets."[23] As Carol Bly put it, referring to the same event: "When the…'Poets Outloud' turn up they arrive in town as seed poets only. In Madison, in fact, they were lucky to get a stanza in edgewise at their own scheduled reading."[24] These were transformative gifts on the move. The troupe stayed overnight with Carol, Robert, and family on their farm.

In ensuing seasons, the Smith Park Poetry Series designation fell away, leaving only Minnesota Poetry Outloud. It became almost strictly a summertime and mostly a rural thing, and Rezmerski took over.[25] Readings happened in parks, libraries, art centers, nursing

---

21   Italics are my emphasis. Quoted in Bob Lundegaard, "Wandering Poets Pursue Their Muse in Countryside," *Minneapolis StarTribune* (11 August 1974).

22   CW to MG, 26 April 2023.

23   Lundegaard.

24   Carol Bly, "If a Thing Is Worth Doing, It's Worth Doing Badly," 27.

25   He organized the tours and did the grant writing. New support came from the Southwest Minnesota Humanities and Arts Council (SWMHAC). There was, however, at least one city event: "The Best of Minnesota Poetry Outloud,"

homes, retirement communities, swimming pools, band shells, correctional institutions, churches, community centers, day care centers, with corn de-tasseling crews, "or any other place where people are interested in listening." In one sense it was a throwback. "The poets are dedicated to reviving the tradition of poetry as an oral art form. They take poetry out of the schools and into public places, to make it live again, for people to enjoy the way it was enjoyed a hundred years ago," Rezmerski wrote.

This again is what Bly had long been stressing. And it jibed perfectly with new programs like Poets in the Schools. "Poetry read out loud is a way of sharing the best of what we are with each other." It was one way of cementing community, and far beyond the Twin Cities. And it represented a rebirth, a return to the past of wandering bards and troubadours rather than a strange innovation. "Our immigrant grandparents had few conveniences and no luxuries. Yet

---

at the Walker Art Center, on November 15, 1975.

poetry was important in their lives and they found time to read it, to talk about it, and even to write it. They knew that poetry is not just a way to show off one's education, but that it can be part of daily life, a kind of entertainment available to everyone."[26] Like in those distant days before radio and television (not to mention the internet). As in Ezra Pound's statement: "poetry is news that stays news."[27]

Other poets joined those mentioned above, including Clayton, Hanson, Michael Harper, Chamberlain, Joe Paddock, Vinz, Knox, and Minczeski. Paddock, for one, has said: "For me, it was a life-changing experience."[28] Holm and Chamberlain coordinated the program for the 1976 season, when the itinerary included the towns of St. Peter, Mankato, Hendricks, Jackson, Luverne, Worthington, Adrian, Pipestone, Montevideo, Benson, Lake Benton, Cottonwood, Milan, Madison, Marshall, Minneota, Willmar, Olivia, Ortonville, Ashby, Hoffman, Alexandria, Glenwood, and Moorhead.

L. to R: John Rezmerski, Howard Mohr, Roger Conover, Bill Holm, Candyce Clayton, Marisha Chamberlain, Phebe Hanson, Roy Moore, Caroline Marshall, John Minczeski

---

26   Rezmerski in Minnesota Poetry Outloud: 2nd Season (1975).
27   So I admit to furthering this common misquotation. He actually wrote: "Literature is news that STAYS news," in *ABC of Reading* (Yale University Press, 1934), 15.
28   Paddock, *Infinity's Edge*, 86.

Holm and Marshall/Rasmussen oversaw the 1977 season. The poets became part of an old-fashioned road show, as from the days of the Chautauqua circuit, with poetry, of course, but also with music and even a little magic (other than the poetic kind) thrown in. Knox refers to the whole crew as "all the gifted and talented oddballs of Southwest Minnesota, Northern Iowa and South Dakota as well."[29] Holm encapsulated the reception of the tour—and its reverberations (not a little fancifully):

> Some sat in wheelchairs eating their napkins. Others clucked their tongues at Lutherans and Catholics or played foosball in the back bar while the traveling troupe laid on them poetry like a circuit rider laying on hands.
>
> Folks thought it was nice, but didn't understand why next winter roosters laid eggs, cattle organized a barnyard union, demanded Beethoven on the radio, no more Johnny Cash, snowbanks arranged themselves elegantly into nude women, didn't melt till after April. Maybe anarchists hiding in corners of old stars, they thought, never dreamt it could have been those nice young poets they invited into town.[30]

Holm also has given another appraisal of his time with Rezmerski:

> His favorite audiences are old people who have lost their fear of showing delight in the magic of language…and children who have not yet developed the fear. John and I have read together on the Poetry Outloud circuit for years, and I have watched faces of nursing home or elementary school audiences as ropes magically reconnect themselves, knots form in

---

29   WKC email to MG, 16 November 2021.
30   Bill Holm, "On Tour in Western Minnesota, the Poetry-Out-Loud Troupe Reads in Four Nursing Homes," *The Music of Failure* (Plains Press, 1985), 21.

mid-air, flowers sprout on the piano player's head. That burst of new life, that twinkle in the eye, was what poetry was always meant to give.[31]

Minczeski reminisces about a couple of the tours he was on:

> It was so much fun. We'd just travel around, go from town to town, usually staying in motels. Rezmerski had a Volkswagen Van, and we puttered around in that. We'd do parks, senior centers, old folks' homes, and sometimes bars. There was a bar in Olivia called The Sheep Shedde. It was packed with people. It was an event. People would show up with poems in their pockets, take them out and stand up and read them. Some of them had written songs… When Bill [Holm] was on the tour, he would play the piano, and once Nancy Paddock was along and we'd do "Now Sam McGee was from Tennessee" ["The Cremation of Sam McGee," by Robert Service]. We would kind of vamp and one of us would recite a poem. Once Bill brought along a book by Rolf Jacobsen that Bly had just translated.[32]

It seems that, in many of these "lost Swede towns" (Fitzgerald's partial misnomer) of western Minnesota, people were able, with some prodding and some uninhibited models, to break the overriding social restraints against feeling, enthusiasm, and the outward show of both. These tours did not succumb to "the pitfall of pasting culture onto the countryside," as Carol Bly put it, but invited participation in the infectious goofiness and joy.[33] They were, as Knox remembers, "the most amazing fun. We really bonded, and Bill [Holm] and the other people with homes and farms out there put us up and helped us get around and put our 'shows' together.

---

31 This in Holm's introduction to Rezmerski, *Growing Down* (Minnesota Writer's Publishing House, 1982), 1.
32 MG interview with JM, 10 July 2020.
33 Op. cit.

Excellent experience with all kinds of groups—what worked and what didn't, how to connect with people, get the message across."[34]

Bly himself said, in a 1975 interview:

> There's a strong hunger in the country for something besides television... These audiences are receptive to poetry. They are scared of poetry because they haven't heard it since their high school teacher gave it to them in a puritanical and hatred-filled voice. But if you read poems aloud, they find that they can bring their own experiences forward, and oftentimes considerable life appears in the room.
>
> This was Neruda's experience in Chile. He said to me, "I have visited every town in Chile many times. It's very exhausting, but we feel in South America that poetry belongs to everyone and I do this. It is my duty."[35]

That about sums it up. A pure and noble gift. And an additional reason for Bly's allegiance to Neruda.

Another effort was made in Southwest Minnesota to build on, it would seem, the early success of Poetry Outloud. *Voices,* an expanded newsletter from the Southwest Minnesota Arts and Humanities Council in Marshall (Polly Mann was a contributing editor), announced A New Chautauqua:

> For the first thirty years or so of this century a wonderful institution, called Tent Chautauqua, flourished in rural America. Great excitement was generated by

---

[34] WKC email to MG, 16 November 2021.

[35] "On the Lack of Thinking in the Left: An Interview with John Maillett and Elliot Rockler," in *Talking All Morning* (University of Michigan Press, 1980), 92-3. A slightly different version of the Neruda quotation is in "The Lamb and the Pine Cone (An interview with Pablo Neruda by Robert Bly)," in *Twenty Poems of Pablo Neruda,* tr. James Wright and Robert Bly (The Sixties Press, 1967), 105.

> the Chautauqua tent with its lecturers, theater, and music. The movement disappeared as we mistakenly came to believe that all truth, beauty, and the good life were to be found by emulating the urban-industrial centers. We now know better. Rural America has its own values; it is full of people who live creatively; each region, and Southwestern Minnesota is one, has its own character and untapped resources for self-education and improvement. So we suggest that our section of rural America create a New Chautauqua. We do not propose to "go to the cities" for talent. Instead, we hope that's through these pages those people and groups who wish to share their talent and ideas be made known to all who are interested.[36]

An excellent idea, it seems, and maybe, if it was even needed anymore, a declaration of independence from the Twin Cities' artistic hegemony. Alas, the endeavor did not succeed.

An alternate and another successful form of the same phenomenon of poetically engaging with communities beyond the Twin Cities, "outstate" in greater Minnesota, and beyond into bordering states, was the Plains Bookbus. This was an offshoot of the Plains Distribution Service in the Fargo-Moorhead area, itself an offshoot of the Plains Bookshop, which Joseph Richardson ran before he and poet, professor, and editor Mark Vinz co-founded PDS. The new project was launched in 1977, with support from the Dayton-Hudson Foundation, the Bush Foundation, and some from arts councils. Richardson also usually drove the bus, which the young, as yet unpublished writer Louise Erdrich, who then was working for him, described as "a fancy traveling RV stuffed with small press books."[37]

---

36   *Voices* (January 1975).
37   "Louise Erdrich, The Art of Fiction No. 208," interviewed by Lisa Halliday, *The Paris Review* 195 (Winter 2010)

As the brochure from the Plains Distribution Service said: "The Bookbus, stocked with over 160 book titles and more than forty magazines, brings a sampling of the flourishing non-commercial literary art of the Midwest to communities in Iowa, Minnesota, North Dakota, South Dakota and Wisconsin." A more detailed description from elsewhere is that it was carrying "material offered by the non-commercial, small press publishers throughout the Midwest," including "numerous books of poetry, fiction, non-fiction, essays, criticism, cooking, and photography," plus "pamphlets, chapbooks, broadsides, posters, and poem cards."

Further, that brochure stated: "The Bookbus can be a dramatic way to excite interest in midwestern writing and the presses and literary magazines who publish in the region. The bus can become the focus for a variety of activities. Communities are encouraged to arrange readings—either by local or visiting writers. PDS will work with community organizations as a 'booking agent' if necessary." It would pull into town for a couple of days, not unannounced. A specific example: On one occasion it also brought a poet, David Martinson of Moorhead, to "conduct a workshop at Vermilion Community College for college and area senior high school students, as well as work with elementary school students at JFK Elementary School in

Ely." In the evening he was slated to "give a poetry reading for the general public and students.... There will be no admission charge."[38]

All told, in the latter 1970s the Bookbus (its program coordinated by Vinz's wife, Betsy) sponsored close to 300 readings, lectures, and workshops around the five-state area. This is very admirable. It was one culmination of the arduous and unremitting process of sowing seeds and building community across the region, for everyone's benefit, for the common good. What follows in the next Chapter is a small representation of some of the many publications the Bookbus scattered.

---

38   *The Ely Echo* (March 5, 1979), 2.

Chapter 14
Small-Scale Farming (A Counterpoetics)

> Wherever new writing has flourished...small presses have appeared in writers' lofts and basements, in bookshops and back rooms. These new outlets were subsidized by writers, their friends and relatives, or by generous patrons of the arts who rarely expected or got any financial return.[1]

To reiterate: In 1958, a young poet from western Minnesota started sowing seeds, by issuing *The Fifties,* a little magazine. But Bly had actually envisioned his own small press before deciding on that.[2] In the decades following, with the rise of regional literary magazines (see Chapters 9 and 12)—sometimes hand-in-hand with them or as a next step—the small press movement arose in Minnesota (just as it had on the coasts). This phenomenon, establishing an alternative, counter to the conglomerate, was very much another sign of the times across the country.

---

  1 Sally Dennison, *(Alternative) Literary Publishing* (University of Iowa Press, 1984), 3. See also, more recently: Matvei Yankelevich, "'Power to the people's mimeo machine!' or the Politicization of Small Press Aesthetics, *Harriet Blog* (Poetry Foundation, February 3, 2020): https://www.poetryfoundation.org/harriet-books/2020/02/power-to-the-peoples-mimeo-machines-or-the-politicization-of-small-press-aesthetics
  2 Inspired, in part, by the inauguration of Lawrence Ferlinghetti's Pocket Poets Book series in 1956. See *Born Under*, 35-7.

Existing, at least at first, on the margins, the work of autonomous small press publishers was one more essential means that, by building and propping up a community of writers, enabled poets to flourish, and to spread the word further. Again, in the Upper Midwest context it was Bly who set the cardinal example, this time with his Sixties (and, later, Seventies) Press, turning out small books that had an outsized impact. The anti-institutional, anti-commercial aspect of the Sixties Press—very far from the center of American publishing—was obvious from its first publication in 1961, a short pamphlet, *A Broadsheet Against the New York Times Book Review*, which announced—for those who didn't yet know his magazine—Bly's presence as a fearless and pugnacious critic, a David taking on a Goliath.[3]

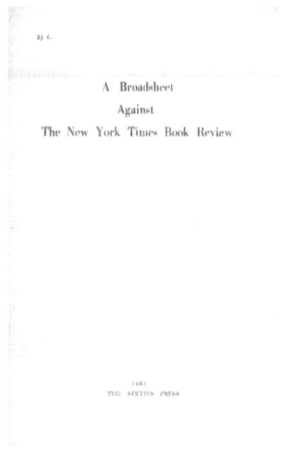

The much more important books that followed were translations, each presenting twenty poems of a poet who deserved more attention from North American poets, including Georg Trakl, César Vallejo, Blas de Otero, Pablo Neruda, Juan Ramón Jiménez, Tomas Tranströmer, Vicente Aleixandre, and Rolf Jacobsen.[4] And *The Sea and the Honeycomb* showcased short poems from around the world.

---

3   See *Born Under*, 101-2.
4   The one exception was Forty Poems of Juan Ramón Jiménez. (The poems

These were, plainly, primers or samplers, small packets of seeds that still packed a wallop.[5]

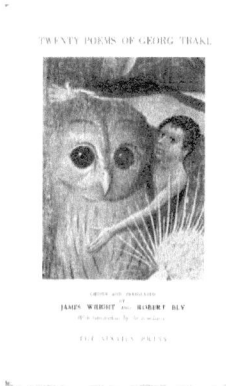  

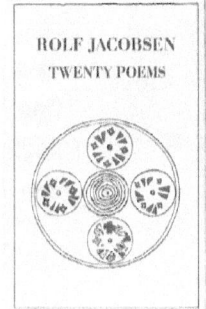   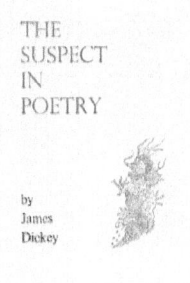

---

5   For details on all of these, and those following, see both my *The Odin House Harvest* and *Born Under*.

The Suspect in Poetry, a series of critical reviews by James Dickey, was in line with Bly's magazine's secondary but acute focus on criticism. Also, as seen in Chapter 4, *The Lion's Tail and Eyes*, a selection of American poems by Bly, Wright, and William Duffy, was meant to showcase the new poetics that Bly was pushing. Coincidentally, it was the only Sixties Press book that highlighted young regional poets—which is what most of the other presses mentioned below in this Chapter did, almost exclusively.

Bly also did some self-publishing in Madison, including *Issa: Ten Poems* (1969), a tiny collection of Bly's versions of Issa's haiku, handed out as a gift (see Chapter 1). Two other publications are germane here. The first, *A Poetry Reading Against the Vietnam War* (1966), a collection of poetry and prose pieces, was assembled by Bly and David Ray in order to provide reading material for antiwar readings across the country. It was published by the American Writers Against the Vietnam War (which the two poets had co-founded) and distributed by the Sixties Press (see Chapter 6).

The second was *The Teeth Mother Naked at Last* (1970), printed on one large sheet of paper folded five times to make twelve pages. This was Bly's most famous antiwar poem, and it too was published first by the American Writers Against the Vietnam War in association with the Sixties Press and with City Lights. This folder came with the prohibition: "Not to be sold. Printed as a gift to the Resistance by Robert Bly, and Lawrence Ferlinghetti for City Lights Books." Another pointedly uncommodified gift on the move.

THE
TEETH-MOTHER
NAKED AT LAST

by

ROBERT BLY

A book can change a life, or the world. Wojahn remembers *Twenty Poems of César Vallejo* (translated by Bly, John Knoepfle, and Wright): "Reading it was life-transforming, and I got interested in Bly's championing of translations of modern international poetry because of it."[6] Many other poets had similar experiences.

Although all Sixties Press books were aimed at a national audience, poets in and around Minnesota were reading them, too. Which is not to suggest they were an immediate, direct influence on the small press printers/editors in Minnesota. Rather, they were examples, originating locally, that pointed the way, showed the possibilities. It's also important to remember that Bly, like all of the small press publishers below, started as an amateur, taking what amounted to a political stance in resistance to the profit-driven publishing business. Following is an illustrated catalog of some of the more important local examples from the period.[7] It was a lively pageant that also opened the door for many women.

---

6   DW to MG, 19 July 2020.

7   Other small presses unmentioned here include Dakota Press (editor, John R. Milton), Juniper Press (ed., John Judson), The Kraken Press (ed., Mike Finley), Scopcraeft Press (ed., Antony Oldknow), Smith Park Press (ed., Caroline Vogel), Truck Press (ed., David Wilk), and Westerheim Press (eds., John Rezmerski and Tom Guttormsson).

The Minnesota Writers' Publishing House (MWPH)

A year after Bly's Seventies Press published his translation of *Twenty Poems of Tomas Tranströmer* (1970), he translated Tranströmer's new short book, *Mörkerseende* (as *Night Vision*).[8] It was originally published by the Författerförlaget, the Swedish Authors' Cooperative Publishing House, a collective begun in 1969, whose stated purpose was to "give the writers influence over publishing conditions of their work, oppose the centralization of power in the publishing world, and attack radically the habit of charging high prices for new work."[9]

Admittedly, the situation in Sweden was different: the number of publishing houses was severely limited, for one thing. Yet Bly, wanting to help validate young writers who were outside of the academy and unacknowledged by commercial publishers, noted similarities in the United States: "the price for new work is too high, houses like Atheneum and Farrar, Straus have a range of possibility so limited it is appalling, and they are not open to younger poets." He continued: "Most of the poets in [Minnesota] will probably have to wait six or seven years, at the present rate of book publishing, before they see their work in print." That could be terribly discouraging. Not only that, "bigger publishers also demand a full book... but a poet in his twenties may not have forty or fifty solid poems."

So, in latter 1972, in discussion with a few other poets, Bly made plans for a much smaller, Minnesota version of the Swedish

---

8   Lillabulero Press, 1971 (and an expanded version from London Magazine Editions in 1972).

9   Published as a separate flyer/press release, and in *North Country Anvil* 3 (December-January 1972/1973) and *The Lamp in the Spine* 6 (Spring 1973). The Swedes had been very intentional, establishing a Swedish Union of Authors, thoroughly laying out how contracts were to be handled, how writers were to be compensated, and also setting up a Writers' Center in Stockholm. See Jan Gehlin, *The Swedish Writer and His Rights* (The Swedish Institute: Stockholm, 1973).

model. This was to be of enormous importance for Minnesota, with many ramifications. Announcing their scheme, Bly wrote: "Fifteen years ago, there were only two or three poets working in Minnesota. The enthusiasm for poetry has increased...since then, and there are thirty to forty poets now in Minnesota alone doing work of high quality." He was looking back to 1957, after he had returned from Norway and just when he was planning in earnest to put together his magazine and start sowing.

As the preceding Chapters have indicated, in those fifteen years the Minnesota literary ecosystem, surely in terms of poetry, had roared to life and was blooming/booming like never before. All eleven issues of Bly's generative magazine had appeared, as had several books of his translations, and his own books, *Silence in the Snowy Fields* and *The Light Around the Body*. He had also spearheaded a poetry-based wing of the antiwar movement.

And, of course—and essential to this telling—he was still living in that red farmhouse just outside of Madison, Minnesota. Quite deliberately he had been going about building a network of poets, not only nationally but also statewide, and he was fostering the growth of other networks and communities by so doing. He had, in this regard, changed the world.

The poets who joined this new collective effort had grand ambitions for it—putting out a book a month, for example. They decided on a format: 1,000 copies, priced at $1.00 each, consisting of twenty poems. (Not by accident; twenty was the usual number in most of Bly's Sixties and Seventies Press books.) Each author would pay $300 to go toward the purchase of printing equipment, paper, and other supplies. That author would then receive a 10 percent royalty (i.e., $100 for the sale of all 1,000 copies). Subsequent reprintings, if any, would help recoup more of that initial investment. One might presume that all the writers were more realistic than to think they might actually come out ahead dollar-wise. The real point was to get their work printed, published, and into readers' hands.

They had bought a used 1250 Multilith press, a plate maker, a light table, staplers, folders, and paper. Tom Hennen, a young poet in Morris, was the printer as they got underway. The small offset press was installed in the basement of his family's house. Cinda, his wife, was enlisted to do the correspondence and distribution. Hennen recalls: "I…put the bunch of us to work. My wife kept order, and the two children assembled the books, with some help, and as long as they felt in the mood." [10]

At the outset, the plan was that Richter and Bitz would design the covers.[11] Bly said: "I am guiding the first ten books through the press, then those first ten poets will be in charge of putting the next ten through the press." That guidance included his editorial help, of course, as many of these poets acknowledge. And so on. In 1973 they began to publish. This was a big step forward. As Lyle Daggett wrote, remembering his first poetry writing class in 1970: "It might actually have been possible, then, to name all of the living poets in Minnesota who had published books, after just thinking about it for a few minutes."[12] All that was about to change.

First, *Raingatherer*, by Franklin Brainard (editor of *Plainsong*), was introduced by an excerpt of an interview conducted by poets Kincaid and Naiden (editor of *The North Stone Review*). Second was *The Well Digger's Wife* by Louis Jenkins, introduced by Dentinger (Jenkins' co-editor of *Steelhead*). We see a pattern of poets supporting one another in more ways than one. In 1974 Hennen's *The Heron with No Business Sense* was introduced by

---

    10   Tom Hennen, "A Thick Skin and a Job You Can Stand," in *Shining Rock Poetry Anthology & Book Review*: https://www.shiningrockpoetry.com/retrospective-essay-by-tom-hennen/ But soon, as Hennen had started a job with the Minnesota Department of Natural Resources, it became too much, as he says: "After printing the first few books I had to quit the printing business."

    11   Richter, in fact, did the first two, but no more.

    12   "Summer Ripening" http://aburningpatience.blogspot.com/2009/04/summer-ripening.html

Rezmerski, and Jenné Andrews' *In Pursuit of the Family*, had introductions by both Brainard and Hampl (co-editor of *The Lamp in the Spine*). It is noteworthy that these were the first books for all four of these poets.

Public readings, reviews in local magazines, and further publications naturally followed as careers were launched. The pattern continues. Bly supplied his own mini-introductions as lengthy blurbs on the back cover of each book. With his imprimatur, he was plainly throwing his not-inconsiderable weight behind these young poets, hoping to further their careers for the ecosystem's benefit. He carefully guided three further books—by Keith Gunderson, McGrath, and Cary Waterman—through the press. Waterman describes the process in her case: "I sent him twenty poems and he accepted ten for the chapbook and told me to write ten more. When the ms. was to his satisfaction he invited me to the farm in Madison where we went through the poems and he arranged them in the order he wanted."[13]

---

13   CW to MG, 26 April 2023.

 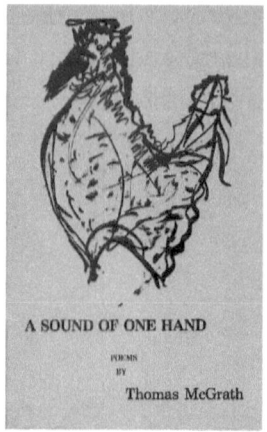 

Then, according to plan, he let others take over the editing. Eight more books followed, as the program gradually withered.[14] The grand vision, however, included more than forty (mostly) young poets.[15] Some of these, McGrath, Rakosi, Fred Manfred, Le Sueur, Vizenor, and Browne, were already established but could always benefit from more exposure. The others would sooner or later become fixtures in the Minnesota scene.

But Bly and these poets had more than just the physical fact of publication and the advancement of individual careers in mind. They intended to use the books to sow seeds among those of a more impressionable age. He said:

> We hope to be able to interest Minnesota high schools in extensive use of the books in class.

---

14 Books by Charles Waterman, Kate Green, Finley, Dentinger, Rezmerski, Dacey, Michael McKeon, and Caroline Marshall.

15 For the rest of the first ten, Bly had first named McBride, Kincaid, Michael Berryhill, and Bitz. The second group of ten, Bly suggested, could include Phil Dacey, Ray Smith, Pam Espeland, Joe Paddock, Caddy, Penelope Suess, Timothy Baland, Richard Waara, Vizenor, and Fred Manfred. A third group, he said, might be Judy Daniel, Rakosi, Don Olsen, Chet Corey, Keillor, Dentinger, Katherine Basham, Stephen Dunn, and Tjepkes. For a fourth group he named Le Sueur, Gunderson, Sarah Shaw, Elmer Suderman, Knox, Browne, Richard Shaw, William Elliott, John Daniel, and Sisson.

High school students, in our state at least, seem most astonished of all that poetry is written by people living in the Middle West, or "in the sticks," or in a small town, near them, or however they phrase the assumption that art is for someone else. If a high school chooses one of the books, there is a good chance also, that, the state not being very large, the poet himself could come to the school and read the poems and talk to the students. This integration of readings with a group of books is something we could offer that a New York publisher could not.

This fits with Holm's stupefaction, when he was in high school, at his initial encounter with Bly's poetry (see Chapter 4). And it fits especially with the mission of the Poets in the Schools program (see Chapter 15).

Nodin Press

Earlier, in 1964, White Earth Anishinaabe poet Gerald Vizenor founded Nodin (an Ojibwe word for "wind") Press in order to publish first his own poetry (starting with *Seventeen Chirps: Haiku in English*), and then traditional Ojibwe poems (*Summer in the Spring: Lyric Poems of the Ojibway*, 1965). In 1967, wanting to shed the burden, he sold the press to Norton Stillman.[16] Subsequent were two more collections of Vizenor's haikus in English (*Empty Swings*, and *Raising the Moon Vine*), plus in 1970, his gatherings of more traditional poetry (*Anishinabe Adisokan: Tales of the People*, and *Anishinabe Nagamon: Songs of the People*).

---

16 Stillman had in 1962 started The Bookmen, Inc., a book distribution business with his cousin Ned Waldman (both of them with the family name Bookman on their mothers' side).

In 1974, Nodin Press put out *25 Minnesota Poets*, an anthology of poems by those who had participated in the Poets in the Schools program (see Chapter 15).[17] A second volume of *25 Minnesota Poets* followed in 1977, pointing to the success of the first, included some of the same poets and several additions.[18] Both of these books obviously did the work of buttressing the poetic community in Minnesota. As Hasse, who was new to the Twin Cities, says, looking back: "I do not understand how I could so rapidly find the writing community in the time before the internet…" But for her, that first anthology was "a way for poets to become visible as a community not only to reader, but to themselves… I studied it and knew about all the writers even if they didn't know me."[19] Each was a directory of the players in the renaissance underway. Nodin Press has been steadily publishing poetry and books with a strong Minnesota connection ever since.

---

17   This is important enough that all should be named: Andrews, Michael Berryhill, Brainard, Breckenridge-Haldeman, Browne, Femi Fatoba, Jeanette Ferrary, Greenberg, Gunderson, Hampl, Hanson, Jenkins, Wallace Kennedy, Stanley Kiesel, Kirkpatrick, Randy Larsen, McBride, McGrath, Moore, Joe Paddock, Rezmerski, George Roberts, Vizenor, Vogel, and James L. White.

18   Additions included: Robert Bly, Cardona-Hine, Dacey, Kate Green, Stephanie Hallgren, Keith Harrison, Hasse, Karr, Knight, Sherry Noethe, Rakosi, Roston, and Cary Waterman.

19   MH email to MG, 10 May 2023.

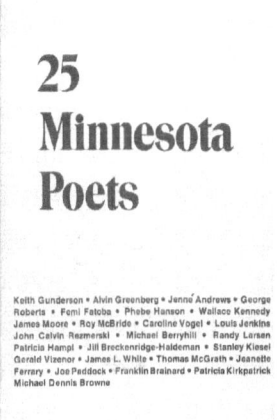

James D. Thueson, Publisher

A librarian at the University of Minnesota and the Minnesota Historical Society, Thueson began to publish poetry by friends and acquaintances in 1965, beginning with Ray Smith, *The Greening Tree,* followed by Frederick Manfred, *Winter Count* (1966). At that point he started putting out Franklin Brainard's little magazine, *Plainsong* (see Chapter 9). More books were from Richard Shaw and John R. Milton. In 1971, he published Freya Manfred's first book, *A Goldenrod Will Grow,* as the first number of a projected Plainsong Poetry Series. The magazine was now defunct, and the series seemed to end there.

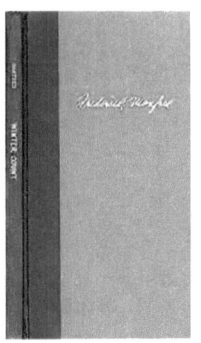

The Territorial Press

Of the local literary magazines that followed in the wake of Bly's, at least a few of them similarly gave rise to a small press. Starting in 1973, *Dacotah Territory*, under the Territorial Press imprint, produced a series of ten poetry chapbooks, all of them by poets living in the local Red River Valley area, thus distinguishing the press somewhat from the magazine's more wide-angle lens.[20] This "cottage industry" (as editor Vinz called it) was showing proud concern for the nearby community and its continued thriving poeticulture. As Michael Moos says of his *Hawk Hover*, number five in the series and his first book: "The publication of that book changed my life. I began taking the process of sending my poems out to other poetry magazines more seriously."[21] Exactly as the MWPH books were meant to function.

---

20 They included James Fawbush, Dale Jacobson, Richard Lyons, David Martinson, Michael Moos, Antony Oldknow, Mary Ann Pryor, Grayce Ray, David Solheim, and Robert Waldridge.

21 MM email to MG, 29 May 2024.

In 1974 Territorial Press also acknowledged its most important forebear by publishing a sizable sampler of fifty of Thomas McGrath's poems entitled *Voices from Beyond the Wall*.[22] And another important book was edited by James L. White in 1976, *The First Skin Around Me: Contemporary American Tribal Poetry*, including work by Leslie Silko, Simon Ortiz, Gerald Vizenor, Joy Harjo, Duane Niatum, and many others (see Chapter 8).

Knife River Press

Steelhead magazine from Duluth, a few years after Jenkins and Dentinger launched it (see Chapter 12), spawned an intermittent series of short chapbooks from the Knife River Press, named after the river and town on the near North Shore of Lake Superior. *The Hockey Poem*, a single prose poem by Bly, was first in 1974, followed by *Cabin Fever* by Jean Alice Jacobson (Jenkins' sister-in-law), and *Running Downhill* by Robert Damsten (Dentinger's friend from college). In 1975 came *Fox* by Browne. *Dreams of Bela Lugosi* by Rezmerski followed in 1977, and then, not surprisingly—given Bly's emphasis on translating—*Some Yellow Flowers: Translations from the Spanish*, by Mara and Ray Smith.[23] These poets were all friends or acquaintances of the publishers, and mostly living in Minnesota.

---

22   Plus, George Roberts, *The Blessing of Winter Rain* (1975) and James L. White, *The Del Rio Hotel* (1975).

23   Others included: *Occasional Uncles* by Timothy Dekin, *Smoke* by Kenneth Fields, and *John Ashbery Reads at the Guggenheim* by Matt Ward.

The Bear Cult Press

From the same region, another press spun off from the magazine *The Great Circumpolar Bear Cult* out of Ashland, Wisconsin. Its one publication was the anthology *Seven Lake Superior Poets* (1979), including the two editors, Rick Penn and Dave Kubach, Kate Basham, Jenkins, and Ray Smith.[24] As the editors remark, echoing themes noted earlier in this book, none of the poets were originally from the area: "They have come for their own reasons to the sort of place that ambitious poets fled, earlier in the century, in pursuit of the broader experience the Londons and New Yorks of their day were supposed to offer. ... And Lake Superior has always been hospitable to exotics." Successful, non-native transplants.

Ox Head Press

On a smaller scale than these last few, considering the physical product itself, but much more long-lived, Don Olsen (who in 1963 had written a Master's thesis for the University of Minnesota on Bly's Sixties Press) began his Ox Head Press in 1966 in Menomonie, Wisconsin. He soon became a librarian and part of the lively community of poets at Southwest State University in Marshall, Minnesota. The

---

24   As well as Lee Merrill and Peter Hoheisel.

bulk of his output in the succeeding decades consisted of small, artfully simple, hand-sewn booklets, often consisting of a single poem and always printed with the obsolete technology of letterpress, using movable metal type. In 1967 he began his run with Bly's *Ducks*, a "book" with only this two-line poem: "Two white ducks waddle past my door / Moving fast: They are needed somewhere!"[25]

Another was a translation of Miguel Hernandez's *El Amor Ascendia* by John Haines, a poet in Alaska pulled along by the magnetic force of his friend Bly's magazine. Other little books in the 1960s and 70s were by Bly (two more), Haines, and Donald Hall, co-translations with Bly of Machado, Neruda, and others. Also, Minnesota poets like Howard Mohr, Al Zolynas, Philip Dacey, Florence Dacey, Bart Sutter, Holm, and Olsen himself.[26] With obvious influence of the prominent parody and satire in *The Fifties/Sixties*, he printed a collection of poetic parodies, *Parodynthology*, including one of Bly, "Counting the Lower-Case Letters (by Robert Sly)."[27]

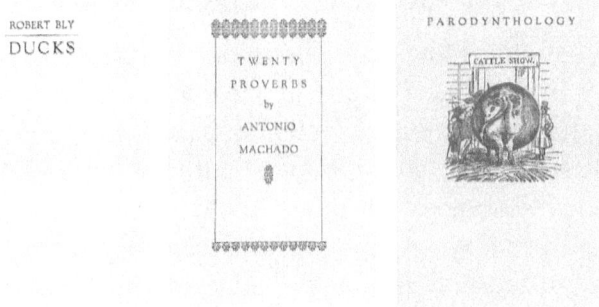

---

25   This book actually went through four editions over the next several years.

26   Many more followed in the 1980s and 90s. And Don Olsen was the primary printing mentor for poet, printer, and publisher Scott King's Red Dragonfly Press.

27   Another Bly parody by Olsen, "The Cowshit Poem," is quoted in Chapter 12. Olsen once told me in conversation that he, too, had considered starting a literary magazine. For more on Ox Head, see Don Olsen, *A Butterfly Sleeps on the Temple Bell: A Reminiscence on the Ox Head Press, 1966-2000* (Cross+Roads Press, 2003).

As Charles Waterman wrote in *The North Country Anvil*: "In a time when most things seem oversize and overdone, the small thing, like a seed, often harbors the most good. This must be the conscious or unconscious realization of Don Olsen, working with carefully handset type and printing these tiny pamphlets with a press, Bly told me, 'no bigger than a waffle iron.'"[28]

Prairie Gate Press

In 1971, as Tom Hennen (not yet involved with MWPH) says:

> I had time to help Jim Gremmels, an English teacher at the little college in Morris to set up a small letterpress in the basement of a campus building… I taught him what I knew about lead type printing, the most important being to keep your hand out of the press when its jaws were closing. Those old hand-fed platen presses had made more than one one-handed printer… Gremmels' printing setup became Prairie Gate Press, and went on to print and publish booklets and small books in limited editions and with the fine look and feel when you

---

28 Review, *NCA* 13 (October-November 1974), 97. Olsen began with a toy printing press on his kitchen table, but in 1967 switched to the (still small) Adana Horizontal Platen Press. The press name came upon learning that the origin of the letter "A" is the ancient Phoenician symbol for the ox. See: Don Olsen, *A Butterfly Sleeps on the Temple Bell: A Reminiscence on the Ox Head Press, 1966-2000* (Cross-Roads Press, 2009), 31-37, 15.

hold it in your hand that only letterpress printing can give.[29]

It seems impossible for Gremmels and Hennen not to have seen and been influenced by the nearby Ox Head Press, with at least a couple of these hand-sewn, letterpress books limited to 100 or 200 copies. *War Poems* consists of two short antiwar poems by Michael Larson and Dick Lee (1972). Next was a bigger book of twenty-four poems, *The Poet in the Next Bed* by Carol Morris (1974), a single poem, *The Fir,* by Bly (1975), *The Hole in the World is Real,* ten poems by Hennen (1976), and another single Bly poem, *Written at the Old Bridge Five Miles South of Morris* (1978).

Vanilla Press

In the mid-1970s the small press tempo really picked up in Minnesota, especially after the Loft (see Chapter 7) got going. Poet Jean-Marie Fisher, Vanilla Press founder and editor, first did the editing, art, and graphics for *Smiling Woman* 1, published by Women Poets of the Twin Cities.[30] Fisher formally started the Vanilla Press

---

29 Tom Hennen, "Thick Skin and a Job You Can Stand," https://www.shiningrockpoetry.com/retrospective-essay-by-tom-hennen/ Gremmels, an English professor and former basketball coach, was one of the original faculty members when the University of Minnesota, Morris, began in 1960.

30 With poems by Fisher, Andrews, Mary Pat Flandrick, and Penelope Suess. It may be debatable that this publication should be considered a little magazine.

in Minneapolis in 1975 with *Smiling Woman* 2.[31] For four years the press published mostly poetry, and mostly by women.

It began at the source, with a collection of Le Sueur's poems, *Rites of Ancient Ripening* (1975), its first "big" book, reprinted several times. The same year, Vanilla Press published an anthology, *Women Poets of the Twin Cities*, an important collection discussed elsewhere (see Chapter 11), with twenty contributors and a preface by Le Sueur. Other publications over these few years included: Wendy Knox, *A Message for the Recluse* (illustrated by Randall Scholes) (1975); Nancy Paddock, *A Dark Light* (1978); Martha Boesing, *Journeys Along the Matrix: Three Plays* (1978);[32] and two chapbooks by men, Thomas Dillon Redshaw, *Lost Bridge* (1976); and Mike Finley, *The Movie Under the Blindfold* (1978).

---

31   Poems by Fisher, Christine Anderson, Susan Hauser, Coco Weber, and Natasha (aka Katy Sheehy). The press name is misleading or overly modest with its connotation of blandness.

32   Boesing was founder of "At the Foot of the Mountain" in 1974, a women's theater collective in Minneapolis, and also an early teacher at the Loft. The book included her plays: "The Gelding," "River Journal" and "Love Song for an Amazon."

Even more importantly, possibly, Fisher also edited the playful, three-volume *A Coloring Book of Poetry for Adults* (1976/77). Subtitled "a sampler of contemporary poetry and art from the Minnesota-Dakotas region," each poem was accompanied by an illustration outlined in black on white, ready to be filled in with crayons or colored pencils. It turns out to be an almost-comprehensive anthology of both urban and rural poets in the area. That is to say, virtually *everyone* from the local scene is in here: Le Sueur, Bly, McGrath and ninety-six others.[33] Fisher wrote: "we hope that the three volumes of our *Coloring Book* will encourage others to look into the poets' and artists' work and, hence, lead to other opportunities for them." She adds, "little would please us more than to find that some of…the poets had been overwhelmed with offers for paid readings and guest poet-in-residence positions."

33 Prominent among the 39 illustrators are Bitz (who does the cover), Leon Hushcha, Gendron Jensen, Ellen Kennedy, Wendy Knox, McBride, Randall Scholes, and Scott Seekins.

Further, in this anthology the poetry and interpretive art are complimentary. "So well have the verbal and the visual merged that, at times, poet and artist seem to have traded spaces—the poet marking depth and breadth as the artist arrays anthropologic and philosophic clues to the mysteries of microcosm and macrocosm."[34] However turgid this expression, it is worth remembering that the melding of poetic and visual art had been inherent in the broadsides from Smith Park Poetry Series (see Chapter 10), and was what got the *Milkweed Chronicle* underway (Chapter 9) a few years later.[35] This time, although the principle was the same, it was done in a much more whimsical fashion.

Vanilla Press, Fisher said, intentionally operated on the "'low-profit'—the real no profit—principle." She described her publishing venture as "dedicated to restoring poetry as the common tongue, art as an everyday occurrence. Dedicated to you who will help it happen." This of course, with its eye on the future, echoes the primary focus of what this book has been about, the effort to spread the word, to get poetry to the people in general—where it belongs, where it had been in the past, or where it is in other cultures.

Red Studio Press

Another endeavor combining the visual and poetic was Red Studio Press in Loretto, a small town just beyond the outer ring suburbs west of Minneapolis. Susan Winter, a wealthy patron of the arts, oversaw operations. In 1975, *Dim Lake* appeared. It had poems and drawings by Bitz, drawings by Leon Hushcha, and poems by Sisson illustrated by Bitz. As noted elsewhere (see Chapter 11), the three of them had formed a collective that they called Fort Mango (which

---

34 This and following quotations from *A Coloring Book of Poetry for Adults,* vols. 1-3, ed. Jean-Marie Fisher (Vanilla Press, 1976-77).

35 This is not to mention Gregory Bitz, the artist and poet who had been combining his drawings and words from the beginning (starting in *Nickel & Dime Quarterly*—see Chapter 9).

had a fairly long life, primarily for visual artists). Browne's *Sun Exercises*, a sequence of poems, was published the next year. Annie Hayes, who had provided illustrations for *The Lamp in the Spine* and for some Smith Park Poetry Series broadsides, has drawings throughout.

Dim Lake **back cover**

And in 1977, two more books. First, *Flight,* a series of photographs (without words) by Richard Olsenius, a staff photographer for the *Minneapolis Tribune.* Second, Bitz's *carrots, as we all know, do not cast shadows.* Virtually indescribable, Charles Fowler gives it a shot in his introduction. "He leads us down the garden path, and beckons us slyly under shadowy ferns among mystical beetle tracks. No one is at home, and the woods are full of little people tinkering with tiny hammers. Branches creak. Choirs of weasels are singing.

A deaf rabbit strolls by. And while you stand there perplexed, Bitz is hiding in the bushes around the side of the house, dressed in an owl suit, chuckling all to himself." With Bitz's singular perspective, the poems are in his facsimile handwriting (as seen first in *Nickel & Dime Quarterly*) and illustrated by his own drawings.[36]

Rusoff Books

One of Marly Rusoff's interests, as her bookstore's stock displayed, was Jungian thought (see Chapter 7). She became friends with the post-Jungian psychotherapist Nor Hall, who had taught a course on "The Eternal Feminine" at nearby Marshall-University High School. Hall was living on the West Bank (and had just completed her PhD in Human Consciousness with Norman O. Brown at the University of California, Santa Cruz). Then she gave a public lecture at the College of St. Catherine in St. Paul in March 1976.[37] Rusoff attended

---

36 Already mentioned several times in this book, Bitz deserves more attention. Mike Finley, in *Poetic Justice – Reviews for the Unreviewed,* has characterized his poems, fables and drawings as "like Brueghel on acid." And Bitz himself as "the jewel. He seemed high, whether he was or not. I never heard him say a single normal thing. But he had style, humor, and a grim surrealistic truth flooding both his drawings and his writings. He was in combat in Vietnam and suffered an egregious bullet injury to his upper left arm…I dug him to bits."

Bitz had done a few earlier books in a similar fashion, including *Watch the Turtle* (Dean Gallery, Minneapolis, 1972) and *Parrot in the Wheat* (Milkweed Press, 1971), both small presses otherwise unknown. He acknowledges the help of Richter for the design of both books, and also Sisson for the first and Robin Raygor for the second. These forces (minus Raygor) had first been joined in Hyde's *Nickel & Dime Quarterly* (see Chapter 9).

37 Hall then participated in Bly's second annual Great Mother Conference—which Rusoff also attended—in northern Minnesota, along with Holm, Knight, and Coleman Barks. It also happens that Hall remembers the first time that Bly showed up at the Archetypal Psychology conference in Chicago in 1976. "I believe it was the moment when the seeds of the men's movement were first planted. Because he met James Hillman at that point, and began to get very involved in the psychology of the post-Jungian movement." From the video, "The Bat of Minerva: Memorial Reading for the *North Stone Review*, Published by James Naiden," https://www.youtube.com/watch?v=4AP1EAJ_34Q

and was so impressed she wanted to publish it. Thus came *Mothers and Daughters: Reflections on the Archetypal Feminine,* with illustrations by poet Ellen Kennedy, the first and only publication of Rusoff Books. So we see yet another way that an amateur's small press, however short-lived, came to be.

Holy Cow! Press

After Jim Perlman and Helge Schjotz-Christensen, co-editors of *Moons and Lion Tailes,* parted ways, Perlman started Holy Cow! Press in 1977, which, long based in Duluth, remains one of the four major independent literary presses in Minnesota and continues its emphasis on regional poetry. *Letters to Tomasito,* a chapbook of short poems by McGrath to his young son, was its first publication. The next year came *at the barre* by Candyce Clayton, a Macalester College graduate who had participated in Minnesota Poetry Outloud and worked for the Poets in the Schools program (see Chapters 13 and 15). Another familiar name, Jenné Andrews, writes the introduction. Of course, McGrath, Clayton, and Andrews had all contributed to Perlman's magazine.

 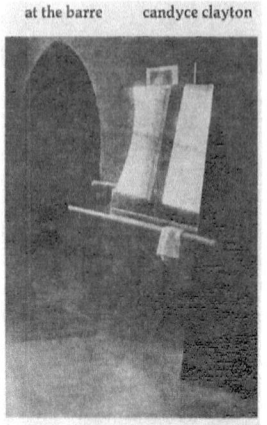 

The third book, *Brother Songs: A Male Anthology of Poetry* (1979), was edited by Perlman (with illustrations by Randall Scholes). In the preface he says he wants to "confront this notion of 'maleness' and how males relate to each other" through the medium of poetry written by living American male poets, poems "that shattered traditional ideas of the male image." The book was meant as a friendly response to the many feminist anthologies of that time, and Perlman hoped to show "That men can have strong, nurturing feelings for the men in their lives."[38] This was a bold move, and it also happens to mirror the direction in which Bly was heading. Bly had started the Great Mother Conference in 1975, examining matriarchy in depth, thinking about women and men. And he was at this time working on poems for *The Man in the Black Coat Turns* (1981), the first book in which he explicitly references his complicated relationship with his father.

Perlman's collection is divided into four parts, "Poems About Fathers," "Poems for Sons," "Poems About Brothers," and "Poems for Friends & Lovers." The first poem in the book is "Finding the Father," by Bly, joined later by his "For My Son Noah, Ten Years Old." Many of the nationally known poets in-

---

38   JP email to MG, 12 December 2020. We might also note that, coincidentally, *Dacotah Territory* 17 (1980) was an anthology titled "Fathers."

cluded were Bly's friends, and there were also many Minnesota poets represented, most of whom had appeared in *Moons and Lion Tailes.*[39]

Ally Press

Paul Feroe was one of the founding editors of a one-shot, student-run literary magazine at St. Olaf College, *Sucking-Stones*, in 1973.[40] That issue included the editors' interview with Bly (who had attended St. Olaf in 1946-47) after his appearance on campus in 1972 (my own first in-person exposure to Bly). Upon graduation, Feroe moved to Denver for a few years, where in 1974 he founded Ally Press, taking its name from Carlos Castañeda's representation of the ally—an incorporeal being, a spirit-helper. At first publishing small books of poems by Martin Booth, Norbert Krapf, Ted Kooser, and Susan Fromberg Schaeffer, plus Ronald Sampson's *The Anarchist Basis of Pacificism,* Feroe maintained the link he had already forged with Bly. He went on to bring out Bly's chapbooks, *Grass from Two Years* and *Let's Leave/Kabir* in 1975, *Kabir, Try to Live to See This!* in 1976, and *Rilke, The Voices* in 1977.

In 1978, Feroe, originally from the Mississippi River town of Lacrosse, Wisconsin, moved "home" upriver to St. Paul, first publishing an impressive anthology *Silent Voices: Recent American Poems on Nature*, including Bly, Philip Dacey, Wright, and many others.

---

39 Including: Browne, Cardona-Hine, Philip Dacey, McGrath, Minczeski,, Mladinic, Moore, Rakosi, Roberts, Charles Waterman, James L. White, and Wojahn. Soon the press moved to Iowa, and then Wisconsin, before settling in Duluth, Minnesota in 1988.

40 Someone had been reading Samuel Beckett's *Molloy.*

In the introduction he picks up on a facet of Bly's outlook already noted (see Chapter 8):

> Only 300 years ago settlers arrived with a cultural system that designated European man as the supreme life-force, a status he felt allowed him to ride rough-shod over the rights of the North American inhabitants. In only a few decades a fixation on economic and territorial growth destroyed the careful balance of nature worked out by previous cultures, and with it the sense of the sacredness of life cherished by the Indians.[41]

Ally's 1979 publication of Bly's translation of Antonio Machado's *I Never Wanted Fame* was letterpress-printed by Allan Kornblum of Toothpaste Press (who also had a little poetry magazine, *Dental Floss*) in West Branch, Iowa (near Iowa City). Kornblum would soon move to Minneapolis and establish his press, then renamed Coffee House, there. The illustration was by Scholes, an artist who had been making his mark in the Twin Cities (as noted above) and would soon, with Emilie Buchwald, found the *Milkweed Chronicle*. Feroe, who also worked briefly at Jim Sit-

---

41 Silent Voices: Recent American Poems on Nature, ed. Paul Feroe (Ally Press, 1978), xi.

ter's book distribution company, Bookslinger, was evidently on to something. Ally Press would be important to Bly and other Minnesota poets for years to come (becoming co-publisher of Bly's own Eighties and Nineties Press).

Finally, for the Loft's Leap Year celebration in 1980, Ally reprinted Bly's by-then famous and influential essay, "Leaping Poetry: Looking for Dragon Smoke," on an easily-pocketed sheet for attendees to take (see Chapter 7). And so, although his mantle had been passed to others, Bly was still scattering seeds, spreading the news, with a lot of help.

New Rivers Press

In the 1960s, C.W. (Bill) Truesdale, a professor and a poet, had been teaching English at Macalester College in St. Paul. When he left and started New Rivers Press in 1968 in Nyack, New York, first as a letterpress operation from a barn in western Massachusetts, intending to publish poetry, he knew where to turn for authors—to Minnesota, that is, where he, and others whom he knew, knew what was happening.

Nevertheless, he claims: "I had no idea what I was getting myself into. I didn't even know in the beginning that there were hundreds of other small presses and literary magazines being thrown together all over America at that time—that, indeed, a kind of renaissance was taking place in this country, a literary explosion that lasted well into the seventies."[42] He first published an anthology, *West of Ely,* including friends and colleagues from Minnesota who had visited his family cabin on Moccasin Lake, Charles Baxter, Alvin Greenberg, John Knoepfle, and others.[43] Soon came Macalester poet-professor Alvin Greenberg's first book, *The Metaphysical Giraffe*. Later, in 1970, the first book of poems by Charles

---

42   *The Talking of Hands,* eds. Robert Alexander, Mark Vinz, and C.W. Truesdale (New Rivers Press, 1998), 17.

43   Also Roger Blakely, Arthur Bradley, John Hiner, and Eric Stokes.

Baxter (then a student at Macalester, on his way to a brilliant literary and academic career), *Chameleon*.

Truesdale adds: "I did not start my own press for political reasons, even though most of the books I was to publish over the next dozen or so years had a strong political basis."[44] In the reflected light of what Bly had been doing with his magazine and press, New Rivers published translations, including *Neruda—The Early Poems* (1969) by David Ossman and Carlos B. Hagen, and translations of Swedish poets by Siv Cedering Fox, of Ivan Lalic (tr. Charles Simic and Truesdale), and of Lars Gustafsson (tr. Robin Fulton). Also, two books by John Knoepfle, a co-translator with Bly and Wright of *Twenty Poems of Cesar Vallejo* (Sixties Press, 1962).[45] These were accompanied by very many other books by an eclectic array of writers.

West of Ely on the left, *Neruda—The Early Poems* next to it

In 1978, near the end of our period, Truesdale moved the press to St. Paul. A decade after New Rivers had begun, now the literary scene was only livelier, of course. Turning his attention back to

---

44   Such as Margaret Randall, *So Many Rooms Has a House but One Roof* (1968), poems out of her visit to Cuba in 1967. She would teach at Macalester, briefly, many years later.

45   Bly's own poetry appeared in two anthologies, *The Sensuous President, by "K"* (including poems by Baxter, Greenberg, Truesdale, Browne, Olsen, and Philip Dacey), and *Toward Winter: Poems for the Last Decade* (James Wright, Baxter, Greenberg, David Ray, et al.).

Minnesotans, in 1979 he published Minczeski's *The Spiders,* illustrated by Alvaro Cardona-Hine. And anthologies of modern Italian and Catalan poetry in translation. Importantly, in 1980 he initiated the Minnesota Voices Project, a competition for first-time publication for new and emerging local poets. This was a great assist to many careers in subsequent years.[46] In 1982, he filed for 501(c)(3) non-profit status, setting a precedent for the several independent presses soon to follow.[47]

* * *

Obviously, from the above accounting, by 1980 the small press movement was well underway, setting the stage for the three independent, non-profit, literary presses in Minneapolis, all still with us and flourishing. Scott Walker, founder of Graywolf Press in Port Townsend, Washington, which began by printing hand-sewn letterpress chapbooks, has tried to explain why he moved his press here in 1985: "This is a very literate, artful, welcoming town." And "This is a city, but it had that small town neighborliness that made it special to me." Fiona McCrae, who became Graywolf's long time director and publisher in 1994, says: "There's an understanding that what we do is important." There is also "a culture of experiment, and risk-taking."[48] There was, in other words, a complex root system already in place, connecting all the outward manifestations of literary culture. As Rulon-Miller says about the early 1980s: "it seemed to me…as if it were one, big extended family, each one's work somehow a part of what the others were doing.

---

46   Madelon Sprengnether, Deborah Keenan, Ruth Roston, Vinz, Chamberlain, Hasse, and DeGrazia were early winners. In a way, this was picking up where the Minnesota Writers' Publishing House had left off.

47   The press flourished at its new home in Moorhead until 2022. Now on (permanent?) hiatus.

48   Both in the video, "Graywolf Press: A World of Voices," (University of Minnesota Libraries, November 12, 2015), https://www.youtube.com/watch?v=d_st871c0rM

None was competing. Everyone shared."[49] Amen to that. And none of this had happened by accident.

In this next period, 1980-2000, what we in retrospect might label the "high" phase of Minnesota's literary renaissance, the key players (the three presses below) and the Minnesota Center for Book Arts would all occasionally give attention to Bly and to many other poets he had directly influenced, at least tacitly acknowledging the one who had set the foundation on which they were building in turn. Toothpaste Press (not yet Coffee House and not yet in Minnesota) in 1980 published Bly's Machado translations, *Canciones* in letterpress (a year after Kornblum had printed Machado/Bly, *I Never Wanted Fame* for Ally Press). In 1982 Scott Walker's Graywolf Press published a letterpress edition of more of Bly's translations of Machado, *Times Alone*. (Graywolf would soon move to Minneapolis, having gained nonprofit status.) We have seen Emilie Buchwald's early awareness of Bly, though his first publication with Milkweed Editions was his translation of Olav H. Hauge's Norwegian poems in 1987, *Trusting Your Life to Water and Eternity*, after a Neruda translation and an essay in the *Milkweed Chronicle* (1986). These facts are incidental, and just beyond our time frame, so raising them may at first seem gratuitous. But they are one more sign of Bly's ubiquity and elementary role in the larger picture of the ever-growing ecosystem.

---

49   Rob Rulon-Miller, *Quarter to Midnight: Gaylord Schanilec & Midnight Paper Sales: A Discursive Bibliography* (Rulon-Miller Books, 2011), 1-4.

Chapter 15
Spreading the Word Farther & Wider

Poetry in Minnesota, stimulated by poets and by publications of this sort, is finding receptive audiences. The intense interest in poetry in this state is evident...[1]
  –Seymour Yenser

In this book's grand view, beyond public readings, various literary organizations, regional literary magazines, and small press publications, a fifth means of pressing on with the process of sowing seeds and building community—and perhaps the most obvious, basic, and enduring of all—is through education. Not education in its looser, more general sense, but specifically as schooling, as teaching and learning in a classroom/institutional setting. Certainly, this often happened in tandem with poetry readings at colleges and universities—the poet, usually well-established (i.e., published) would also visit a class, run a workshop, meet with students individually, give a talk on the craft of poetry, or sometimes all of the above. Such practice became more common as more schools instituted creative writing programs.

But there was another, bigger audience, and one surely more malleable—high school and even elementary school students. They

---

[1] In the preface to *25 Minnesota Poets #2* (Nodin Press, 1977).

could be reached in two ways: 1) by approaching them directly and trying to inculcate a love of or at least an openness to and awareness of poetry, even enabling them to write it themselves, thereby demystifying it; 2) by enlisting their teachers to make poetry less inaccessible and forbidding, more interesting and relevant to their students in the world and times in which they were living.

Bly, to say it again, was a poet on the side of the future. The seriousness with which he took education in poetry was made loud and clear and often. As with all of his concerns, we discover that this was not a matter originally limited to Minnesota. In November 1966, he was invited to the annual meeting of the National Council of Teachers of English in Houston, Texas, with some 6,000 teachers in attendance. The published account of what happened there begins this way:

> Robert Bly, it was, who lunged from his place in the front row among the dozen gathered poets, turned to the NCTE audience at the 1966 Convention, and—quite expectedly—blew the top off...
>
> Richard Eberhart as main convener and speaker for current American poets had just finished his opening lecture... The general drift had been that poetry draws on the wellsprings of life and that we should all accommodate to various kinds of poetry and be happy to bring students into such a rich heritage.
>
> "Not at all!"—from the front row. And—alive and kicking—the assembled ingredients went critical. Robert Bly did not accept easily some kinds of poetry. Further, he contended that poets and all others present should never blur immediate first issues that their society faced—namely, for the American people, the war in Viet Nam.
>
> It was not the usual convention that followed.[2]

---

2   William E. Stafford, "A Poetry Happening," *English Journal* 56.7 (October 1967), 951-2.

Bly was there with fellow poets Stafford, Merwin, Hall, Creeley, and Snyder. He had spent much of that year involved with a group he co-founded, American Writers Against the Vietnam War, sometimes including these five, as they took their antiwar message to colleges and universities (see Chapter 6). He was not about to accede to the view that high school students should somehow be protected from poetry that took contemporaneity, present-day realities into account.

In early 1968, a federal grant from the Academy of American Poets through the National Endowment for the Arts and Humanities brought nine major poets to Minneapolis to give Saturday workshops for high school teachers of poetry. The nine were Galway Kinnell, Donald Hall, Louis Simpson, Denise Levertov, W.D. Snodgrass, May Swenson, and three residents of Minnesota, Tate, Berryman, and Bly. (Bly was especially close to the first four.) These sessions were held at the Bell Museum of Natural History on the University of Minnesota campus, moderated by Roland Flint from the English Department and John Caddy, an instructor at Marshall-University High School in Dinkytown.

Speaking to a local news reporter, Bly indicated that he had been involved with a similar project in 1967 in Detroit. There he learned that "the students were more interested in us as poets than in hearing poems. They were extremely surprised to find out that we were not all living in castles—that we had problems, money problems, women problems, that we were like them. In high school the assumption is that the poet is like Shelley, infinitely far away."

He shifts his (typically—for the day—male-centered) concerns from students to teachers:

> It's my opinion that the teaching of poetry in high school is going to be drastically revised. Perhaps one year in which the classics of English and American poetry are taught, if they want to teach the high school students some Shakespeare, Milton and Keats. But

> the main study should be of modern poetry: Ferlinghetti, Ginsberg, Galway Kinnell. What we're trying to do is read poems to high school teachers in such a way that they'll understand that for the poet the poem is not an intellectual exercise but an attempt to talk about things about which he feels passionately and deeply. Poetry cannot be taught as you teach airplane mechanics.[3]

But the most important and remarkable part of the program in Minnesota was not the star power of well-known poets from elsewhere. Rather, it was the enthusiasm and approachability of young Minnesotan poets who would visit junior and senior high classrooms to hold readings and discussions—over 100 visits in all, sometimes returning to the same groups two or three times, and including a select few elementary schools. The poets involved include Keillor, Gunderson, Caddy, Flint, Richard Shaw, Peter Welter, and June Meyer.

A year later (and what a year!—with the Tet offensive in Vietnam, the assassinations of Martin Luther King., Jr. and Robert Kennedy, the demonstrations, the "police riot" and bloodshed at the Democratic National Convention in Chicago, and the election of Richard Nixon as President), the program was put on again. Ginsberg participated, speaking on "The Beat Poets and Their Appeal to Students." Raymond Patterson spoke on "Black Poets and Poetry." Bly spoke on "The Poet as Social Commentator." Other poets from elsewhere included Kenneth Koch, Hall, Creeley, Simpson, and David Ignatow. (Bly and his contemporaries/friends were heavily represented here; Tate and Berryman and their generation not at all.) They visited school classrooms at Marshall-University High School. Again, Keillor, Gunderson, Caddy, Shaw, Welter visited other schools throughout the district, as did Tjepkes (who came to mine).

Bly's involvement in such educational efforts was not merely concentrated in a narrow time frame of a year or two; this was an on-

---

3   Bob Lundegaard, *Minneapolis Star* (January 9, 1968).

going concern. For example, in 1972, he and McGrath were judges for a poetry contest including all the high schools in Fargo, North Dakota. Gaylord Schanilec came in second place for "Ragweed Mourning," an important early validation that put him on his own singular road as poet and then artist, engraver, printmaker, book illustrator, and printer extraordinaire beginning in the late 1970s. (Now for several decades he has been a key part of Minnesota's literary ecosystem.[4]) Also, in 1973 Bly participated in a Minnesota Forum on KSJN-FM radio entitled "The State of English," a special report on another meeting of the National Council of Teachers of English, along with Margaret Mead, Jonathan Kozol, and Murray Kempton.

Being future-oriented necessarily meant focusing attention on young people. This was fresh, fertile ground. At the same time, from one poet's viewpoint, in the latter 1960s and early 70s, the poetry scene was "unraveling, as rock songs displaced poems as soul food for young hearts and minds."[5] Maybe true up to a point, but Bly's focus on getting contemporary poetry to young people, relevant to their lives, was hardly immaterial or ineffective. It was another way of feeding their souls, furthering the growth of poetry, and expanding their ability to appreciate it.

PITS

Simultaneous with all of the above was a most consequential related development. In 1966, the Poetry-in-the-Schools program (PITS), a pilot effort from the National Endowment for the Arts, began under the broad direction of Leonard Randolph, the director of Literature Programs for the NEA. As he put it, the program:

---

4 Primarily, in the end, via the magnificent work in his own Midnight Paper Sales Press. See Rulon-Miller, *Quarter to Midnight, passim.*

5 Peter Schjeldahl, "The Art of Dying," *The New Yorker* (December 23, 2019). Schjeldahl, once a Minnesotan and a student at Carleton College, was included among the second generation of the New York School poets—long before becoming art critic for the *New Yorker*.

is a return to the most fundamental elements of learning. It attempts to inspire children to write out of their own experience, to seek their own imaginations and, through this process, to encourage them to appreciate the writing of others. Most of the work with students is done on a nearly one-to-one basis... In rather remarkable and successful ways, it is nearly a re-creation of the one-room school some of us remember from the past.[6]

Another throwback, one of so many in this book, and thus part of the wider rebirth.

Minnesota PITS began in 1967 in Minneapolis, under the direction of Molly LaBerge. It was a stunning success and became a model for the rest of the country. By 1973 it involved fifty schools all over the state, reaching over 50,000 elementary and secondary school students. That year there were four poets-in-residence at work in the state, and thirteen other poets who participated part-time. By exposing children and youth to contemporary poetry and encouraging them to express themselves in their own words, the hope was that they would become aware of the possibilities of language. This was something done for the common good, not to make poets out of everyone. As Randolph said, this was a "return" to fundamentals. Positive effects were noted on students, even "unteachable" ones, in terms of increased confidence in general, leading to higher interest in all areas of learning. This was sowing seeds at its radical best.

But it was also "work" involving remuneration for the poets, thus putting food on the table and enabling them to go about their important unremunerative "labor" of writing poetry.[7] Initially, the poets, including Keillor and James L. White, were all men. Margaret Hasse and Kate Green were the first two women hired to teach for PITS. Their mentor

---

6   *American Poetry Review* (May/June 1974), 61. Bly, for one, surely remembered his own one-room schoolhouse experience.

7   I owe this distinction to Lewis Hyde, *The Gift,* 50.

was "master teacher" John Caddy, who taught them how to teach, how to bring poetry to the classroom.[8] Andrews writes of her work in the St. Paul Public Schools: "It involved going into schools three weeks a month and getting kids worked up about language, with one week off to write. I got this job and my contract was renewed for four years."[9]

Different arms of the literary community lent their support to the ongoing enterprise. In 1974, Nodin Press published *25 Minnesota Poets*, an anthology of poets who had participated in the program (see Chapter 13). Another non-financial benefit for participants—in the form of publication—came in 1975, when the entire issue of *Dacotah Territory* 11 was a "Minnesota Poets in the Schools Anthology," edited by Vinz with help from Moore, Rezmerski, and White. That issue was also distributed to schools throughout the state. And a second volume of *25 Minnesota Poets* followed in 1977, bringing more recognition, with some repeat appearances and many new additions.

DACOTAH TERRITORY 11
SPECIAL ISSUE: MINNESOTA POETS IN THE SCHOOLS ANTHOLOGY

8　So Hasse says in the video made of the November 2016 memorial reading for the North Stone Review and James Naiden. https://www.youtube.com/watch?v=4AP1EAJ_34Q&t=133s Also, MH email to MG, 9 May 2023. Fuller appreciation of Caddy can be found in *John Caddy: 2012 Distinguished Artist* (McKnight Foundation, 2012).

9　Jenné Andrews, "Loquaciously Yours, Memoir and Ruminations: Time and the Poet," https://loquaciouslyyours.com/2010/03/22/time-and-the-poet/

COMPAS

In 1974, the PITS program incorporated and was renamed Community Programs in the Arts (COMPAS), though still run by Molly LaBerge, moving beyond poetry alone to include theater, music, drama, and visual art. (This move shows the sway of the success of Wallace Kennedy's Urban Arts Program [1970-78] in the Minneapolis Public Schools, a pioneering initiative that linked high school students with mentors, including Hasse, who were professional artists, actors, and musicians.) There were workshops in studios, in theaters, in concert halls, and museums. It, too, soon became a national model. COMPAS quickly expanded and took a giant step—moving beyond schools and young people to those on the margins, the incarcerated, the elderly, persons with disabilities, and the neurodivergent. New support was found as well.[10]

Arts in Corrections

Before working for COMPAS, Margaret Hasse taught writing workshops, functioning as a "circuit rider" between Stillwater Prison, St. Cloud State Reformatory, the Lino Lakes Detention Center, and Sauk Center Home School (for teenagers, and where Bill Meissner also taught). This was through a new federally funded Arts in Corrections program. She writes that the classes could be "very intense. Much more than three hours' worth of insight, challenge, intelligent response, communication, poetry, feeling, conversation went in and came out of the sessions." She adds, in solidarity with the prisoners: "We needed the language of symbols and emotion to experience our

---

[10] The program still lives: "Today - Our artist roster boasts 100+ professional musicians, visual artists, performers, writers and the like. COMPAS has become an experienced innovator in the field of creative, art-filled learning for people of all ages, and has been recognized for excellence from organizations such as the National Endowment for the Arts, the President's Committee on the Arts and Humanities, and the Minnesota Department of Education." In 2009, COMPAS merged with Young Audiences of MN. https://www.compas.org/mission

reactions to the prison scene and to the people who had gotten hurt because of our past acts."[11]

She also got Roy McBride, whom she had met at a reading, involved: "He wanted the experience of teaching in prison, so I applied for a visitor's pass for him to come to my class at Stillwater."[12] She recalls:

> One of the years…the administrator, a woman named Merle Minda, helped organize a reading in the prison with the students in my writing workshop and local poets. Michael Dennis Browne was there, and… Franklin Brainard… We sat in a large circle and went around, like an AA meeting; each poet—both prisoners and from the outside—read a poem.[13]

This is remarkable, a clear precursor to the current Minnesota Prison Writing Workshop, founded in 2011, "now the largest and most enduring prison-based literary organization in the country."[14]

* * *

Beyond the benefits of all these opportunities for the student/participants were the practical benefits for the poet/teachers. This was, as Patricia Hampl has put it, "the golden age of arts support for the virtually unpublished! …these COMPAS gigs were lifesavers. I worked for Poets in the Schools…and did some freelance editing and teaching. Some COMPAS jobs: I had a poetry class for the elderly at the St. Paul Jewish Community Center, and worked for several years there, then at Little Sisters of the Poor, the Sholom Home, the Presbyterian Home. These jobs kept the wolf from the door."[15]

---

11 Margaret Hasse, "Passing Time and Making Time," *Sez* 1 (Winter 1978), 2-3.
12 MH email to MG, 9 May 2023.
13 MH email to MG, 10 May 2023.
14 https://mnprisonwriting.org/
15 PH email to MG, 19 February 2020.

Here also is John Minczeski's summation of his experiences working to allow the continuance of his poetic labors:

> Poets in the Schools residencies lasted a week, I had occasional longer terms at schools through the Minnesota State Arts Board's Arts in the Schools program, and in some freelance situations. I began teaching at the youth correctional facility at Lino Lakes through New Focus: Arts in Corrections, a COMPAS program. I visited Home of the Good Shepherd, a kind of halfway house for young women once a week, sponsored by the Ramsey County Extension of the U of M, part of its inner city 4-H programming.[16]

As one physical manifestation, a wealth of anthologies came from the various communities served by these programs: *Poetry is a Lady* (1975), by inmates at the State Reformatory for Men at St. Cloud (illustrations by Ta-Coumba T. Aiken); *Writings from the COMPAS Artists and the Aging Project* (1976), Hampl at the Jewish Community Center in St. Paul, and Jim Moore at the Minnesota Veteran's Home in Minneapolis; *The Joy of Memory or The Pig in the Garden: Writings from Wilder West* (1977), Bill Holm's work with residents at a nursing home in St. Paul; *See My Message and Come Home* (1978), Hasse with elementary and high school students.

Another anthology was the long-running *Angwamas Minosewag Anishinabeg (Time of the Indian)* (1979).[17] In the foreword to this, the ninth issue, David Martinson (as "Writer-in-Residence

---

16   MG interview with JM, 25 June 2020. He did more than education work, as he adds: "Making a living as a poet for me involved a lot of part time jobs—I was an early adopter of the gig economy. … I also worked in the want ads department of The Pioneer Press, did typesetting at Vanilla Press, in the attic of Jean-Marie Fisher's home, on a Compu-Graphic machine. Several years later I acquired a used AM Varityper machine and set type for New Rivers Press and other small publishers." His typesetting service was called Peregrine Cold Type.

17   See Chapter 8 for an earlier issue edited by James L. White.

for the Minnesota Chippewa Tribe"), part of the Fargo-Moorhead poetry contingent, reflects on his work with youth: "Everywhere I worked there were people who opened their homes to me, fed me and made me welcome. Oftentimes my work took me to places at the literal end of the road. Throughout the year I learned anew that poetry is community. And the writers, you have given what is real. Like the water birds you dive and fly and swim. Your poems have made me over and I am stronger because of them." Nicely put, and we note also that the layout of the book was designed by Gaylord Schanilec, and "produced" by Hasse. Beyond the edification of the classes and their experience of writing poetry, it's not hard to imagine the thrill, the sense of accomplishment, and the confidence boost for many of the participants in seeing their own poems and names in print for the first time.[18]

---

18 Others include *Friend to Deep Water* (1977), Jenné Andrews and elementary school kids, and *A Box of Night Mirrors* (1980), Caddy and more student writing.

One outgrowth of this slate of community programs was the weekly writing workshops at NorHaven, "a private, community-based residence for mentally retarded adults in St. Paul" (so described in the terminology of the time). Marisha Chamberlain edited *Shout, Applaud*, a collection of the participants' poems, for COMPAS in 1976. Mary Karr, and Mary Logue (who also worked with PITS and COMPAS) led more workshops with thirty-one NorHaven women, and Logue edited the anthology to come out of that, *Thief of Sadness* (PLS Press, 1979). The Norhaven Poetry Collective also staged a public reading at the Court House in downtown St. Paul.

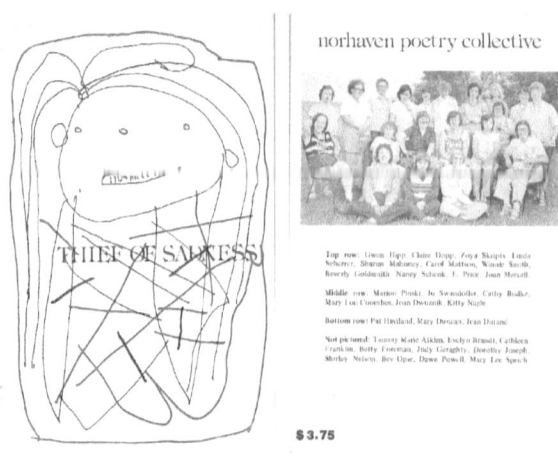

Similar things were happening elsewhere around the state. For example, in 1976 Joe and Nancy Paddock edited *Something to Remind Us,* made up of poems by people in the town of Olivia, Minnesota. Administered by COMPAS in St. Paul, it was funded by the NEA, the Minnesota State Arts Council, and the Southwest Minnesota Arts and Humanities Council. They continued as poets in residence for the region, comprising many small towns, until 1978. (See Chapter 13)

Many poets did make enough money to make ends meet and to keep writing. It was especially good when those jobs involved planting in receptive but otherwise easily overlooked soil. Who knows how many lives were changed for the better? As Knox said of McBride: "He was with Poetry-in-the-Schools for years and influenced a LOT of young people and writers of all kinds."[19] Moos gives a testimonial:

> I essentially made a living doing Poetry residencies in schools, community centers, libraries, etc., for about ten years. It was hard work, but so very rewarding. It was in this venue that I learned to teach. Poetry had changed my life, and it became my mission to take that love of poetry as a way to express myself, a way to survive, a way to understand to young students, adults, and the elderly.[20]

Finally, the words of Lynn Lohr, Director of Programming for COMPAS: "Poets in the Schools is a process marked by energy—the energy of the poet who is teaching from the heart of his or her life, the energy of the teacher who seeks the experience for students because of a belief in the power of language, the energy of the students liberated to see that words are accessible, and a way in and out of the lonely places of the spirit."[21] This, ultimately, regardless of the age, circumstances, or identity of the student, is the gift of sowing seeds.

19　WKC email to MG, 16 November 2021.
20　MM email to MG, 29 May 2024.
21　Lynn Lohr, "Introduction," in *See My Message and Come Home*, edited by Margaret Hasse (COMPAS 1978),

Postscript

Fast forward to the present. Suffice it to say, literary life in Minnesota is still flourishing. It has continued to change, to grow, to generate, to fructify, to diversify. We are now well past the "early" renaissance (the subject of this book) and even past the so-called "high" renaissance (laid out in the preface), now solidly grounded in what we can guess might eventually be called the long "late" phase of the still ongoing renaissance. As this book has shown, that process of rebirth began more than six decades ago, not by accident. There was a vision at the start, although hazy. While the precise outline was, of course, unknown and unknowable, it was by no means unconcerned with future developments or oblivious to the possibilities.

Poetry and poeticulture together formed the basis at the start of the Minnesota literary revival. Even as literary life around here has developed and expanded to include all genres of writing, poetry remains at its heart. And while so much has changed, much has stayed the same. Therefore, I think it cogent to let a single poem do the work of wrapping up (not encapsulating) this literary history; an example, chosen not at all randomly, but deliberately, just one out of a vast array of possible choices. And a poem of place, as that, too, is where this history began.

Consider "i'm going back to Minnesota where sadness makes sense" by Danez Smith, from their book *Homie* (winner of the Minnesota Book Award for poetry in 2021):

> o California, don't you know the sun is only a god
> if you learn to starve for her? i'm over the ocean
>
> i stood at its lip, dressed in down, praying for snow.
> i know i'm strange, too much light makes me nervous
>
> at least in this land where the trees always bear green.
> i know something that doesn't die can't be beautiful.
>
> have you ever stood on a frozen lake, California?
> the sun above you, the snow & stalled sea—a field| of mirror
>
> all demanding to be the sun, everything around you
> is light & it's gorgeous & if you stay too long it will kill you.
>
> it's so sad, you know? you're the only warm thing for miles
> the only thing that can't shine.

So much has stayed the same. Amazingly, here we are, still in the snowy fields, but in an entirely new way. This poem, with its clear-eyed, honest focus on place, encompasses the outer world and the inward one. Smith, standing on a frozen lake, imparts the experience of an epiphany. Elegiac in mood—reflecting on mortality and the consolation of beauty, acknowledging and accepting our impermanence, and embracing solitude/silence. All the while the poet finds comfort in the seasons and especially in the ice, snow, and bitter cold of winter in Minnesota, and feels at home here, despite the pull of the West Coast, of California.

So much has changed. From external information, not explicitly from the poem itself, it is certain that this is not Minnesota from the point of view of a then mainstream, white male poet and performer who was raised on a farm there in the early twentieth century. Rather, a poem by another successful and brilliant poet and performer, who was born in St. Paul, a member of the Dark Noise Collective who now in the twenty-first century identifies as Black, Queer, and Poz. The center has shifted. Smith also finds meaning, depth, and satisfaction in the place that they're from and where they have chosen to remain.

Smith's poem is a gift. It's almost uncanny how it fits, except we know. We don't need to intellectualize, to apply force in order to see and feel it. Also fitting, and unsurprising, that it is published by Graywolf Press, a key player in our literary scene.

Whether or not Smith, whose freewheeling poems are more often intent on love, desire, friendship, family, race, gender, everyday survival and resistance, was conscious of Bly in this instance, it was Bly's both disruptive and generative work, starting some sixty years ago, well before Smith's birth—Bly's long-range foresight leading to and affording the constant regeneration and evolution of poeticulture here in the Upper Midwest—that makes it possible to identify Smith's poem as part of Bly's legacy. There is an irregular lineage, but a traceable through line, linking the two.

To reprise lines from Chapter 1: "It is not going too far to say that poets in Minnesota today are his heirs across the generations, unwittingly or not. Or that all the participants in the literary scene here and now are indebted and linked creatively to him." As Whitman says in the last lines of "Song of Myself": "If you want me again look for me under your boot-soles. /You will hardly know who I am or what I mean, / But I shall be good health to you nevertheless." Bly is an ancestor, unacknowledged though present as a ghost.[1] But the mere and

---

1   Only after I had envisioned using Smith's poem here did I recall these lines from Bly's 1993 poem, "Gratitude to Old Teachers": "When we stride or stroll across the frozen lake, / We place our feet where they have never been. / We walk upon the unwalked. But we are uneasy. / Who is down there but our old teachers? / Water that once could take no human weight—/ We were students then—holds up our feet, / And goes on ahead of us for a mile. / Beneath us the teachers, and around us the stillness."

wonderful existence of Smith's poem is acknowledgment enough.

From this vantage point, the literary future in Minnesota looks very good. May it be so. And long may the renaissance run, reinforced by appreciation of its history, its origin story.

Acknowledgments

First I want to acknowledge Robert Bly† (*requiescat in pace*) for a thousand things. He was unfailingly generous with and encouraging to me.

Especial thanks to Jim Lenfestey, who, without warning, assigned me the task of delivering the introduction at the Minneapolis celebration in 2019 for the publication of Bly's *Collected Poems*. And to Eric Lorberer, for subsequently printing that talk in *Rain Taxi Review of Books*. Thus was born the idea for this book.

I am grateful to all these interviewees who graciously replied to my questions either in person (before the onset of Covid) or via telephone and email:

> Michael Dennis Browne, Phil Dentinger, Paul Feroe, Mike Finley†, Patricia Hampl, Margaret Hasse, Mike Hazard, Lewis Hyde, Louis Jenkins†, Garrison Keillor, Patricia Kirkpatrick, Wyndy Knox Carr (aka Wendy Knox), Mary Logue, John Minczeski, Jim Moore, Michael Moos, Marilyn Nelson, Jim Perlman, Marly Rusoff, Laurie Savran, Gaylord Schanilec, Jim Sitter, David Unowsky, Mark Vinz, Cary Waterman, David Wojahn, Ray Young Bear, Carolyn Zniewski

Decades ago, long before this particular book was conceived, I corresponded with Bill Holm† and talked/corresponded with Don Olsen† on overlapping subjects. I remain grateful to them both, now gone.

Thanks to the staff of the Gale Family Library of the Minnesota Historical Society, where some of my research took place. Also to the staff of the Andersen Library at the University of Minnesota, which houses the Upper Midwest Literary Archives.

For permission to reprint published poems I thank the following:

> Ruth Bly (Robert Bly†)
> Jane Dickerson
> Rachel Frazin (Mike Finley†)
> "Plains Poet" by Meridel LeSueur ©Meridel LeSueur, used with permission from the Meridel LeSueur Family Circle. All Rights Reserved.
> Freya Manfred
> Lacinea McBride (Roy McBride†)
> Tom McGrath (Thomas McGrath†)
> Danez Smith, "i'm going back to Minnesota where sadness makes sense" from *Homie*. Copyright © 2020 by Danez Smith. Reprinted with the permission of The Permissions Company, LLC on behalf of Graywolf Press, Minneapolis, Minnesota, graywolfpress.org
> Mark Vinz
> Anne Wright (James Wright†)

And for other help, thanks to Lucinda Anderson, Bridget Bly, Mary Bly, Peter Campion, Danny Klecko, Thomas R. Smith, Sandy Spieler, Connie Wanek, and Tim Young.

Readers of Rebecca Solnit's *Orwell's Roses* may note the devices I have adopted from that fine study.

I thank my publisher, Ian Leask, for his faith in and support of this book, and Gary Lindberg, who helped wrangle it into shape.

For persistent support through my own recent trials and days, I am grateful to family and friends: Hannah & Hope Campbell Gustafson, Joan & Marc Cox, Dan Bergeson, Ron Skidmore, Mike Crump, Dan Soneson, Phil Johnson, Mustafa, and Axel.

Finally, thanks above all to my *sine qua non*, Sarah Campbell.

Index

A

Abbe, Mary, 4, 205 n. 19, 227, 230 n. 19
Academy: A Journal of the Liberal Arts, 175, 195 n. 39
Aeschylus, 36, 156
African-American Cultural Center, 120, 232 n. 24
Agee, Jonis, 189 n. 28, 239
Aiken, Ta-Coumba T., 232 n. 24, 328
Aleixandre, Vicente, 176, 188, 288
Alexander, Jerri, 119
Allen, Paula Gunn, 162
Allende, Salvador, 134, 144
Allison, Mose, 87
Ally Press, 143, 313-5, 318
Altany, Alan, 263 n. 30
Amazon Bookstore, the, 240-1
American Flyer & Other Suspensions, The, 187
American Indian II, 161-2
American Indian Art: Form and Tradition, 165-7
American Indian Center, the, 167
American Indian Movement (AIM), 152-3
American Indian Speaks, The, 158-9
American Poetry Review, 273-6
Amussen, Diana, 138
Anderson, Christine, 306 n. 31
Andrews, Jenné, 182 n. 15, 189 n. 28, 190, 194, 206, 212-5, 218, 221, 222, 224 n. 7, 226, 233, 254 n. 17, 266, 295, 298 n. 17, 305 n. 30, 311, 325, 329 n. 18
Angwamas Minosewag Anishinabeg, 164-5, 328-9
Arndt, Tom, 205, 226-7
Arts in Corrections, 119, 326-8
Ashbery, John, 55, 246 n. 4, 301 n. 23
At the Foot of the Mountain Theater, 31 n. 9, 96, 209, 306 n. 32

Augsburg College, 114, 129, 239

B

B. Dalton Booksellers, 142
Baland, Timothy, 179, 266 n. 4, 296 n. 15
Baldwin, Christina, 138
Banks, Dennis, 152-3
Baraka, Amiri, 232 n. 24
Barks, Coleman, 232, 310 n. 37
Barsness, John, 162
Basham, Katherine, 254-5, 296 n. 15, 302
Baxter, Charles, 56 n. 18, 203, 315-6
Beach, Joseph Warren, 49
Bear Cult Press, the, 302
Beckwith, Nancy, 224 n. 7
Beddowe, Jeff, 217
Beggar's Bowl, the, 261, 263 n. 30
Bell, Marvin, 106
Bellamy, Lou, 122
Bellecourt, Clyde, 152
Bellow, Saul, 49
Belvo, Hazel, 227
Bemidji State College, 159, 161, 256
Benn, Gottfried, 8, 11 n. 15, 102
Benson, Gov. Elmer, 28, 112
Bergie, Astrid, 226
Bergie, Sigrid, 191
Bernstein, Maury, 90
Berry, Wendell, 8, 40
Berryhill, Michael, 179, 296 n. 15, 298 n. 17
Berryman, John, 34, 49-51, 106, 251, 321, 322
Bieler Press, 240
Bitz, Gregory, 57, 137, 176, 177, 180, 182 n. 15, 191 n. 32, 205, 206, 209, 218, 226-7, 266, 294, 296 n. 15, 307 n. 33, 308, 309-10
Black Elk, 151
Black Flag: Poems for the Resistance, 116, 161 n. 25, 178-9, 249 n. 9, 253, 266
Black Market Book Fair, the, 120
Black Panthers, the, 93, 128, 153
Blake, William, 7, 38

Blakely, Roger, 56 n. 18, 315 n. 43
Blazek, Doug, 186 n. 22, 189 n. 28, 251 n. 12
Bly, Carol, 8, 77, 79, 193, 212 n. 35, 268, 272, 276, 278, 282
Bly, Carrie (Nelson), 9
Bly, Jacob, 9, 272
Bly, Robert, *passim*
Boesing, Martha, 94, 96, 136, 306
Boesing, Paul, 94, 96
Bookmen, Inc., the, 133, 187, 238, 297 n. 16
Bookslinger, 238, 315
Bradford, James, 263 n. 30
Brainard, Franklin, 151, 174-5, 179, 185, 188, 193, 194, 198, 203, 206, 207-8, 215 n. 41, 218, 251 n. 12, 260 n. 24, 263 n. 30, 266, 294, 295, 298 n. 17, 299, 327
Breckenridge-Haldeman, Jill, 138 n. 24, 143, 189 n. 28, 224 n. 7, 254 n. 17, 298 n. 17
Brennan, Dan, 138
Brewer, Dick, 226
Brooks, Cleanth, 51, 215 n. 39
Brooks, Gwendolyn, 120
Brother Songs: A Male Anthology of Poetry, 250, 312-13
Brown, Hugh, 87
Browne, Michael Dennis, 76, 78, 125, 131, 136-7, 139-40, 143, 144, 183 n. 15, 187, 206, 211, 215 n. 41, 254 n. 17, 255, 257, 296, 298 n. 17, 301, 309, 313, 316 n. 45, 327
Bruchac, Joseph, 167-8, 251 n. 12, 256
Bryant, Linda, 229
Buchwald, Emilie, 191 n. 30, 195, 216 n. 43, 314, 318
Burke, Herbert, 108
Burke, Lar, 191
Bush Foundation, 141, 284

C

Caddy, John, 175, 179, 186, 203, 205, 206, 215 n. 41, 260 n. 24, 266 n. 4, 296 n. 15, 321, 322, 325, 329 n. 18
Caesar's Bar, 90
Caesura, 209
Campbell, Douglas, 36, 106
Camus, Albert, 199
Cardona-Hine, Alvaro, 189 n. 28, 211, 237 n. 40, 246, 298 n. 18, 313 n. 39, 317
Carleton College, 34, 55, 114, 202, 323 n. 5
Carleton Miscellany, the, 55, 173 n. 5, 261
Carruth, Hayden, 182
Casson, Ann, 106, 108
Cedar-Riverside People's Center, the, 143, 235
Chamberlain, Marisha, 188, 194, 224 n. 7, 237 n. 40, 247 n. 5, 254 n. 17, 280, 317 n. 46, 330,
Char, René, 8, 11 n. 15
Chautauqua, 115, 281, 283-4
Chekov, Anton, 89
Cherry, Kelly, 239
Children's Theatre Company, the, 94
Church of Saint Vincent Van Gogh, the, 228-30
Clayton, Candyce, 189 n. 28, 224 n. 8, 237 n. 40, 260 n. 24, 280, 311
Clepper, P.M, 83
Coffeehouse Extemporé, the, 93, 207-8, 217, 223
Coffee House Press, 1, 240, 314, 318
College of St. Catherine, the, 227, 239, 240, 310
Collins, Cyn, 81 n. 1, 90 n. 27
Coloring Book of Poetry for Adults, A, 216 n. 43, 307-8
Community Programs in the Arts (COMPAS), 230, 271, 326-31
Connolly, Carol, 140, 192 n. 33
Conover, Roger, 280
Corey, Chet, 177, 179, 186 n. 22, 260 n. 24, 266 n. 4, 296 n. 15
Corso, Gregory, 55, 252
Coyle, Brian, 57 n. 20, 126
Craig, Earl, 112
Crawford, John, 116-17
Crazy Horse, 148-50, 244-8
Creeley, Robert, 55, 112, 169, 203, 251, 321, 322

D

Dacey, Florence, 192 n. 33, 270 n. 13, 303
Dacey, Philip, 61, 211, 246-7, 251 n. 12, 253, 256, 257, 260 n. 24, 263 n. 30, 270 n. 13, 296 nn. 14-15, 298 n. 18, 303, 313, 316 n. 45
Dacotah Territory, 163-4, 248-52, 261, 263 n. 30, 300, 312 n. 38, 325
Daggett, Lyle, 208, 229-30, 294
Dakota Arts Quarterly, 252 n. 16.
Dakota Press, 162, 291 n. 7
Damsten (Waara), Richard, 161 n. 25, 178, 217, 253, 266 n. 4, 296 n. 15
Damsten, Robert, 186 n. 22, 254 n. 17, 255, 301
Dania Hall, 89, 93
Daniel, John, 188 n. 22, 218, 296 n. 15
Daniel, Judy, 296 n. 15
Davidov, Marv, 86 n. 18, 87, 96, 113, 115, 127
Dayton-Hudson Foundation, 141, 284
Dean Gallery, 310 n. 36
DeGrazia, Emilio, 260, 262, 317 n. 46

Dekin, Timothy, 301 n. 23
Dellinger, David, 116
Deloria, Jr., Vine, 147, 152
Deming, Barbara, 114 n. 30
Dental Floss, 314
Dentinger, Phil, 182 n. 15, 186, 189 n. 28, 251 n. 12, 252-4, 255, 256, 260 n. 24, 294, 296 nn. 14-15, 301
De Otero, Blas, 288
Derleth, August, 175
De Vlaminck, Maurice, 39
Dewey, John, 39
Dickerson, Jane, 116 n. 35, 122
Diego, Gerardo, 253
Dochniak, Jim, 116-20, 122, 138, 140, 142, 187, 189 n. 28, 211, 229, 235, 239
Dorn, Ed, 239
Drantell, Jan, 224 n. 7
Duffy, Ella, 45
Duffy, William, 46 n. 4, 48, 68 n. 15, 73, 74-5, 290
Dunn, Stephen, 189 n. 28, 206, 296 n. 15
Durrell, Lawrence, 73
Dworkin, Richard (Dickie), 126-7
Dylan, Bob, 8 n. 9, 45, 51, 81-4, 86-8, 103, 129, 257

E

Eberhart, Richard, 29, 320
Edson, Russell, 189
Eide-Tollefson, Kristen, 85 n. 15, 86 n. 16
Ekelöf, Gunnar, 8, 11 n. 15, 61, 248 n. 6
Electric Fetus, the, 93, 205
Eliot, T.S., 7, 12 n. 15, 41, 43, 50, 63, 202
Elkin, Stanley, 239
Elliott, Ramblin' Jack, 84
Elliott, William, 159, 256, 261, 296 n. 15
Emerson, Ralph Waldo, 67
Engman, John, 182 n. 15, 186 n. 22, 211
Erdrich, Louise, 168 n. 36, 284
Erikson, Erik, 15
Espeland, Pam, 296 n. 15
Etter, Dave, 263 n. 30

F

Falk, Margaret, 208, 224 n. 7
Fatoba, Femi, 206, 298 n. 17
Fawbush, James, 246, 261, 300 n. 20
Felien, Edwin, 57, 96, 126-8, 131 n. 10, 134
Ferrary, Jeanette, 189 n. 28, 224 n. 7, 298 n. 17
Ferlinghetti, Lawrence, 252, 287 n. 2, 290, 322
Feroe, Paul, 313-15

Fields, Kenneth, 301 n. 23
Fifties, the, 11, 16 n. 23, 35, 41, 46-7, 51, 52, 54, 55, 61, 68 n. 15, 86, 87, 99, 100 n. 3, 101 n. 5, 130, 171-2, 176 n. 7, 186, 200, 245, 259, 287, 303
Finley, Mike, 182 n. 15, 188, 191 n. 32, 195 n. 39, 208-9, 215 n. 41, 217, 229, 256, 260, 291 n. 7, 296 n. 14, 306, 331 n. 36
Firehouse Theater, 94
First Skin Around Me, The, 168, 301
First Unitarian Society, the, 197, 203, 217
Fisher, Jean-Marie, 224 n. 8, 305-08, 328 n. 16
Fitzgerald, F. Scott, 29, 282
FitzPatrick, Kevin, 191
Five Corners Saloon, the, 90
Flaherty, Doug, 179, 263 n. 30
Flanagan, Barbara, 110
Flandrick, Mary Pat, 207, 218, 224 n. 7, 305 n. 30
Flint, Roland, 57, 88, 174, 321, 322
Forché, Carolyn, 189 n. 28, 251 n. 12
Fort Mango, 206, 226-7, 308-9
Foster, Sarah, 53
4-H Club, the, 9, 275 n. 18, 328
400 Bar, the, 90
Four Indian Poets, 162, 166
Fox, Siv Cedering, 255, 263 n. 30, 316
Free People's Poetry Workshop, the, 231-5
Frumkin, Gene, 251 n. 12
Future Farmers of America (FFA), 9-10

G

Gallo, Philip, 186 n. 22
Galt, Francis, 57, 106, 182 n. 15
Galt, Margot Fortunato, 158 n. 19, 191, 227
Gardner, Isabella, 50
Georgeville Commune, the, 126, 127
Ghosh, Amitav, 11 n. 11
Giles, Ivory, 229
Ginsberg, Allen, 55, 81, 110, 140, 183, 203, 205, 245, 246 n. 4, 252, 322
Glover, Tony, 57, 86, 88, 90, 92, 204 n. 17
Gold Flower, 226
Goldbarth, Albert, 182
Gomsrud, Lowell, 115
Good Sky, Harold, 152-3
Graywolf Press, 1, 169 n. 37, 317, 318, 335
Great Circumpolar Bear Cult, the, 255-6, 302
Great Mother Conference, the, 130 n. 8, 232, 310 n. 37, 312
Great River Review, the, 262-3
Green, Kate, 140, 192 n. 33, 233, 296 n. 14, 298 n. 18, 324

Greenberg, Alvin, 56 n. 18, 186, 189 n. 28, 206, 215 n. 41, 237, 261, 298 n. 17, 315, 316 n. 45
Gremmels, Jim, 304-5
Grika, Herb, 226
Gruchow, Paul, 7, 11, 18, 21, 22, 24, 40, 138, 194, 221, 258
Guenther, Charles, 55
Guest, Judith, 140
Guild of Performing Arts, the, 205, 207, 222
Gunderson, Keith, 106, 176, 179, 189 n. 28, 203, 205, 206, 218, 263 n. 30, 295-6, 298 n. 17, 322
Gustafson, Mark, 110-11
Gustavus Adolphus College, 114, 129, 201, 271
Guthrie, Tyrone, 35-6, 234
Guthrie, Woody, 84
Guthrie Theater, the, 35-6, 106, 156, 203-5,
Gutknecht, David, 110, 180 n. 11
Guttormsson, Tom, 291 n. 7

H

Hagedorn, Jessica, 235
Hagen, Tom, 249
Haines, John, 253, 303
Hall, Donald, 12 n. 15, 36, 45, 48, 203, 231, 303, 321, 322
Hall, Nor, 138, 232, 310
Hallgren, Stephanie, 298 n. 18
Hamline College, 114, 240
Hampl, Patricia, 17-18, 20, 50, 57-8, 70, 71, 75-6, 78, 106-7, 129, 132, 135, 136, 137, 138, 139, 140, 176, 177, 180-4, 189 n. 28, 193-4, 197, 198, 206, 212 n. 35, 215 n. 41, 222, 224 n. 7, 226, 237 n. 40, 238, 251 n. 12, 268-9, 295, 298 n. 17, 327-8
Hamsun, Knut, 89
Handeen, Dale, 224 n. 7, 229, 237 n. 40, 269
Hanson, Phebe, 138, 140, 189 n. 28, 215, 217-8, 222, 223, 224 n. 7, 269, 270 n. 13, 280, 298 n. 17
Hanson, Warren, 126-7
Harjo, Joy, 164, 168, 301
Harper, Michael, 236 n. 35, 280
Harrison, Jim, 19-20
Harrison, Keith, 206, 298 n. 18
Hart, Robert, 254
Hasse, Margaret, 117-9, 121, 140, 189 n. 28, 191 n. 32, 192 n. 33, 206, 211, 218, 224 n. 8, 256, 263 n. 30, 298, 317 n. 46, 324, 326-7, 328, 329, 331 n. 21
Hasselstrom, Linda, 116 n. 35, 263 n. 30
Hassler, Jon, 257
Hastings, Linda, 255
Hauge, Olav H., 318
Hauser, Susan, 257, 306 n. 31
Haycock, Todd, 162, 166, 206
Hayes, Annie, 216, 309
Hayes, Terrance, 233
Hazard, Mike, 140 n. 27, 194, 197 n. 2, 198 n. 5, 237 n. 40
Heddan's Book Store, 86 n. 16
Hedin, Robert, 18 n. 27, 73 n. 28, 189 n. 28, 256, 262 n. 29, 263
Heins, Sam, 57 n. 20, 97 n. 36, 180 n. 11
Hennen, Tom, 20 n. 32, 72 n. 26, 77-8, 175, 179, 186, 187, 188, 194, 203, 254 n. 17, 260 n. 24, 266, 270 n. 13, 294-5, 304-5
Hernandez, Miguel 19, 48-9, 303
Heyen, William, 203
Heyer, Shirley, 226
Hinkley, Bill, 90, 137
Hitchcock, George, 176 n. 7, 189
Hoheisel, Peter, 302 n. 24
Hollo, Anselm, 185, 270
Holm, Bill, 40 n. 30, 58, 63-4, 70, 79, 101, 186, 201-2, 232, 247 n. 5, 263 n. 30, 267, 269, 270, 276-7, 278, 280-2, 297, 303, 310 n. 37, 328
Holy Cow! Press, 189, 250, 311-3
Honeywell Project, the, 96, 113, 128
Hughes, Barbara, 211
Hugo, Richard, 39, 48 n. 6, 251 n. 12
Humphrey, Hubert, 110, 112
Hundred Flowers, 96, 116, 126-8, 131, 134
Hungry Mind Book Store, the, 235, 236-9, 240, 241
Hushcha, Leon, 206, 226-7, 307 n. 33, 308-9
Hyde, Lewis, 15-7, 20, 21, 57-8, 106, 125-6, 135, 147 n. 2, 155-6, 175-7, 180, 182 n. 15, 183-4, 186, 188, 194 n. 37, 267-9, 310 n. 36, 324 n. 7

I

Ibsen, Henrik, 37 n. 21, 89-90
Ignatow, David, 183, 186, 189, 203, 205, 246 n. 4, 251 n. 12, 253, 322
Igoe, Ann, 232
In the Heart of the Beast Puppet and Mask Theatre, 31 n. 9, 95
Inti-Illimani, 144
Issa, Kobayashi, 16-7, 245, 290
Ithunn Apple Occasional Poets Collective, the, 226
Ivins, Molly, 113
Ivory Tower, 56-9, 88, 96, 97, 106, 126, 135, 137,

J

175-6, 180, 182 n. 15, 187 n. 25, 188, 193, 212 n. 35, 269

Jacobsen, Rolf, 5, 61, 203, 282, 288-9
Jacobson, Dale, 122, 179, 189 n. 28, 246, 249, 300 n. 20
Jacobson, Jean Alice, 301
Jarrell, Randall, 49
Jenkins, Louis, 69, 78, 130, 139-40, 182 n. 15, 186, 189 n. 28, 194, 215 n. 41, 251 n. 12, 252-6, 260, 266, 278, 294-5, 298 n. 17, 301, 302
Jensen, Gendron, 307 n. 33
Jiménez, Juan Ramón, 8, 268 n. 8, 288-9
Johnson, Jan, 223
Jones, Seitu, 232 n. 24
Joyce, James, 38, 132
Judson, John, 251 n. 12, 263 n. 30, 291 n. 7
Jung, Carl Gustav, 11, 67, 130-1, 138, 144, 154, 232, 273, 276, 310
Juniper Press, 291 n. 7
Justice, Donald, 106, 246 n. 4

K

Kachinske, Timothy, 254
Kane, Patricia, 56 n. 18
Karr, Mary, 189 n. 28, 211, 229, 233-5, 237 n. 40, 298 n. 18, 330
Kedemi, 195 n. 39
Keenan, Deborah, 237 n. 40, 317 n. 46
Keillor, Garrison, 40, 56-7, 70-1, 78-9, 81, 85, 90, 92, 97 n. 36, 106, 131, 137, 180 n. 13, 182 n. 15, 193, 205, 206, 209-10, 212 n. 35, 218, 227, 296 n. 15, 322, 324
Kempton, Murray, 323
Kennedy, Ellen, 140, 192 n. 33, 216, 224 n. 8, 237 n. 40, 307 n. 33, 311
Kennedy, Wallace, 298 n. 17, 326
KFAI, 119, 210
Kiesel, Stanley, 206, 211, 237 n. 40, 298 n. 17
Kimmerer, Robin Wall, 21
Kincaid, Michael, 175, 179, 185, 186, 191 n. 32, 197, 203, 205, 206, 218, 254 n. 17, 260 n. 24, 261, 266 n. 4, 294, 296 n. 15
King, Scott, 303 n. 26
Kinnell, Galway, 106, 112, 183, 203, 233, 234 n. 32, 235, 251, 321, 322
Kirkpatrick, Patricia, 3 n. 4, 41 n. 31, 69, 70, 76, 102, 154 n. 11, 182 n. 15, 194, 212 n. 35, 215 n. 41, 222, 224 n. 7, 298 n. 17
Kissinger, Henry, 134 n. 15

Klein, Carl, 87
Klein, Irwin, 88
Kling, Bill, 193
Knapp, Martha, 120
Knife River Press, 252, 301
Knight, Etheridge, 117, 141, 168, 195, 215, 229, 231-5, 298 n. 18, 310 n. 37
Knoepfle, John, 55, 291, 315, 316
Knox, Wendy (aka Wyndy Knox Carr), 136, 183 n. 15, 189, 192 n. 33, 208, 211, 215 n. 41, 218, 222-3, 224 n. 7, 225, 226, 237 n. 40, 269, 280-2, 296 n. 15, 306, 307 n. 33, 331
Koch, Kenneth, 322
Koerner, John, 57, 82, 84, 86, 90, 116, 204 n. 17
Kolstad, Papa John, 90
Kooser, Ted, 61, 182, 251 n. 12, 313
Kornblum, Allan, 186, 240, 314, 318
Kozol, Jonathan, 323
Kraken Press, 209 n. 28, 219 n. 45, 291 n. 7
Krug, Michael, 210
Kubach, David, 255, 302
Kuzma, Greg, 182, 263 n. 30

L

LaBerge, Molly, 164, 324, 326
Lake Street Review, the, 143, 191-2
Lake Superior Journal, a, 254-5
Lakewood Community College, 240, 269
Lamantia, Philip, 182
Lamp in the Spine, the, 135, 179-84, 188, 193, 261, 292 n. 9, 295, 309
Lamppa, William, 261
Lange, Gerald, 240
Larsen, Randy, 298 n. 17
Larson, Judy, 90, 137, 223
Larson, Michael, 305
Leadbelly, 82, 86
Lee, Dave & Muriel, 83, 90
Lee, Dick, 305
Lenfestey, James, 17 n. 25, 41 n. 31, 206
Le Sueur, Meridel, 31-4, 115, 116 n. 35, 117 n. 36, 119, 140, 144, 175, 183, 187, 192 n. 33, 194 n. 37, 208, 213, 214, 225, 258, 260, 296, 306, 307
Letter to an Imaginary Friend, 31, 40 n. 29, 121, 149, 214
Levertov, Denise, 55, 182, 183, 189, 203, 233, 321
Levine, Philip, 189
Levis, Larry, 246
Lewin, John, 36, 156 n. 15
Lewis, Sinclair, 27, 28-9, 34, 265, 272

Lifshin, Lyn, 207
Linnerson, Beth, 94
Linsner, Steve, 229
Lipp, Barbara Meyer, 190
Little Crow (Ta Oyate Duta), 63 n. 2, 147, 154-5
Little Sandy Review, the, 84, 87 n. 21
Loft Literary Center, the, 1, 22, 96, 117, 125-45, 192, 195, 199, 210, 211-2, 239, 262, 305, 306 n. 32, 315
Logan, John, 55
Logue, Mary, 189 n. 28, 194 n. 37, 210-1, 226, 233, 256
Lorde, Audre, 186 n. 24, 233-4, 239
Loonfeather, 256-7
Love from Women Poets, 224-5
Lowell, Elizabeth, 224 n. 7
Lowell, Robert, 49, 110
Lundegaard, Bob, 88-9, 278 n. 21, 322 n. 3
Lynd, Staughton, 114 n. 30
Lyons, Richard, 174-5, 246, 260 n. 24, 300 n. 20

M

Macalester College, 56 n. 18, 71 n. 23, 80, 96, 113, 114, 175, 198, 200, 203, 208, 212 n. 35, 222, 233, 236-7, 239, 269, 311, 315-6
Machado, Antonio, 8, 66, 102, 189 n. 28, 253, 303, 314, 318
Machete, 143, 195 n. 39
Magler, Ruth, 229
Magrane, Jan, 96
Manfred, Frederick, 29, 31, 82 n. 5, 174-5, 270 n. 13, 296, 299
Manfred, Freya, 29 n. 7, 80, 189 n. 18, 206, 215 n. 41, 254 n. 17, 260 n. 24, 263 n. 30, 299
Mann, Polly, 121-2, 283-4
Many Corners, 195 n. 39
Marks, Melissa, 137
Marshall (Rasmussen/Vogel), Caroline, 212 n. 36, 215 n. 40, 218, 222, 280-1. 296 n. 14
Martinson, Dave, 164, 182 n. 15, 186 n. 22, 215 n. 41, 249 n. 9, 254 n. 17, 285-6, 300 n. 20, 328
Martinson, Harry, 253
Martinson, Sue Ann, 138, 191 n. 32, 192
Matthews, William, 182
Mayday Festival, 95, 229, 230
Mayhew, Jonathan, 77
McAnally, Mary, 116 n. 35, 117, 119, 229, 231
McBride, Roy C., 56 n. 18, 119, 140, 179, 197-8, 203, 205, 206, 208, 211, 215, 228-30, 233, 235-6, 237 n. 40, 266 n. 4, 296 n. 15, 298 n. 17, 307 n. 33, 327, 331

McCarthy, Eugene, 110, 140-1, 195 n. 38
McClure, Michael, 252, 317
McCosh's Books, 84-6, 89, 90, 96, 139, 174, 237
McCrae, Fiona, 317
McCrorie, Edward, 7 n. 4
McGee, Alphonse, 115
McGrath, Thomas, 29-32, 34, 40, 103, 115, 116 n. 35, 119, 121, 122, 143, 148-9, 163, 179, 183, 187, 188, 194, 206, 213, 214, 218, 237 n. 40, 244-6, 249, 250, 251 n. 12, 252, 254 n. 17, 260, 263 n. 30, 266, 268-9, 295-6, 298 n. 17, 307, 311, 313 n. 39, 323
McKeon, Michael, 296 n. 14
McKiernan, Ethna, 191 n. 32, 224 n. 8
McLuhan, Marshall, 99
Meacham, Stewart, 114 n. 30
Mead, Margaret, 323
Medicine Man, the, 190-1
Meissner, William, 189 n. 28, 263 n. 30, 326
Menand, Louis, 13-4, 19
Merrill, Lee, 302 n. 24
Merwin, W.S., 183, 251 n. 12, 321
Meyer, June, 322
Micawber's Books, 238 n. 44
Michaux, Henri, 11 n. 15
Midnight Paper Sales Press, 323 n. 4
Midwestern Writers' Festival & Book Fair, the, 230, 239-40
Milgrom, Al, 129 n. 7, 195 n. 39
Milkweed Chronicle, the, 195, 216 n. 43, 228, 308, 314, 318
Milkweed Editions, 1, 191 n. 30, 194-5, 318
Milkweed Press, 310 n. 36
Miller, Jack, 259, 265
Milton, John R., 150, 157 n. 17, 158-9, 161-2, 174-5, 251 n. 12, 291 n. 7, 299
Minczeski, John, 119, 136, 138, 140, 187, 189, 191 n. 32, 206, 216, 231, 233, 260 n. 24, 280, 282, 313 n. 39, 317, 328
Minda, Merle, 327
Minneapolis Free Press, 128 n. 6
Minneapolis Institute of Art, the, 166
Minnesota Center for Book Arts (MCBA), the, 1, 318
Minnesota Daily, the, 56, 92, 112, 187, 208, 210, 222 n. 2
Minnesota Literature Newsletter, the, 209
Minnesota Educational Radio (MPR), 193, 212
Minnesota Mama, 175
Minnesota Poetry Outloud, 212-5, 271-2, 277-83
Minnesota Prairie Poets Association, 266
Minnesota Review, the, 53-6, 173 n. 5, 174, 261

Minnesota State Arts Board (Council), 138, 230, 141, 209, 211, 212, 271, 328, 330
Minnesota Writers' Publishing House (MWPH), 187, 188, 193, 260, 261, 266, 267, 292-7, 317 n. 46
Mixed Blood Theatre, 96, 122, 139
Mixers Bar, the, 90 n. 28, 97
Mladinic, Peter, 138 n. 24, 186 n. 22, 256, 260 n. 24, 313 n. 39
Mohr, Howard, 247, 251 n. 12, 278, 280, 303
Momaday, N. Scott, 151-2
Monaghan, Patricia, 194, 222 n. 2, 223-4
Moons and Lion Tails, 187-90, 261, 311, 313
Moore, Jim (James), 20, 32, 34, 43, 57, 69, 78, 106, 123, 129, 131-2, 135-41, 171, 176-7, 180-4, 186, 189 n. 28, 193, 194, 206, 210, 215 n. 41, 237 n. 40, 238, 251 n. 12, 254 n. 17, 258 n. 20, 260, 267, 268-9, 298 n. 17, 313 n. 39, 325, 328-9
Moore, Roy, 280
Moorhead State College, 148, 237, 244, 251
Moos, Michael, 76-7, 130, 182, 215, 246, 249, 251, 300, 331
Moppet Players, the, 94
Morgan, J.P., 63-4, 101, 200, 202
Morris, Carol, 186 n. 24, 305
Morrison, George, 158, 165 n. 32, 166, 167
Morse, Julie, 240-1
Morton, Dave, 86-7, 89 n. 23
Mueller, Lisel, 239
Murphy, Willie, 90, 204 n. 17

N

Naiden, James, 79, 114, 184-6, 191 n. 32, 206-9, 218, 223, 251 n. 12, 260-1, 294
Natasha (aka Katy Sheehy), 224 n. 7, 306 n. 31
National Endowment for the Arts (NEA), 141, 142 n. 30, 164, 211, 269, 270, 321, 323, 326, 330
National Poetry Festival, 168, 233
Neihardt, John G., 151
Nelson, Marilyn, 192 n. 33, 211, 233-5
Nelson, Paul, 84
Neruda, Pablo, 11 n. 15, 32, 79 n. 43, 102, 109, 126, 133-5, 144, 176, 183, 194 n. 37, 201, 275, 283, 288, 303, 316, 318
New Riverside Café, the, 93
New Rivers Press, 191 n. 30, 315-7, 328 n. 16
New World Writing, 63
Niatum, Duane, 164, 168, 186 n. 24, 301
Nickel & Dime Quarterly, the, 125, 175-7, 179, 180, 182 n. 15, 183, 188, 269, 308 n. 35, 310

Nixon, Richard, 93, 114, 129, 134 n. 15, 322
Nodin Press, 8 n. 8, 133 n. 14, 150, 238 n. 44, 297-9, 325
Noethe, Sherry, 298 n. 18
Norris, Kathleen, 263 n. 30
North Country Anvil, the, 116, 119, 128, 256, 257-61, 292 n. 9, 304
North Dakota State University (NDSU), 174, 244, 246, 252
Northeast, 263 n. 30
North Stone Reading Series, 206-9
North Stone Review, the, 143, 184-6, 207, 261, 294
Northland College, 255
Northland Cultural Workers' Conference, 119-20
Nurmi, Earl "Pete", 116 n. 35, 117, 119

O

Oakwood, 263 n. 30
O'Connor, Frank, 66
Odetta, 82
Odysseus, 8
O'Fallon, David, 95
Oldknow, Anthony, 291 n. 7, 300 n. 20
Olds, Sharon, 251 n. 12
Olsen, Don, 2-3, 49 n. 9, 186, 201-2, 203, 247, 253, 254 n. 17, 296 n. 15, 302-4, 316 n. 45
Olsenius, Richard, 309
Olson, Charles, 55
Olson, Don, 240-1
Olson, Floyd B., 28
Olson, Tom, 88-9
ONE, 187
One Groveland, 210
Oppenheim, James, 107
O'Rourke, Kevin, 229
Orr, Gregory, 24 n. 43, 182
Ortiz, Simon, 158, 164, 168, 301
Owen, Mary Gwen, 200
Ox Head Press, 198 n. 4, 253, 302-4, 305

P

Paddock, Joe, 130-1, 183 n. 15, 186, 194 n. 37, 247 n. 5, 260 n. 24, 269-70, 280, 296 n. 15, 298 n. 17, 330
Paddock, Nancy, 189 n. 28, 192 n. 33, 247 n. 5, 270, 282, 306 n. 31, 330
Palmer's Bar, 90, 205
Pankake, Jon, 84
Patterson, Raymond, 322

Peacock, Thomas, 164, 168, 211
Penn, Rick, 255, 302
Pentagram Press, 240
Penumbra Theatre, 122
People's Pantry, the, 96
Perine's Campus Book Store, 86 n. 16, 177, 186 n. 23
Perlman, Jim, 119, 138, 187-90, 210, 311-3
Piercy, Marge, 182, 189 n. 28
Pillsbury-Waite Cultural Arts Center, 226, 229
Pinochet, Augusto, 134, 144
Plainsong, 151, 174-5, 294, 299
Plains Bookbus, the, 284-6
Plains Distribution Service, 284-5
Poetry in the Schools (PITS), 211 n. 33, 230, 323-6, 330, 331
Poindexter, Tom, 246
Pound, Ezra, 7, 12 n. 15, 19, 41, 43, 51, 99, 280
Powderhorn Puppet Theatre, 95, 209
Prairie Gate Press, 304-5
Preview, 193-4, 212 n. 35, 213 n. 37, 258 n. 20
Pucci, Linda, 115
Puente, Nic, 115
Pryor, Mary Ann, 300 n. 20

R

Rago, Henry, 55, 243 n. 1
Rain Taxi Review of Books, 1
Raisin Bread, 128 n. 6
Rakosi, Carl, 34, 108, 186, 189 n. 28, 194, 206, 260 n. 24, 296, 298 n. 18, 313 n. 39
Randall, Margaret, 316 n. 44
Randolph, Leonard, 164, 323, 324
Ransom, John Crowe, 49, 51, 102
Rapson, Ralph, 98 n. 36
Rasmussen (Marshall/Vogel), Caroline, 212 n. 36, 281
Ray, Dave, 57, 86, 88, 90, 204 n. 17,
Ray, David, 78, 105, 160, 179, 182, 251 n. 12, 290, 316 n. 45
Ray, Grayce, 211, 300 n. 20
Ray (Bly), Ruth, 268
Raygor, Robin, 205, 218, 266 n. 4, 310 n. 36,
Red Dragonfly Press, 303 n. 26
Red Studio Press, 308-10
Redden, Nigel, 206
Redshaw, Thomas Dillon, 182 n. 15, 186 n. 22, 260 n. 24, 306
Region, 87-9, 116, 128, 173 n. 5
Replansky, Naomi, 182
Reuler, Jack. 96, 122,
Rexroth, Kenneth, 252, 256
Rezmerski, John Calvin, 140, 183 n. 15, 189 n. 28, 215 n. 41, 218, 247 n. 5, 254 n. 17, 255, 260 n. 24, 266, 267 n. 7, 271, 278-82, 291 n. 7, 295, 296 n. 14, 298 n. 17, 301, 325
Richardson, Joseph, 284
Richter, Franz Allbert, 57, 106, 176-7, 182 n. 15, 183, 188, 193, 269, 270 n. 13, 294, 310 n. 36
Richter, Rosina, 240-1
Richter's Drugs, 93
Rilke, Rainer Maria, 7, 55, 143, 183, 249, 256, 313
Rites of Ancient Ripening, 31, 306-7
Road Apple Review, the, 179, 263 n. 30
Roberts, George, 189 n. 28, 237 n. 40, 256, 298 n. 17, 301 n. 22, 313 n. 39
Rolvaag, O.E., 65 n. 8
Rose, Jacqueline, 114
Rosenwald, John, 232
Roston, Ruth, 190, 191 n. 30, 192 n. 33, 298 n. 18, 317 n. 46
Rothenberg, Jerome, 15
Rubin, Jerry, 113, 116
Rulon-Miller, Rob, 3 n. 4, 317-8
Rummel, Mary Kay, 191 n. 32
Rusch, Tom, 91
Rusoff, Marly, 125-6, 129-37, 142, 144, 310
Rusoff & Co., 132-3, 142, 237
Rusoff Books, 310-1

S

St. John's University, 108, 114, 193
St. Louis, Ray, 95,
St. Olaf College, 114, 158, 313
Salinger, Wendy, 182 n. 15, 183, 268
Sanchez, Sonia, 186 n. 24, 231 n. 23
Sander, Polly, 190
Sanders, Ed, 112
Saunders, Jeff, 162, 166, 206
Savran, Bill, 82, 90, 92, 130, 133, 236
Savran, Laurie, 92, 126
Savran's Paperback Shop, 90-3, 126, 129, 177, 186 n. 23, 236, 237, 239
Savran-Rusoff Bookdealers, 129, 186 n. 23
Schanilec, Gaylord, 323, 329
Schjeldahl, Peter, 323
Schjotz-Christensen, Helge, 187-9, 311
Scholes, Randy, 195, 216 n. 43, 306, 307 n. 33, 312, 314
Schuler, Robert, 251 n. 12, 263 n. 30
Schutte, Betty, 190
Seekins, Scott, 226, 307 n. 33
Seuss, Diane, 199

Seventies, The, 11, 41, 143, 182, 186, 231, 261
Seventies Press, the, 12, 188, 267-8, 288, 292, 293
Seward Café, the, 235
Sez, 117-22, 143, 173 n. 5, 327 n. 11
Shapiro, Karl, 49, 106
Shaw, Mary Ellen, 119, 194, 195 n. 39, 215 n. 41, 218, 224 n. 7, 226, 237 n. 40
Shaw, Richard, 57, 88, 179, 186 n. 22, 203, 266 n. 4, 296 n. 15, 299, 322
Shaw, Sarah, 57, 179, 186 n. 22, 266 n. 4, 296 n. 15
Shepard, Sam, 94
Shope, Rick, 140, 204 n. 17
Shumaker, Rita, 232
Sibley, Mulford Q., 106, 108
Silence in the Snowy Fields, 12, 32 n. 11, 62-71, 72, 74, 75-6, 102, 109, 112, 153, 172-3, 175, 189 n. 27, 201, 253, 268, 293
Silent Voices: Recent American Poems on Nature, 313-4
Silko, Leslie Marmon, 168-9, 301
Simpson, Louis, 189, 203, 251 n. 12, 321, 322
Sing, Heavenly Muse, 143, 192
Sisson, Jonathan, 57, 88, 106, 176, 177, 182 n. 15, 186, 191, 194 n. 37, 195 n. 39, 206, 218, 226, 253, 260 n. 24, 296 n. 15, 308-9, 310 n. 36
Sitter, Jim, 235, 237-40
Sixties, the, 11, 16 n. 23, 41, 51, 54-5, 58, 89, 101-2, 130, 134 n. 16, 171, 176 n. 7, 177, 181-2, 245, 253
Sixties Press, the, 12, 74-5, 134 n. 16, 175, 188, 202, 253, 283 n. 35, 288-91, 293, 302-3, 316
Sklar, Morty, 263 n. 30
Sleepers Joining Hands, 12, 156, 157 n. 16
Smith, Danez, 333-6
Smith, Mara, 260, 301
Smith, Patti, 92, 205
Smith, Ray, 151, 174, 260, 261, 296 n. 15, 299, 301, 302
Smith Park Poetry Series, the, 115, 190, 212-6, 228, 236, 240, 271, 291 n. 7, 308, 309
Smith Park Press, 224
Snodgrass, W.D., 12 n. 15, 321
Snyder, Gary, 12 n. 15, 38, 179, 183, 251 n. 12, 252, 256, 321
Solheim, David, 300 n. 20
South Dakota Review, the, 38 n. 24, 149-50, 158-9, 161, 173 n. 5, 174-5
Southern Theater, the, 143
Southwest Minnesota State College, 206, 246, 270, 278 n. 25, 302

Southwestern Minnesota Arts and Humanities Council (SMAHC), 141, 263 n. 30, 283, 330
Spieler, Sandy, 95
Spirit That Moves Us, the, 263 n. 30
Spitz, Bob, 84-5
Sprengnether, Madelon, 206, 317 n. 46
Stafford, William, 39-40, 186, 203, 251, 254, 270, 320-1
Starbuck, George, 106
Steelhead, 182 n. 15, 252-4, 261, 294, 301
Stegner, Wallace, 43
Stein, Gertrude, 27
Stenvig, Charles, 129
Stillman, Norton, 133, 150, 187, 238, 297
Storlie, Eric Fraser, 82 n. 7, 90 n. 28, 97 n. 36
Strindberg, August, 36, 55, 89, 90 n. 25
Stryk, Lucien, 37 n. 22, 265
Sucoff, Marge, 224 n. 7, 261
Suderman, Elmer, 296 n. 15
Sukov, Marvin, 251
Suess, Penelope, 218, 221, 224 n. 7, 296 n. 15, 305 n. 30
Sunday Clothes, 263 n. 30
Sutter, Bart, 189 n. 28, 246, 260 n. 24, 303
Swanson, Roy Arthur, 56 n. 18
Swenson, May, 321
Synge, John Millington, 66

T

Tarachow, Michael, 240
Tate, Allen, 34, 49-56, 77, 102, 243 n. 1, 321, 322
Tate, Muriel, 115
Ten O'Clock Scholar, the, 82, 84, 86, 90, 94
Territorial Press, the, 168 n. 36, 300-1
Terry, Megan, 94
The Branch Will Not Break, 48-9, 72-6
The Light Around the Body, 12, 63 n. 3, 105 n. 30, 109, 112, 115, 153-6, 198 n. 3, 293
The Lions Tail and Eyes, 74-5, 188, 290
Theatre in the Round, 90, 94, 96, 223
Thomas, Dylan, 131
Thueson, Publisher, James D., 80 n. 44, 174-5, 299
Tjepkes, Michael. 176, 179, 185, 189 n. 28, 203, 205, 206-7, 218, 260 n. 24, 261, 266 n. 4, 296 n. 15, 322
Todd, Helen, 107
Toothpaste Press, 240, 314, 318
Trakl, Georg, 8, 11 n. 15, 55, 72, 288
Tranströmer, Tomas, 61, 188, 200, 203, 253, 288-9, 292

Triangle Bar, the, 89 n. 23, 90
Troupe, Quincy, 204 n. 17, 233
Truck Distribution Service, 239
Truck Press, 291 n. 7
Truesdale, C.W. (Bill), 56 n. 18, 315-7
25 Minnesota Poets, 298-9, 325
25 Minnesota Poets #2, 298-9, 319 n. 1, 325
Twin Cities Book Festival (TCBF), 1
Twin Cities Draft Information Center (TC-DIC), 96, 110-1

U

Unger, Leonard, 49
University of Minnesota, Duluth, 254-5
University of Minnesota, Minneapolis, 2, 29, 34, 36, 45, 49-51, 54, 71, 76, 81-2, 89, 125, 144, 150, 157, 200, 201, 212, 232 n. 25, 238 n. 44, 299, 302, 321
University of Minnesota, Morris, 29, 266, 304, 305 n. 29
University of South Dakota, 150
Unowsky, David, 236-9
Upper Midwest Writers Conference, 159, 258
Urban Arts Program, the, 326
Utne, Tom, 126
Uzzano, 263 n. 30

V

Vallejo, César, 8, 11 n. 15, 19, 55, 72, 79 n. 43, 102, 246, 288, 291, 316
Vanilla Press, 216 n. 43, 224, 228, 305-8, 328 n. 16
Viking Bar, the, 90
Vinz, Mark, 37, 130, 163-4, 182 n. 15, 186, 189 n. 28, 237, 246, 247 n. 5, 249-52, 253, 256, 257, 260 n. 24, 280, 284, 286, 300, 317 n. 46, 325
Vizenor, Gerald, 115, 150, 151, 164, 166-7, 168, 203, 206, 260 n. 24, 296, 297-8, 301
Vogel (Marshall/Rasmussen), Caroline, 140, 186 n. 22, 188, 212-3, 215, 221, 224 nn. 7-8, 226, 254 n. 17, 271, 277-8, 291 n. 7, 298 n. 17
Vold, Jan Erik, 253
Volk, Craig, 117, 119, 120, 211
Voss, Carl, 115

W

Waara (Damsten), Richard, 178 n. 8, 217, 253, 296 n. 15
Wakoski, Diane, 112, 205

Waldman, Ned, 238, 297 n. 16
Waldridge, Robert, 300 n. 20
Walker Art Center, the, 92, 165-6, 199, 203-6, 224, 279 n. 25
Walker Methodist Community Church, 209
Walker, Scott, 317, 318
Walker, Thomas Barlow, 209 n. 30
Wanek, Connie, 254 n. 18, 256
Ward, Matt, 301 n. 23
Warren, Robert Penn, 49, 51, 202
Waterman, Cary, 20, 109, 116 n. 35, 43 n. 35, 194 n. 37, 255, 260 n. 24, 278, 295, 298 n. 18
Waterman, Charles, 109, 122, 189 n. 28, 247 n. 5, 255, 260, 296 n. 14, 304, 313 n. 39
Weaver, Will, 187 n. 25
Weber, Coco, 138, 210, 226, 306 n. 31
Weber, Harry, 55-6
Weil, Suzanne, 166, 204-6
Welch, James, 158, 161, 168
Welter, Peter, 322
West End, 116-7
Westerheim Press, 291 n. 7
White, Bukka, 87
White, James L., 78, 164, 168, 211, 261, 298 n. 17, 301, 313 n. 39, 32
Whitman, Walt, 7, 24-5, 71, 335
Whittemore, Reed, 34, 55, 243 n. 1
Wiebe, Dallas, 55
Wilk, David, 239, 291 n. 7
Williams, Beryle (Bea), 192 n. 33, 222-4, 226, 261
Williams, William Carlos, 39, 51
Winter, Susan, 308
Woessner, Warren, 185, 186, 253, 256
Wojahn, David, 19, 20, 76, 78, 93, 136, 138, 142, 173, 175, 189 n. 28, 200, 203, 209, 210-1, 233, 234, 238, 254 n. 17, 256, 291, 313 n. 39
Wolfe, Diana, 190-1
Women Against Military Madness (WAMM), 121-2
Women Poets of the Twin Cities (WPTC), 31 n. 9, 190, 206, 211 n. 33, 221-5, 226, 228, 305-6
Women Poets of the Twin Cities, 224-5, 306, 307
Women's Art Registry of Minnesota (WARM), 224, 227-8
Woolf, Virginia, 180
World Famous Poets, 210-1
Wright, Franz, 189 n. 28
Wright, James, 34, 45-9, 51-3, 55, 61, 72-7, 78-80, 86, 97 n. 36, 101, 160, 169, 173, 175, 183, 189, 233, 246, 257, 267, 290, 291, 313, 316

Y

Yeats, W.B., 7, 39, 101
Yenser, Seymour, 319
Young Bear, Ray, 159-61, 164, 179, 256

Z

Zniewski, Carolyn, 92-3
Zolynas, Al, 255, 278, 303

About the Author

Mark Gustafson lives in Minneapolis. The breadth of his interest in contemporary literature is evident in the many reviews he has written for *Rain Taxi Review of Books* and for the *Minneapolis Star-Tribune.* His focus on Robert Bly's influence and accomplishments is reflected in long-form essays in *Antioch Review, Catamaran Literary Reader, Great River Review, Kenyon Review, Michigan Quarterly Review, Middle West Review, Rain Taxi Review of Books,* and in *Robert Bly in This World,* in the bibliography he compiled, *The Odin House Harvest,* and in his book, *Born Under the Sign of Odin: The Life & Times of Robert Bly's Little Magazine & Small Press.* In 2012, Bly designated Gustafson as his biographer. That massive task is ongoing.

Gustafson's professional life has been as a Classics professor, teaching for thirty years at colleges and universities in Minnesota, Iowa, Indiana, and Michigan. His scholarship on tattoos in Greco-Roman antiquity, recognized by the *New York Times* in 1997, continues, with presentations in Berlin in 2014 and Erlangen-Nuremberg in 2025.

Over his lifetime, sabbaticals have enabled him to live in Indonesia, Beirut, Rome (twice), Istanbul and London. Still, he is always happy to retreat to his rustic cabin on Leech Lake.

www.ingramcontent.com/pod-product-compliance
Lightning Source LLC
Chambersburg PA
CBHW020218170426

43201CB00007B/255